The RESCUERS

Laura Greaves is a multi-award-winning journalist, author and proud 'crazy dog lady'. She has spent more than twenty years writing for newspapers and magazines in Australia and around the world and is the former editor of *Dogs Life* magazine. Now a freelance writer, Laura has written extensively for countless dog and pet-specific print and web publications. She is the author of the collections *Incredible Dog Journeys* and *Dogs with Jobs*, as well as three romantic comedy novels, *Be My Baby*, *The Ex-Factor* and *Two Weeks 'Til Christmas*, all of which feature an extensive supporting cast of cheeky canines.

Also by Laura Greaves

Incredible Dog Journeys
Dogs with Jobs

The RESCUERS

INCREDIBLE STORIES OF LIFE-SAVING DOGS

LAURA GREAVES

MICHAEL JOSEPH
an imprint of
PENGUIN BOOKS

MICHAEL JOSEPH

UK | USA | Canada | Ireland | Australia
India | New Zealand | South Africa | China

Penguin Books is part of the Penguin Random House group of companies whose addresses can be found at global.penguinrandomhouse.com.

Penguin
Random House
Australia

First published by Penguin Random House Australia Pty Ltd, 2018

Cover design by James Rendall © Penguin Random House Australia Pty Ltd
Cover photograph courtesy P.j. Regan
Typeset in Sabon and Brandon Grotesque by Midland Typesetters, Australia
Printed and bound in Australia by Griffin Press, an accredited ISO AS/NZS 14001 Environmental Management Systems printer.

NATIONAL LIBRARY OF AUSTRALIA
A catalogue record for this book is available from the National Library of Australia

ISBN: 978 0 14378 734 1

penguin.com.au

MIX
Paper from responsible sources
FSC® C009448
FSC www.fsc.org

For Tex, my rescuer

AUTHOR'S NOTE

The rescue dogs in these stories are not trained 'search and rescue' working dogs. For the purposes of this book, a rescue dog is one that has had more than one home. He wasn't purchased by his owner directly from a breeder or pet shop, but adopted from a shelter or rescue group, or given away via a classified advertisement, or found on the street, or placed with his human by a charity.

A dog is the only thing on earth
that loves you more than you love yourself.
– Josh Billings

CONTENTS

INTRODUCTION

A funny thing can happen when you write books about remarkable dogs. You can start to think that your own dog is a little, well, ordinary.

That's not to say that all dogs aren't magical, wondrous love bugs that human beings clearly do not deserve. Obviously they are. Every single pooch on the planet fits that description.

But when you're meeting people whose four-legged friend has literally saved their life you could be forgiven for seeing your own pup snoozing on the couch, or hearing him licking his nether regions in the middle of the night (why *always* in the middle of the night?), and thinking, *What have you done for me lately?*

Would *my* dog save me from a burning building, as Buddy the labrador did for Judy Scrivener? Would she throw herself in the path of a speeding motorcycle to stop it from hitting me, like street dog Kabang did for two little girls in the Philippines?

Would she give me the impetus to stick with recovery from addiction, like Clove the pit bull does for P.j. Regan?

Personally, I don't know about that. My dogs are pretty lazy. I'm just not sure there's room for rescuing in their busy schedules of napping, eating, harassing my guinea pigs, and producing the enormous fur balls that seem to occupy every corner of my house.

But here's the thing I've learned while writing three books about amazing canines: *dogs are rescuing us even when we don't realise it.*

All dogs are rescuers. Sometimes, as many of the stories in this book demonstrate, they save us in the most literal sense. But even if they're not physically standing in the way of death or disaster, our dogs are saving our souls in tiny ways every day.

Sounds a bit highfalutin, doesn't it? But I can prove it.

I have two dogs, Nova Scotia duck tolling retrievers called Tex and Delilah. Tex has always been my 'problem child'. From a young age, he's had a laundry list of illnesses and ailments that would have bankrupted me if not for the wonders of pet insurance. When he was just three I learned he had arthritis. Next came a diagnosis of hypothyroidism, for which he takes twice-daily medication (and will for the rest of his life). When Tex was six he had what I can identify with the benefit of hindsight as something like a mental breakdown. With the support of an incredible veterinary behaviourist who diagnosed an anxiety disorder, and also with daily anti-anxiety medication, we helped Tex make sense of the world, calmed his behaviour and gave him back his quality of life.

Tex is now eleven years old and, at the time of writing, has just been diagnosed with both cancer and epilepsy. I know – when is this dog going to catch a break?! He may have a couple more years with us, he may only have a few more months, but today, at this very moment, he is well and he is happy.

He is *so* happy. That's what is really remarkable about Tex. Even on days when he must be feeling physically terrible, or when his head starts to spin in a cycle of worry and fear, he manages to find contentment. I'll spy him sitting in a patch of sunshine in the garden, a beatific expression on his handsome face. Or he'll roll into 'roach' position mid nap – lying on his back with all four feet in the air – and let out a long, satisfied sigh. And in those moments I think, *This dog knows how good he's got it.*

So what, you may ask, does this have to do with me? *Is she trying to say that this sickly, neurotic dog has somehow rescued her?*

Yes. That's precisely what I'm saying.

You see, I also struggle with anxiety. I've also battled depression. I've had my share of strange health issues. I have felt like an outlier, a misfit, a weirdo. Sometimes I have real problems with being 'present'; with enjoying where I am instead of worrying about what lies ahead.

Like many of us, I've had days where I have felt overwhelmed. Many times I've wanted to throw my hands up in the air and wail, 'I give up!'

But I don't give up. And I won't give up. Because my dog has shown me that giving up is not an option.

No matter what life throws at him, Tex finds the good. He pinpoints the beauty and he surrounds himself with it. He loves fiercely and he knows he's loved in return and he doesn't question it.

Helping Tex with his issues allowed me to identify my own. In choosing me to be his person, Tex has saved me from myself. He's saved me from worry, from frustration when life is challenging, from being ashamed of my own idiosyncrasies. He has saved me from the exhaustion and sadness that comes from feeling uncomfortable in your own skin. Tex has rescued me from a life spent apologising for my perceived flaws, because Tex doesn't apologise for who he is. Tex is Tex, and frankly, he doesn't care what anybody thinks about that.

As the musician Moby reportedly said, 'Dogs have boundless enthusiasm, but no sense of shame. I should have a dog as a life coach.' I think that perfectly sums it up.

It was Tex's cancer diagnosis that made me realise all this. Every day with both of my dogs has been a joy, but knowing that Tex is here for a good time, not a long time, has thrown his impact on my life into sharp relief. He's been rescuing me for a decade and I didn't even know it.

So I'll say it again: all dogs are rescuers. The dogs in this book are remarkable, and all dogs are remarkable. Dogs are superheroes in their own wonderful ways.

They will save us if we let them.

How incredibly lucky are we?

Laura Greaves
2018

KHAN

RESCUED HUMAN: CHARLOTTE SVILICIC

Ask any international visitor to Australia what they know about our country, and our vast array of venomous, poisonous and just plain massive animals often tops the list. From snakes, spiders and insects to great white sharks, blue-ringed octopuses and those famously fearsome boxing kangaroos, it may indeed look to the uninitiated like our wildlife, by and large, wants us dead.

Australians, of course, like to think we take a more pragmatic view. We tend to be raised with a healthy – and necessary – respect for the dangerous creepy crawlies we share a continent with, but we know the truth of the matter is that very few deaths are caused by deadly native animals. As the well-known Australian proverb goes, 'She'll be right, mate.'

According to a 2017 study, between 2000 and 2013 there was an average of two fatalities per year from snakebites across Australia. Jellyfish were responsible for an average of one death every four years, while spiders claimed no lives. Drownings and car accidents accounted for a far greater loss of life during the same period, as they do every year.

For the most part, these critters fear us more than we fear them. It's not that we're blasé about the potential danger posed by, say, funnel-web spiders or box jellyfish. We know they're out there, it's just that there's really not a lot we can do about it.

Unless, that is, you're a rescued Dobermann with a curious little girl to look after. In that case, you might think there's a *whole lot* you can do about it. You might, in fact, do whatever it takes to keep her safe.

Much like a snake or a spider, the Dobermann is a breed that has had its fair share of less-than-glowing press. Sadly, every generation seems to have a designated 'bad breed'. Today it is the pit bull, but in the 1980s, when Catherine Svilicic was growing up, it was the Dobermann. The breed had long been unfairly stereotyped as ferocious and aggressive, and, like it did for many others, that narrative convinced Catherine.

'Like most people, I had always misunderstood the Dobermann. They are a greatly misunderstood dog,' she says.

Catherine grew up in Mareeba, a small town in Far North Queensland. Her bush childhood sparked a lifelong passion for animals. 'I was raised by parents who always had pets, and then I became a vet nurse and started a veterinary science degree,' she says.

It was while working as a vet nurse in a local clinic that Catherine first had her ideas about the Dobermann challenged. 'At the surgery where I worked, the vet, Phil, had a real soft spot for Dobermanns. He would say, "Once you get to know a good Dobermann, they're hard to pass up."'

The Dobermann was developed around 1890 by Karl Friedrich Louis Dobermann, a German tax collector who also ran the local dog pound. Tax collecting was a dangerous profession and Dobermann wanted a dog that was large, looked intimidating and would fearlessly guard and defend him in the dicey parts of town. This dog would need to be intelligent and biddable, possess great strength, speed and endurance and, above all else, be loyal. Dobermann used dogs from the local pound including German pinschers, Rottweilers and Weimaraners to create his ideal breed, which was named in his honour after his death in 1894.

While the Dobermann *was* originally bred to be fierce and frightening – it has been used extensively in police work and was the official war dog of the United States Marine Corps during World War II – more than 120 years later the breed is entirely different. Today's Dobermanns are known for their even and good-natured temperament, energy and obedience. The only thing that hasn't changed is that famous protective streak – the 21st century Dobermann remains as watchful and loyal as ever, as Catherine would soon discover.

In 2007, Catherine and her husband, Alan, decided the time was right to get a dog. The couple had met at university in Brisbane and later moved to Atherton, in Far North Queensland, with their first daughter, Charlotte. They had previously owned a sweet little shih tzu–Maltese mix and figured a similar breed would be the best addition to their growing family – Charlotte was then seventeen months old and the couple hoped to have more children down the track.

But before she could start her search for a pint-sized four-legged friend, Catherine found herself chatting with Kerry Kinder, a local boarding-kennel owner and breeder of Dobermanns, who was a client at the vet surgery.

'I went to meet Kerry and see her dogs and just fell in love. I was surprised by how placid Dobermanns are, the "gentle giant-ness" of them,' she says. 'Dobermanns are guard dogs; they're not attack dogs. There's a running joke that a Dobermann will let you into the house but they won't let you out.'

Almost before she knew it, Catherine had said to Kerry, 'I'm going to come and get a puppy.' But Kerry had a proposal of a different sort: she had just rescued an adult Dobermann and he needed a new, loving home.

The dog's name was Khan. 'He was originally one of Kerry's – she had bred him and sold him to a guy, but I think that he wanted a guard dog, a vicious dog, and he misread the breed that he'd bought,' Catherine says. 'In an attempt to get a vicious dog he beat Khan, and it didn't work.'

Kerry was tipped off about the man's behaviour and, furious, immediately jumped in her car. She reportedly drove for two days to retrieve the helpless dog she had entrusted to the man's care. 'She said to the guy, "I won't call the cops if you give the dog to me right now," and he did. I wouldn't want to mess with Kerry,' says Catherine.

So Khan was safe, but he was in a very bad way. He'd been starved and had injuries. And that was just the physical damage – Kerry knew there could be deep psychological wounds, too. Who knew just how much abuse and neglect the young dog had suffered, and what it had done to him? But in her heart, Kerry felt that Khan deserved a second chance at a happy life with a family that treasured him.

And that family, she decided, was the Svilicic clan.

'Kerry said, "I've just got this guy from a bad situation – if you take him you can have him for free,"' Catherine recalls.

Though she and Alan had by now agreed on a Dobermann and were well aware how large a fully grown dog would be – up to 45 kilograms for males and 35 kilograms for females – they had planned to get a puppy that would grow *with* their young family. Catherine wasn't sure whether tossing a large adult dog with a sad history into a house with an active toddler was the right way to go.

'We had Charlotte and I thought, *Do we really want a great big dog with a tiny baby?*' she says. Charlotte may have been little, but she was already a dynamo. 'She was walking really young and she was a bolter: we ended up having to buy one of those kiddy leashes that everyone hates.' Catherine wasn't sure she had the energy to manage both her go-getting daughter and a 'damaged' dog.

The family's first meeting with Khan didn't exactly go according to plan either. 'Kerry brought Khan out to meet us, and another dog, Phoenix, was in the kennel. Khan decided to have a fight with him on the way and Kerry was holding his collar screaming, "You're embarrassing me!"'

There was also the not-insignificant fact that Khan was enormous. Even his name sounded warlike and imposing. 'Each of Kerry's litters, their names started with the same letter. Phoenix's litter were all P's and Khan's were all K's,' Catherine says. 'We thought about changing it, but it actually really suited him.'

At first glance this dog seemed like he could be a handful. But then something rather magical happened. As Catherine and Alan stood chatting with Kerry, Charlotte the eternal explorer slipped away from her parents. She took off across the paddock – and promptly fell over. Without missing a beat, 'Khan took off after her and picked her up,' says Catherine. 'He really had such a sweet nature.'

Any doubts she'd had about adopting Khan vanished in that instant. 'We agreed to take him. I didn't think it would pose a problem at all. I just had a lovely feeling from him,' she says.

A feeling that, just four days later, would prove to be very well founded indeed.

*

Late October may technically still be spring in Australia, but in Far North Queensland it might as well be the middle of summer. The daytime temperature frequently tops 30°C and the humidity hovers around a steamy 60 per cent. In other words, it's hot.

It was particularly warm on October 29, Catherine remembers. It was a Monday and Khan had joined the family the previous Friday. As his quick thinking in Kerry Kinder's paddock had suggested, Khan had already decided that Miss Charlotte Svilicic was his number one girl; the committed canine had barely left her side since arriving at his new home.

'If Khan and Charlotte were out in the garden together and someone walked down the street he'd stand right at the gate, in front of her, and just stare at them,' says Catherine. 'Dobermanns have got those piggy little eyes – they don't have the lovely big eyes that other breeds have – so when they want to give you the hairy eyeball, they really can.'

Khan was next to his favourite girl on that stifling Monday when Catherine took Charlotte into the garden for some fresh air.

'I was just in the house doing boring mother things and Charlotte wanted to go outside and run around. It was really hot, I remember that. I remember it like it was yesterday,' she says. 'She just had a pair of joggers on and a nappy. We were just cruising around the garden, looking at flowers and all that good stuff. Khan was with her.'

The family's home was an old Queenslander, a classically charming architectural style that's ubiquitous across the state, as well as in parts of northern New South Wales. Queenslander houses are made from timber, with a corrugated iron roof and at least one large verandah. They are usually single storey, but raised up off the ground on 'stumps' – a clever trick that helps to protect the building from termites and other pests, but mainly serves to keep the house cool via ventilation through the airy, dark under-floor void.

While some homeowners choose to use the under-floor space as a carport or extra living area, for Catherine and Alan it was handy extra storage. The entire perimeter was decoratively screened with timber palings, with a small gate for access. As is often the wont of small children, Charlotte soon tired of playing in the expansive garden and instead homed in on the padlock on the gate.

She seemed fascinated by it, Catherine recalls. 'She was flapping the padlock back and forth and it was banging on the gate,' she says. She thought Khan, who was naturally right next to Charlotte, might be startled by the jarring noise, but he seemed unfazed by it.

That was until, entirely without warning, he became very fazed indeed. An unearthly sound began to emanate from the normally placid dog. It chilled Catherine to her core.

'Khan suddenly started making this noise from the depths of his chest, this growl,' she says. 'His whole chest puffed up and his hair stood up and he lowered his head. He continued to make this guttural growl.'

As Catherine watched, Khan seemed to double in size. For a terrifying moment, she was convinced her early concerns about adopting Khan were about to be proven correct. 'He kept trying to nudge her. I was right next to Charlotte – no more than a metre away – and I thought, *He's going to kill her*. His chest was bigger than he was long – he was a monster of a dog,' she says.

Time seemed to slow down as Catherine lunged desperately for her daughter.

But Khan saw her approach, and he got to Charlotte first.

'I went to grab Charlotte and he saw me coming. I don't know if he thought, *This is one too many people*, or what he was thinking, but he grabbed her by the back of the nappy and threw her over his shoulder into the garden,' says Catherine.

Of all the outcomes Catherine's racing mind had envisioned in those few seconds, Khan tossing Charlotte like a rag doll was not one of them. 'I turned and looked and she was just sitting there in a pile of mulch.'

But the drama was far from over. Still not certain whether Khan's bizarre behaviour was some sort of attack on her child, Catherine raced to pick up Charlotte, who was completely unharmed, and take her inside to safety.

'As I turned to flee into the house, this big brown snake came out from between the palings and got Khan right in the chest,' she says. 'He screamed like he'd been stabbed.'

In an instant, it all made sense. Whether he had seen it or smelled it, Khan had somehow sensed the deadly Eastern brown snake lurking under the house, right behind the palings where his human best friend was playing. His menacing growl had been an attempt to scare away the reptile, which is most active during spring. When that didn't work, and he saw Catherine approaching, Khan knew he had to act. That primal Dobermann drive to protect had kicked in at the absolute right moment. The devoted dog hadn't been trying to hurt Charlotte at all – Catherine felt ashamed that she had ever entertained the thought. Just four days after meeting the little girl, he had been trying to *save* her.

And he had succeeded – but not before the snake had struck a potentially lethal blow.

'I ran Charlotte into the house. She was screaming and I was saying, "You can shush now, you're fine,"' Catherine says. Moments later, Khan staggered into the house. It was obvious the snake's potent venom was already beginning to take a terrible toll. 'He came in and lay on the carpet going *pant, pant, pant*. He was just really flat, lying on his side like he was really, really tired. I think he was feeling pretty terrible.'

While deaths from snakebite are generally rare in Australia, the Eastern brown snake is responsible for about 60 per cent of all snake-related fatalities. It is notorious for its speed and aggression – celebrated Australian naturalist David Fleay reported that the snake could outpace a person running at full speed – and is considered to be the second-most venomous terrestrial snake in the world (only the inland taipan has a more toxic bite; it's also native to Australia). An envenomed bite can be fatal within minutes. Symptoms of a bite include weakness, convulsions, renal failure, paralysis and cardiac arrest.

According to a study published in the *Australian Veterinary Journal*, dogs in NSW (and likely the other eastern states) are bitten by the Eastern brown snake more often than any other snake species except the red-bellied black snake.

Khan was in grave danger. He needed veterinary attention – and fast. There literally wasn't a moment to lose.

But Catherine had another problem. She was home alone. How on earth was she going to manoeuvre a distressed toddler *and* a desperately sick, 45-kilogram Dobermann into the car without help? And she didn't even want to think about the possibility that the snake still lurked beyond the front door.

'I rang the local vet – not the vet I worked for – who was literally two minutes away from me. She jumped straight in her car and rushed to the house,' she says. 'It was late morning, creeping up to lunchtime, and she looked at him and said, "He looks okay now, but come midnight he'll be dead." That's the way the venom works.'

His only hope, the vet said, was a shot of antivenin. Catherine felt helpless. For all her personal and professional experience with animals, she had never dealt with a snakebite before.

'I was only working at the vet clinic one day a week at that stage, so I only saw whatever cases Phil, the vet, had in on that Friday,' she says. 'I had no experience with snakebites at all, so I just deferred to the vet and said, "Do what you've got to do to save this dog."'

Even in the frantic aftermath of the incident, there was no doubt in Catherine's mind that Khan had saved her daughter's life. Had the brave dog not literally thrown Charlotte from the snake's path and used his own body as a shield, she knew the outcome would have been very different.

'By the time the vet arrived and I told her what had happened, it was starting to sink in that Khan had saved Charlotte. The vet just looked at me, gobsmacked, and I went, "Okay, this situation is bigger than I thought it was."'

With Catherine's help, the vet was able to get Khan into her car. She raced him back to her clinic and administered the life-saving medication. It was touch and go for a day or two, but Khan soon made a full recovery. 'He was absolutely fine and came home after a couple of days,' Catherine says. 'It was just astounding.'

Khan knew he had to make it home – he had a little girl waiting for him, after all.

The second half of 2007 was traumatic in terms of major events in Australia and around the world. In July, nearly 200 people died in a plane crash in Brazil, while an earthquake in Peru claimed at least 450 lives in August. In September, Queensland Premier Peter Beattie abruptly resigned and retired from political life. The same month, a three-year-old toddler was abandoned by her father at Melbourne's Southern Cross train station after he murdered the little girl's mother and fled to the United States. Then, in early October, severe thunderstorms lashed the Queensland coast for nearly a week, causing widespread damage.

By the end of October, still counting her blessings after Khan's life-saving feat, Catherine thought the local community might appreciate some good news.

'At the time, everything in the world was really crap. There was just a lot of really bad news about, so I called the *Cairns Post* and said, "You might want to run this story to cheer people up,"' she says.

The newspaper duly printed an article about Khan's incredible heroism and, says Catherine, 'it was off like wildfire'. In no time at all, the story of the rescue dog that rescued a little girl went around the world. It was picked up by media outlets as far afield as the US, the UK and Korea. Australia's rival breakfast television shows, *Sunrise* and *Today*, became embroiled in a bidding war for Khan's story.

The RSPCA even encouraged Catherine to nominate Khan for a Purple Cross, which is an honour awarded to animals that have demonstrated bravery and service.

The public's response to Khan's brave deed was heartwarming. 'One lady sent us a cheque for twenty dollars. I don't know how she found us, but she wanted to help pay for Khan's vet bill. She wrote, "I don't have much money, this is all I've got,"' Catherine says. 'I just thought, *No, I'm not going to cash that*. It's in Charlotte's baby book.'

In an incredible twist, Catherine says Khan's breeder, Kerry Kinder, revealed that the hero dog's grandfather had also saved a child in similar circumstances.

While the interest in her courageous canine may have been overwhelming, for Catherine it wasn't particularly surprising. 'I wasn't surprised that the story touched so many people, to be honest. What Khan did was pretty amazing. He saved Charlotte's life, quite literally,' she says. 'I remember at the time a lot of people saying to me, "Oh God, I needed to hear that."'

She never saw the snake again, but says she wouldn't have wanted it harmed under any circumstances. 'I wouldn't have killed him even if I could have found him. There's no point killing snakes. Even the venomous ones are transient creatures. We lived between a creek and a river – he would've just been cruising under the house to get where he was going. It was that time of year,' she says.

'That snake was in the wrong place at the wrong time. For a snake to bite, they've got to be afraid. He didn't want to be there; Khan didn't want to be there. It was a bit of bad luck on all fronts.'

Neither did the near miss make Catherine and Alan restrict their children's freedoms. Charlotte and now her siblings – Harper, Giselle, and Bear – are still encouraged to spend as much time as possible in the great outdoors, even during snake season (which, let's be honest, is essentially all year round in Australia).

'It didn't make me more cautious about the kids' safety. I was raised in the bush. You've just got to live, otherwise you're afraid all the time,' says Catherine.

His brush with death didn't change Khan's fundamentally sweet personality either. He remained the big love bug he'd always been. 'He was just a big, lovely, soft, lazy, gorgeous thing,' Catherine laughs. 'He thought he was a small dog. He'd try to get in your lap when you were watching TV. He was just a sook.'

In 2013, the Svilicic clan packed up and moved to Western Australia. Catherine had suffered severe postnatal depression after the birth of son Bear and wanted to be closer to family. Alan's parents live in Perth and the kids are very close to their cousins there.

Khan, of course, also made the move west. By then ten years old, he was billeted with Alan's parents, who had a much bigger backyard for him to enjoy – but he was constantly in the company of at least one of the Svilicic kids or an equally doting cousin.

'They used to ride him like a horse, the little ones. I've got photos of them sitting on his back. We had a pony by proxy,' Catherine laughs.

But there was no question about which of his junior playmates was Khan's favourite. Though she has no memory of the day her rescue dog rescued her, the experience proved formative for Charlotte nonetheless. Put simply, 'she and Khan were soulmates', says Catherine. 'They were inseparable forever.'

'The impact of the whole thing isn't lost on her. She feels profoundly grateful and extremely proud,' she says. 'I think she feels really privileged to be able to tell people this really cool story about this wonderful animal in her life.'

In fact, Khan's selfless act has inspired in Charlotte a deep desire to give back. At the age of just twelve, she launched a grassroots initiative that collects used spectacles for vision-impaired people in Indonesia. She received an

Aussie of the Month Award from the WA Australia Day Council for her efforts. 'She's grown up to be an amazing kid. She's a unique little person and she's going to do some good things,' says her proud mum.

Sadly, even the strongest, most fearless dogs can't live forever. In 2016, the Svilicic family made the heartbreaking decision to have Khan peacefully put to sleep after excruciating hip problems limited his mobility and impacted his quality of life.

Two years on, the whole family still misses their beautiful, gallant boy. They dote on their other pets – Catherine is a foster carer for a Perth-based rescue organisation and has a steady stream of cats and kittens to look after – but Khan was truly one in a million.

'The kids were just so devastated. We still have a lot of tears at bedtime. Charlotte has Khan's photo by her bed. She used to call him Khany-bear,' Catherine says. 'If his hips hadn't gone, I don't know how long he would have lived. I said to Alan, "We'll never get another dog like this."'

It's hard to imagine ever being that lucky again. But then, they never dreamed of being lucky enough to love a dog like Khan either.

COLT

RESCUED HUMAN: JANAYE KEARNS

March 29, 2016 was going to be a good day for Janaye Kearns. She could feel it.

With her ever-present roster of chronic pain, mobility problems, dizziness, fainting spells and seizures, most of Janaye's days recently had been of the 'bad' variety – but today felt different. The constant throbbing in her head was bearable and she was steadier on her feet. On a day like today, Janaye could just about believe she felt active, energetic, excited to go out into the world and have an adventure. She could almost imagine her life was like it used to be almost four years earlier, before a traumatic brain injury (TBI) changed everything.

Janaye called to her labrador–Weimaraner mix, Colt, to fetch his red service dog vest. It was a beautiful early spring afternoon in Colorado, where Janaye lives, and she was determined to enjoy it. It was time to take a walk.

Almost invariably, Janaye would take somebody with her whenever she left the house. She often used crutches and occasionally a wheelchair, and her history of TBI made it impossible to predict when she would need a steadying hand or someone to dial emergency services. It was just easier – and certainly safer – to have someone there, whether at the supermarket or the dog park. Usually Janaye's partner, Garrett, would go with her, or perhaps a friend or neighbour.

'Almost every time I go out I have someone with me. I also have tracking apps on my phone and if I don't make contact within a certain time it sends out an emergency text to my family. I have my support system that I'm very thankful for,' Janaye says. 'I used to be extremely active and I try to continue to be as active as possible. I do go on walks a lot. I have to take a lot of safety precautions, but I still go.'

Today, though, she was confident the ever-watchful Colt would be precaution enough. He was her right-hand man after all. With Colt by her side, what was the worst that could happen?

The inseparable pair made their way to a large, historic park not far from Janaye's home. The picturesque park is one of the busiest local green spaces, home to sports fields, basketball courts, playgrounds, picnic areas, a greenhouse and even a 100-year-old public swimming pool.

The park also boasts almost 7 kilometres of walking trails – and conquering part of these was Janaye's goal that day. She and Colt strolled happily for hours, enjoying the weak sunshine after a long, frozen winter. Their progress was slow but steady, and Colt – though never one to shirk his duties – had ample opportunity to follow his nose wherever he pleased.

Deep into a 3.5-kilometre section of trail, Colt suddenly became fractious, pawing frantically at Janaye. After nearly three years together, she knew immediately what her faithful rescue dog was telling her: *Get ready – there's a seizure on the way.*

Janaye turned and headed for home. If she could take her anti-seizure medication quickly, there was a chance she might stave off the seizure all together. But there was no way of knowing precisely how long she had: sometimes Colt alerted her to an imminent seizure hours in advance, while at other times it was just minutes. She hoped for the best, but suspected time was not on her side on this occasion.

'He alerted while I was pretty far along the trail. I knew I wasn't going to make it back in time. I was just going to lie down and have a seizure in the grass. I've done it before; it's not the end of the world,' says Janaye. 'Every time I'm not with somebody and I'm going to have a seizure, I call someone and they stay on the phone with me. I called my friend Anne,* lay down and we were talking.'

Janaye may have been matter-of-fact about her predicament, but the situation was concerning. She and Colt were all alone. To make matters worse, it was growing dark and

---

* Name has been changed.

the daytime temperature was plummeting as the shadows lengthened. While seizures are generally short, the postictal state – the period when the brain is effectively 're-booting' afterwards, when speech and movement are limited – could last fifteen minutes or more. Janaye knew she could be facing a long stretch of unconsciousness out there, by herself, in the cold, dark night.

And yet, with Colt beside her, she felt strangely calm. 'I actually feel calmer when Colt lets me know a seizure is coming, I think because I know how it feels to have a seizure when I *don't* know it's going to happen,' the 25-year-old says. 'And I completely trust Colt with my life, so that helps.'

Moments after Janaye called Anne, the seizure that Colt had sensed hit – hard.

'I had my seizure and Anne said Colt started barking, which is not normal. It means something's wrong,' she says.

In fact, something was very wrong. Janaye's trust in her service dog was about to be put to the test.

To call Janaye an animal lover would be a gross understatement. Today, as well as Colt, she shares her home with several cats, a ferret and a snake, but pets of all persuasions have been an integral part of Janaye's life as far back as she can remember.

Growing up, her family bred German shepherds, whose smarts and aptitude for training led many into careers with the military and police. Janaye was training dogs herself at a young age.

'We would do all the basic training, as well as more intensive training – everything up until "college" for the dogs. We weren't doing bomb detection or anything like that, but it wasn't just "sit" and "stay",' she says.

'So I grew up around that and I've also had a lot of animals in my family just as pets. I did a lot of rescue and rehabilitation. I've had bats, hummingbirds, ducks and Canadian geese – all sorts of things. I love animals so much.'

When she moved into her own apartment, Janaye knew it was only a matter of time before she would add a tail-wagging companion to her menagerie once again. But she never could have imagined just how that dog would come into her life.

In 2012, aged nineteen, Janaye was always on the go. She played soccer and volleyball, and enjoyed horse vaulting and figure skating. She had even spent five years working on a horse ranch. She had recently started dating Garrett and was excited for their future together.

That summer, as she had done countless times before, Janaye spent a warm weekend with family at a lake in Michigan, close to where her mother was living at the time. While riding atop an inner tube being towed by a speedboat, she was hit by a jet ski and flung into the water. Unconscious and suffering a severe head injury, Janaye then drowned. The rider of the jet ski left the scene amid the commotion and was never found; Janaye isn't sure they even realised she'd been hit.

She was brought onto a boat and resuscitated, but Janaye's fight for survival was only just beginning. Rushed to a local medical centre, she was later flown to a larger hospital, where she underwent an emergency craniotomy – surgery to relieve pressure on her brain and remove the pooled blood. She was in a coma for about two weeks.

Once her recovery from the initial head trauma and surgery was on track, she faced another uphill battle. The drowning and oxygen deprivation had damaged Janaye's brain, meaning she was forced to spend a year in in-patient rehabilitation to re-learn basic skills that most people take for granted.

'I had to learn to do everything again: walk, talk, read and write. It was very intense, teaching me how to brush my teeth all over again. I was very weak,' she says.

She doesn't remember the accident or those first few months in the hospital at all. 'Initially I didn't remember anything about that first year. I'm not sure where my memory starts, whether it was in the hospital or later. I don't know if it was just because it was so traumatising.'

Even when she was finally well enough to return home in August 2013, every day was a struggle for Janaye. She had to learn to use a wheelchair, crutches and the array of adaptive equipment – such as temperature-controlled taps that would prevent her from scalding herself – that now filled her home. 'The frustration level was super high. I couldn't even control my muscles the way I wanted. I knew how to pick up a cup, but I'd go to pick it up and my arm wouldn't do what I wanted it to do,' she says.

'Just basic dexterity, like putting coats on and stuff, had to be learned again. Some days I was okay and I could walk, but on hard days I could barely do anything myself. I'd struggle trying to get a jacket off and get frustrated. I can't control my body temperature and get overheated really fast. It'll be the middle of winter, snowing, and I'll be telling people I'm too hot.'

The right side of Janaye's body is completely numb due to impaired communication with her brain, and she has delayed sensation on the left side. Depending on the day, she may battle intense head pain, dizziness or crippling muscle spasms. She can lose consciousness and pass out with little or no warning, meaning potentially catastrophic falls are an ever-present possibility.

Her poor short-term memory can also cause injuries, such as minor burns sustained when Janaye forgets she recently used the stove and that it's still hot.

Perhaps most difficult to deal with in the early days following her accident, however, were the changes to her mood. As she began to accept that her injuries were lifelong, Janaye fell into a deep depression, which would sometimes manifest as angry outbursts.

'I used to be a super active, productive, happy-go-lucky person and I turned into a Negative Nancy. Not all the time, but I'm definitely not as positive as I used to be. I just felt so angry at the world,' she says. 'I pretty much felt like a burden all the time.'

She worried her fledgling relationship with Garrett wouldn't survive her new circumstances – but she needn't have. 'Garrett was my boyfriend for only two months before my accident happened and suddenly he's having to carry me to the shower and bathe me and help me do a lot of things,' says Janaye.

'I have really bad, angry outbursts that I can't really control. I would always be screaming at him or crying. I have learned a lot of different coping skills over the years but in the beginning it was like, *This poor man*. It's crazy that he stayed even though he barely knew me, but he did stay and he just loves me.'

And Janaye was about to meet another young gentleman who would love her just as fiercely.

Almost a year after the accident that had nearly claimed her life, Janaye was ready to add another tool to her recovery kit. Working so closely with dogs throughout her childhood and right up into her teenage years, she was more than familiar with the myriad ways canines can assist humans. She began to wonder whether a service dog might be able to help bolster her independence.

While seizures have been a fact of life for Janaye since her first TBI, they have worsened over time. When her brain was still in repair mode in the early days following the jet ski accident, the seizures were manageable. She knew there were service dogs that would alert their owners to an approaching seizure, but her priority early on was finding and training a dog that could assist with mobility.

'The point of getting a dog was hopefully mobility support and basic assistance – things like opening doors, getting my meds and going to get help if I wasn't able to do it myself,' Janaye says.

Like most people seeking the services of a loyal four-legged helper, Janaye's first ports of call were the dozens of organisations across the United States that provide fully trained service dogs to people with disabilities. But while she was impressed with the skills those dogs offered, Janaye struggled to find an organisation that could supply a dog with the multitasking abilities she needed. Her canine companion had to be able to assist with mobility *and* perform practical daily tasks *and* be able to get help when a seizure occurred. It was a big ask.

Even if she could find a dog that could cater to her complex needs, buying a ready-to-roll service dog would cost thousands of dollars upfront. The alternative was to wait at least a year to be allocated a dog by a not-for-profit organisation, but if she was going to continue to make progress in her recovery and regain more independence, Janaye needed an assistance dog as soon as possible.

That's when inspiration struck. Janaye realised she had a secret weapon, honed over many years of helping her family prepare German shepherds for life as military and police operatives: her training ability.

US law allows experienced people to train their own service dogs, which can legally accompany their owners virtually anywhere, from supermarkets to hospitals. 'You can't just watch YouTube videos, but if you have a good amount of experience you can do it,' Janaye explains.

She had that experience in spades. And as she has proven with her tenacity and persistence every day since the accident, Janaye isn't one to shy away from a challenge. Determined to find and train her perfect service dog, she set about contacting local breeders of Weimaraners.

She felt it was important to have an impartial professional opinion on the various dogs' potential aptitude for assistance work, not only because she knew she would want to take home every puppy she saw, but because mobility assistance dogs can be hard to assess as puppies, since they generally don't begin to do the 'heavy lifting' their role entails until around two years of age. So she paid an animal behaviourist to accompany her on her visits to breeders. 'We looked for a dog for months,' she recalls.

'You have to wait until they're two before you can even know if they can physically do the necessary tasks – at that point they can have x-rays to make sure they're skeletally sound,' she says. 'If you're getting a mobility dog it can be scary because you can wait all that time and then the dog can turn out to be not able to do it. '

As a long-time fan of Weimaraners, Janaye had a gut feeling the hard-working breed would make an ideal service dog. Originally bred in the early 19th century for hunting large game such as boar, bear and deer, the Weimaraner is an athletic and robust gun dog known for its energy, endurance and stamina.

Though she figured a breeder would be her best bet when it came to finding a puppy, Janaye also contacted local rescue groups and explained what she was looking for. To her surprise, after months of meeting countless purebred puppies, it was a rescue that called with promising news.

'A local Weimaraner rescue called and said, "We just had, like, seven litters come in."'

While specific details were scarce, it seemed some sort of disaster had struck a local breeder, leaving him with no option but to immediately shut up shop and find new homes for his breeding dogs and their puppies.

'Apparently he loved both English labrador retrievers and Weimaraners, so he bred them together and had been doing it for years. He knew each breed had great qualities that, when combined, would make them perfect for hunting and working situations,' says Janaye. 'The rescue normally just takes in Weimaraners, but they were generous enough to take in these dogs. There were six or seven litters of all different ages – some not old enough to leave their mum yet, some a bit older – plus all the breeding dogs.'

Though the possibility that her perfect dog might be among the homeless pups was exciting, Janaye was also saddened by the situation. 'I was kind of upset with that breeder. I felt like they should have had something set up in case something happened to them. I wish they were more responsible. When you have so many animals depending on you, it's so important to have a back-up plan. I have no idea what happened to the other dogs. It's so sobering.'

Nevertheless, these dogs needed homes – and Janaye was hopeful that, for one of them, it might be hers. 'I felt awful that something bad had happened for the breeder, but even in the midst of tragedy, good things can happen,' she says. It was a truth Janaye had reminded herself of every day since her accident.

She called the animal behaviourist she'd enlisted, and together they went to meet the puppies. First impressions were encouraging.

'I was looking for the youngest possible dog, because that's best for training, but it was great to meet the older dogs and see that they had an amazing temperament. The behaviourist was like, "This is great to see because we know what these puppies are going to turn into,"' she recalls. 'I wanted to take them all home right then because I was so in love, but I had to be patient.'

One puppy in particular caught Janaye's eye: a male, wriggling ball of brown fluff who was happy-go-lucky, yet calm. But she wanted the behaviourist's expert opinion before she officially decided he was The One.

'The behaviourist said two of the youngest litters showed great promise, and this little puppy was in one of them, so we waited until they were old enough to go to their new homes. She re-checked them and said, "This is right, this is the dog for you."'

Happily, the dog the behaviourist had identified was the one that had stolen Janaye's heart. She brought him home in the summer of 2013, but the little fluff ball remained nameless for a while. We called him "Puppy" for a long time, and he still responds to it. But he just grew so fast that we were like, "Gosh, he's going to be like a horse,"' she says.

'Garrett and I grew up on ranches, so we both had a lot of experience with horses and shooting. We'd be doing housework and Garrett would lean over and say, "What about Winchester?" or "What about Remington?" but once Colt was brought up it was just perfect.'

Colt's training as Janaye's right-hand man began in earnest right away. In no time at all, the eager young pup had mastered everyday tasks like bringing his mistress her shoes, unzipping her jacket and pulling the sleeves to help her take it off, and opening the change compartment of her purse. He learned the different names of Janaye's various medications, so that he can bring her the right one when she asks for it. Janaye even trained him to operate a special push-button adaptor for the phone that connects directly to a dispatch centre that can call emergency services.

'We have a device where you just push one button and they have all my personal information,' she explains. 'They say, "Janaye, are you there?" and if I don't answer they can send paramedics.'

A few months before she rescued Colt, Janaye's seizures had suddenly stopped. Her doctors explained that her brain had healed enough to prevent them, paving the way for a greater degree of independence for her and the dog who, at that stage, was still a dream.

Having Colt in her life had another, less outwardly obvious benefit, too: he helped to calm her anxiety and stress and alleviate depression.

'Because of my brain injury I get really overstimulated. When I'm grocery shopping, for example, or if I'm in a restaurant and there's music playing, my brain is overwhelming itself and going a bit crazy trying to understand basic information that other people don't really think about,' Janaye says.

She's often unaware when she's getting worked up – but Colt is always on the ball. When he picks up on cues that suggest Janaye's stress levels are rising, such as certain breathing patterns or her leg shaking, Colt performs Deep Pressure Therapy (DPT); he uses his weight to apply pressure to her body in places that typically elicit a calming effect. To the untrained eye, it may simply look like cuddling, but its benefits are profound. 'If I start breathing in a way that suggests I'm upset, he'll lean up against me or start pawing at me and I'll go, *I need to calm down*. I don't always notice that I'm getting that way, but Colt knows before I do.'

It wasn't long before Colt had many of his commands down pat, and even though Janaye wouldn't know for more than a year whether he'd be equally adept at mobility work, she was confident that her eager-to-please canine would be both the service dog and the companion she had so wanted.

'He was just amazing. He was a blessing and I was so thankful that he was willing to learn all that for me,' she says.

But then, when Colt was around five months old, the unthinkable happened. Without warning, he started to display strange, potentially dangerous behaviour. He would ignore commands, bark uncontrollably and leap up at Janaye, and nothing she did seemed to help.

'He was jumping all over me, barking and going crazy and not listening at all. By that time he had all his training down and then all of a sudden he'd lose his mind. We were like, *What is wrong with this hormonal little teenager?*' she says. 'This was unprofessional behaviour for a service dog in training. He was coming into stores and stuff to train, but we were like, *We can't take him places if he's going to act like that whenever he feels like it.*'

Even more concerning was the threat to Janaye's safety. Colt's wild behaviour was frightening enough when he was a small puppy; once he reached his fully grown weight of approximately 38 kilograms, there was a very real risk his antics could harm his loving handler. 'He wasn't yet fully grown and he was going to get bigger. We were scared that him jumping on me would knock me over.'

Worse news followed: Janaye had begun having seizures again – doctors suspected they were triggered by scar tissue forming in her brain – and they were more frequent and unpredictable than ever before. She tried taking daily medication to keep them at bay (in fact, her doctors would experiment with different cocktails of anti-seizure medication for more than four years), but it didn't help.

'We tried different doses, this one and that one, and it never worked. My doctor explained that it's most likely my metabolism,' she says. 'If the medication is given to me immediately before a seizure it does work, but it won't stay in my system long enough to be effective as a daily preventative.'

For two months, Janaye tried everything she could think of to discourage Colt's worrisome outbursts and reinforce all the positive behaviours he'd picked up so readily. But nothing worked. With her service dog apparently out of control and debilitating seizures now an almost daily occurrence, a heartbroken Janaye began to consider whether the plucky pooch she'd so hoped would change her life for the better would be happier living with someone else.

'We didn't know what he was doing. We were looking into asking family and friends if they were willing to take him. We almost got rid of him,' she says. 'My life was pretty difficult and he was driving me nuts. He was so attentive and so good most of the time, but he'd have these random freak-outs.'

Then, just as it looked like the end of the road for Janaye and Colt, the penny dropped. Janaye realised that, just as he could sense her rising anxiety, Colt could somehow sense when a seizure was imminent.

He wasn't naughty or out of control. He was simply – desperately – trying to warn the woman he loved more than anything that she needed to find a safe place to wait out an approaching seizure.

Just how a dog detects a seizure has never been fully explained by science. Some researchers think these clever canines pick up on tiny changes in their human's behaviour or scent before a seizure strikes. What is known, however, is that seizure detection seems to be an innate ability – some dogs have it, some dogs don't – and the behaviour is not breed, age or gender specific.

A study by the University of Florida College of Veterinary Medicine found that just three of 29 dogs whose owners had seizures at least once a month would alert to an impending seizure. Those dogs generally gave their owners about three minutes' warning.

But Colt was different. As well as the fact that she'd enjoyed a long period with no seizures at all, the key reason Janaye initially failed to connect Colt's behaviour with seizure alert was that he would 'go crazy' up to *two hours* before a seizure struck.

'We didn't notice because it was so far in advance. It could be anywhere from thirty minutes to two hours in advance and we just never put two and two together,' she says.

With Colt at last receiving credit for his incredible superpower, Janaye was able to train him to alert in a more low-key fashion. Now, when Colt knows a seizure is looming, he paws at and makes eye contact with Janaye. 'He looks at me like, *This is not good*,' she says.

When the seizure begins, depending on whether she's had time to get to a safe place or not, Colt may wedge his shoulders under Janaye's head to keep her from banging it on the floor. Or he'll use his body to push her onto her side, which significantly reduces the chance she will choke on saliva and stop breathing.

If neither of those measures is necessary, Colt will simply stay by Janaye's side, comforting her throughout the seizure – which generally lasts no more than ninety seconds – and the disorientation of the postictal period. 'He knows when a seizure is done. He'll get up and comfort me or he'll lick my face to bring me around. It always brings me around faster than if he's not here,' she says.

Sometimes, thanks to Colt, Janaye is able to avoid a seizure all together. Once she realised he was alerting well in advance, she was able to send Colt to fetch her anti-seizure medication. She also taught him to follow up with a second alert, if necessary, immediately before the seizure starts. Depending on how far in advance he gave the first alert, the medication may kick in to prevent the seizure and a second alert won't be needed.

'I didn't want to have to lie on the couch for two hours, waiting for a seizure to come, so we worked to train him to alert again right before it's going to happen,' she explains. 'It takes about an hour for the meds to pierce the blood–brain barrier, so about fifty per cent of the time I'll have no seizure because of him alerting.'

Colt saves Janaye's life most days like it's no big deal. And then some days – like 29 March 2016 – it's a very big deal indeed.

As soon as she heard Colt start barking at the other end of the phone line that dark night, Anne Evans knew the situation was grave. Trouble was, while Anne knew exactly where Janaye was within the nearby park, she struggled to describe the specific location to the emergency services dispatcher.

'Colt normally doesn't bark when Janaye has seizures. He usually lays down next to her, so I knew at that point that something was wrong. I kept saying, "Janaye, Janaye," and my son looked at me and said, "Mom, I think you need to call 911,"' Anne later told a local news station.

Anne's instincts were correct: this was no ordinary seizure. Janaye's tonic clonic seizures, also known as grand mal seizures, were coming in life-threatening clusters.

'I was told later that I wasn't even coming fully out of one seizure before going straight into the next one. Having cluster seizures, and having them for more than five minutes, is very dangerous,' she says.

It took emergency services an hour to find Janaye. 'I was told there were ambulances, fire trucks and police cars all driving through the park with spotlights,' she says.

Not that she saw those lights. In fact, Janaye has virtually no memory of the entire incident – but Colt sure saw them. Fighting every instinct that told him to stay by Janaye's side during a seizure, he ran out into the darkness, determined to find the help she so desperately needed.

As Officer Jeff Rymer from the Colorado Springs Police Department searched for the young woman who'd been reported missing in the park, he was surprised when his torch beam picked up the reflection of a pair of gleaming eyes.

'Using my spotlight, I saw the dog's eyes reflect off my light, but couldn't see [Janaye] at first,' Officer Rymer told KRDO NewsChannel 13. Nevertheless, when Colt turned tail and ran, the policeman took off in pursuit. 'When I got a little bit closer, I found her laying on her back. She was having a seizure.'

When the seizure finally stopped, Janaye wasn't breathing – probably, she thinks, because she had rolled onto her back and aspirated saliva when Colt left his bolstering position to guide the officers to her location – so

Officer Rymer quickly performed life-saving measures. Paramedics arrived soon after and administered medication that helped to stabilise her condition, though Janaye was told she continued to have seizures in the ambulance en route to the hospital.

As she recuperated in hospital, the enormity of what had happened started to sink in. Had the quick-thinking police officer not followed Colt, Janaye may not have survived. And if loyal, brave Colt hadn't courageously decided to leave her side in order to seek help, Officer Rymer would likely not have been able to locate her in the darkness.

Once again, Janaye realised, her rescue dog had rescued her. Colt had unquestionably saved her life.

'Later on, the local news contacted me and wanted to hear about Colt. I said I wanted to be able to thank the officer who helped saved my life. Officer Rymer and I were on the news together and I got to hug him and it was really cool,' she says.

The news appearance wasn't Colt's first taste of the spotlight, however. Shortly after Colt was trained and helping Janaye live independently, she had started an Instagram account (@servicedogcolt), which now has more than 10 000 followers, as well as a YouTube channel (Service Dog Colt), which today has almost 20 000 subscribers. The social media platforms not only showcase her daily life with Colt, but also raise awareness about living with TBI and the challenges faced by service dog teams.

The latter is something Janaye is especially passionate about. In the US there is an epidemic of 'fake' service dogs – untrained canines that people falsely claim are service animals in order to be able to take their pets with them into places like shops and restaurants. It's a real problem for genuine service dogs and their handlers, says Janaye. It can set back a real service dog's training and even be life threatening if the dog is distracted from his duties.

'People are lazy and they don't take responsibility and that's where the problem lies. You go to Walmart, for example, and you're going to see at least two fake service dogs every time. It's frustrating,' she explains.

Some of Janaye's social media videos have gone viral and been shared by other high-profile websites including The Dodo, whose heartwarming animal videos are viewed more than 80 million times every month.

'I love my dog and he's spectacular to me, but other people finding him so fascinating as well is really moving,' she says.

The thing about traumatic brain injuries is that suffering one makes subsequent injuries much more likely. 'I've since had multiple brain injuries and it's not just because I'm a huge klutz,' Janaye says. 'Once you have one, you're more susceptible because your brain tissue is damaged.'

Thanks to her seizures, dizziness and fainting spells, Janaye falls frequently, sometimes hitting her head – though Colt's vigilant presence means it's fortunately not as common as it could be. The most severe recent fall happened in November 2016, resulting in another TBI and requiring a third emergency brain surgery. That incident effectively took Janaye back to square one in recovery terms. Once again, she was forced to re-learn many basic tasks.

This time, however, she had Colt by her side, along with a wheelchair, crutches and other helpful medical aids. 'I was mostly out of the wheelchair when I got Colt, and he wasn't yet two so I couldn't test his aptitude for mobility assistance. After my second brain surgery I had to train him to do the mobility work from my wheelchair,' she says. 'What he did before all of that was enough, then suddenly I'm back in the wheelchair and he has to learn how to walk appropriately, how not to let the chair run him over, how to let me brace on him when I'm getting up or down, how to retrieve it – so if the chair is across the room he can pull it to me. He's pretty bomb proof.'

Two years on from her most recent TBI, Janaye is again able to walk most of the time with crutches or using Colt, now five, to provide forward momentum. Her seizures continue and, though she's hopeful they will once again lessen or disappear altogether, there are no guarantees.

Janaye has no doubt there was some sort of divine intervention that led her to rescue her amazing life-saving dog. Not a day goes by that she doesn't count her blessings – and her furry four-legged saviour is always top of the list.

'Sometimes I feel so unlovable. I can just randomly drop into a gloom where I feel like my life isn't worth it, but with Colt I constantly have that support, whether I'm sad or angry or sick in bed. He always looks at me the same, with the same care. He doesn't treat me any different,' Janaye says.

'He's given me such freedom and so much love. Such unconditional love. Everybody says, "I love my pet," but I don't think they could fully understand the bond that happens between you and a service dog, especially one that saves your life. It's a deep, deep connection.'

KABANG

RESCUED HUMANS: DINA BUNGGAL AND PRINCESS DIANSING

The story of Kabang is truly a tale like no other. Destined for the dinner table, but allowed to become a much-loved family pet instead, Kabang was indeed rescued from a terrible fate. Then she returned the favour by rescuing two little girls from certain death, suffering horrific injuries in the process.

But the real story is what happened after that. It's a story about a defenseless stray that became a global celebrity, inspiring the kind of frenzied hero worship usually reserved for movie stars or sporting legends. It's also about the kindness of strangers – specifically a group of animal lovers and cutting-edge veterinary surgeons on opposite sides of the world who somehow found each other and moved heaven and earth to rescue the rescue dog a second time.

And it all starts with a motorcycle.

*

The Philippines is a motorcycle-mad nation. The quickest and cheapest way to traverse the narrow, vehicle-choked streets of its major cities is undoubtedly on two wheels. There are nearly five million registered motorcycles across the country, accounting for more than half of the vehicles on the road.

Some days, it can feel like at least four million of those are in Zamboanga City.

Located some 1300 kilometres south of Manila, the teeming metropolis of Zamboanga City is the sixth most populous city in the Philippines. ZC, as the locals call it, is home to nearly a million people squeezed into just 1400 square kilometres. (By comparison, Sydney, Australia, sprawls over 12 000 square kilometres and is home to five million.) Its major industries are sardines and seaweed, so the transportation and delivery of goods by road is a 24/7 fact of life.

The total number of deaths due to road crashes in the Philippines has been increasing nationwide since 2006. Motorcycle riders make up the largest proportion of those killed, closely followed by pedestrians. Sadly, more than 500 children are killed in road accidents every year. According to the Philippines Statistics Authority, motorcycles are involved in more than two-thirds of all reported transport incidents.

So it's fair to say that braving the traffic in ZC – or indeed anywhere in the Philippines – is not for the faint hearted. There isn't a parent in the city who doesn't grip their child's hand a little tighter whenever they need to cross the street or walk beside a major road.

But kids can be stealthy creatures. Sometimes all it takes is a moment of inattention – a split second of looking in the wrong direction – for a young child to step straight into the path of disaster. That's what happened to eleven-year-old Dina Bunggal and her three-year-old cousin, Princess Diansing, in late 2011.

On 14 December, the girls were attempting to cross Nunez Extension, a busy road near Dina's humble shanty home, when they walked in front of an oncoming motorcycle. As the speeding bike bore down on them, catastrophe seemed inevitable. The girls hadn't seen the bike, and there was simply no way the rider could avoid colliding with them. In that instant, they seemed fated to become another set of sad statistics.

But Dina and Princess had a guardian angel on their side that day. Or rather, they had a guardian askal.

There are hundreds of thousands of homeless animals across the Philippines. Between 2007 and 2012, the country had the second fastest-growing population of dogs and cats in the world. The Philippines Animal Welfare Society (PAWS) describes the typical Philippines stray as a domesticated dog that is thrown out onto the streets when its owner can no longer afford to feed it, or when it gets sick and the owner is either unwilling or unable to pay for its treatment.

Many of these dogs are askals, a sort of 'native breed' of mongrel traditionally used to guard property. They are frequently seen wandering the streets – even owned askals are trusted to roam around their neighbourhoods to socialise with other dogs – hence their name: askal means 'street dog'.

When they are part of a family, askals are known for their loyalty and protective nature, particularly towards children.

In an effort to remove stigma and improve public perception of the street dogs, PAWS encourages the use of the alternative name aspin, short for asong pinoy, meaning 'Filipino dog'. The organisation estimates that around 98 per cent of the calls it receives about cruelty and abuse involve aspins.

Whether an askal or an aspin, the guardian angel looking out for Dina and Princess on that steamy afternoon was known to those who loved her by another name: Kabang.

Dina's father, Rodolfo 'Rudy' Bunggal, had found Kabang abandoned in heavy rain in a swamp near his home in 2008; she was just a few weeks old. He had previously raised dogs for meat, and took the pretty puppy intending it to be a meal, not a pet. He fed her mostly coffee creamer to fatten her up; she rarely got milk because it was so expensive.

According to the United States–based Animal Welfare Institute (AWI), between 300 000 and half a million dogs are killed for food in the Philippines every year. Historically, says the AWI, consumption of dog meat was a cultural practice associated with celebratory events and rituals of mourning, and only affected a small number of dogs. However, in recent decades, the dog-meat trade has rapidly increased for commercial rather than cultural reasons.

The killing and selling of dogs for food was banned nationwide in 1998, but the illegal dog-meat trade still thrives. Dogs are rounded up off the streets – many are owned dogs, still wearing collars and identification tags – and transported in inhumane conditions to slaughterhouses, where they are brutally killed.

It may be difficult for dog lovers in more developed nations to comprehend, but for Rudy, as for many other Filipinos who live in poverty, consuming dog meat was simply normal. Rudy worked as a 'vulcaniser', earning less than five dollars a day repairing punctured tyres. Water spinach harvested from the swamp was the main staple of the family's diet; meat was a rare luxury. 'The dogs we raised did not last longer than three months. I slaughtered them. It's our only way of eating meat,' Rudy told the *Philippine Daily Inquirer* in a 2012 interview. 'Life is difficult and I have to feed my family.'

But there was something about this friendly fawn-coloured canine; some indefinable quality that set her apart as special. He knew he could not bring himself to end her life. His quarry became a rescue instead.

Rudy named his new pet Kabang – meaning 'spotty' in the Visayan dialect – and promptly fell in love with her.

He told the *Inquirer* that he couldn't explain what led him to spare the dog. His then wife, Christina, was also baffled by his change of heart.

'Rudy became a different person when Kabang came. He became humane to animals. It was maybe because we treated her differently. Of all the dogs we raised, she was the only one we fed Coffee-mate and milk. None of the other dogs we had raised spent the night in the same space with our daughter,' Christina told the newspaper. 'If she went out of the house, it would be with the children.'

Kabang may have trod a precarious path to find her

family, but she was soon a treasured member of it. Rudy described her as a sweet dog that loved cuddles. She was protective, too: she would sit on Rudy's vulcanising tools to safeguard them from thieves.

Dina and her cousin Princess, who lived with the Bunggals, also adored Kabang. The little dog and her little girls were rarely apart.

Which is why Kabang was hot on Dina and Princess's heels when they ran into the path of the motorcycle. Just as it was about to hit the girls, Kabang threw herself at the motorcycle, knocking it over.

An eyewitness, Jovito Urpiano, told local media it was as if the dog had appeared from nowhere. 'I thought somebody threw the dog on the motorcycle, but I could not see anyone who might have done that,' he said, adding that he only realised later that Kabang had intentionally blocked the motorcycle's path to save the girls.

The children were spared – neither they nor the rider suffered anything more severe than bruises. All three were taken to hospital but were soon discharged.

But Kabang had been gravely injured. Her head had landed directly on the front wheel of the motorbike, which trapped her snout as it rolled. Her nose and upper jaw were torn off by the impact.

'The bones holding her upper snout were crushed, and we could not do anything to save it,' said Rudy, who quickly arrived at the scene.

Rudy didn't know what to do. Surely Kabang couldn't survive such a terrible accident? And even if he could get her to a veterinary clinic, how would he pay for treatment? Rudy's family was desperately poor. He didn't have much in the way of formal education, but he didn't need to be a vet to know that saving Kabang's life – if it was even possible – would cost more than he had. Her injuries were so severe that Rudy almost couldn't bear to look at his adored little dog.

And yet Kabang had just saved the lives of his daughter and niece. She had acted without a moment's thought for her own safety. Rudy shuddered to think what might have happened if she had leapt just half a second later. He felt she deserved a chance to fight, no matter what it took.

He debated the best course of action as he worked frantically to pull Kabang's head from the wheel. But the instant she had been extracted from the mangled wreckage of the motorcycle, Kabang made Rudy's decision for him.

She fled.

Shocked, terrified and undoubtedly in terrible pain, Kabang disappeared into the crowd that had gathered around the accident scene. There was no way anybody could catch her amid the chaos. There are few faster creatures on earth than a scared dog.

In the days after the accident, as Dina and Princess recovered from their frightening near miss, Rudy looked for Kabang. He searched his neighbourhood, the swamp and the surrounding areas, but there was no sign of her. As the days dragged on, he feared the worst. There was surely no way she could be out there somewhere, still alive, with half her face missing. When a week had passed since the accident, Rudy was forced to concede the obvious: Kabang must have had hidden herself away somewhere and succumbed to her injuries. He was devastated, but remained deeply grateful to the little dog for saving Dina and Princess. Kabang had performed a miracle and he would never forget it.

And then, two weeks after the accident, a second miracle occurred.

Kabang turned up on Rudy's doorstep.

She was in a terrible state. She was weak and hungry, and her face looked like something from a horror film. Her gaping wounds, left untreated for a fortnight, were clearly infected. But she was alive, and somehow she had made it home.

This time, Rudy didn't think twice. He took Kabang straight to a nearby vet hospital. The hospital's chief veterinarian was Dr Anton Lim. He was away in Manila when Rudy arrived with Kabang.

'My staff saw her and took a photo of her, so the first time I saw her was from pictures they sent me. I saw the infected wound and immediately asked my staff to bring her to my clinic for cleaning and massive antibiotic treatment,' says Dr Lim.

He hurried back to ZC and when he first saw Kabang in the flesh, he wasn't optimistic about her chance of survival. 'The first time I saw her I thought she would weaken, but after three days she improved a lot. That's when I knew she would survive.'

Incredibly, even with her mouth all but destroyed, Kabang was still able to eat and drink. Dr Lim says that's probably what kept her alive during those first two weeks, even as infection set in.

'At that time I did not know of her story. It was a week after we started treating her that I found out about her story from Rudy,' he says. 'That's the time I was more determined to help her. It was the least we could do to pay her back.'

There was no doubt that Kabang had a powerful will to live. Everyone who came into contact with her loved her. Dr Lim believes she understood that she had a whole team of people on her side. 'She was her jolly self the whole time. She was friendly and very cooperative and would be very happy when my staff picked her up from Rudy to be brought to my clinic,' he says.

The only time Kabang wasn't particularly pleased was when cameras were pointed in her direction. And that happened *a lot*. As word of her incredibly heroic act and against-the-odds survival spread through ZC and then around the Philippines, Kabang was hailed a national hero and started to assume bona fide celebrity status.

'She was a star! She befriended the media people by always wagging her tail and posing for the camera, but she would always hide her face,' says Dr Lim.

As the weeks passed, Dr Lim and his colleague, Ed Unson, did their level best for Kabang. They continued to keep her wounds clean and free of infection. They also took a holistic approach, feeding her nourishing food and supplements designed to promote tissue repair.

The vets knew that surgical repair of her wounds would mean a significant improvement in Kabang's quality of life, but they had gone about as far as they could within the confines of available veterinary facilities and surgical expertise in the Philippines. Plus, there was the expense: any surgical option was going to be wildly beyond the Bunggal family's reach.

They weren't sure what step to take next for her continuing care. Kabang's life had been spared, and that would likely have to be enough.

Little did they know that 14 000 kilometres away lived a woman who didn't believe it had to be enough.

Not by a long shot.

Ask Karen Kenngott what made her so sure she could get Kabang the help she needed and her answer is simple: 'It's called I'm-too-German-and-Irish-for-my-own-good-and-I'm-a-redhead,' she laughs. 'Don't tell me no. Don't tell me it can't be done without even trying.'

It was a dark, snowy Friday afternoon in Buffalo, New York, when Karen first learned about Kabang. She even remembers the date: it was 24 February 2012, more than two months after Kabang's accident.

'The wind was howling and the snow was blowing and I thought, *I'm not going anywhere today – I'm just going to stay home and drink my cup of tea and catch up on email,*' she recalls.

A lifelong animal lover, Karen's inbox was full of digital newsletters from animal welfare and rescue groups around the world. She's not sure exactly how it happened, but one link led to another and another, and before she knew it she was reading about a heroic street dog from the Philippines.

'All of a sudden, in the lower right corner of my screen, I saw a headline: DOG LOSES FACE SAVING CHILDREN. When I clicked on that link and saw the picture of Kabang I was simply aghast. I was like, *Is this real? Is it a scam?*' she says.

Karen's background is in critical care nursing. She works in hospital intensive care units with open heart surgery and transplant patients, some of whom are children. The incredible story she was reading piqued both her personal and professional interests.

'You can't show me a headline like that and expect me to not be interested,' she admits. 'My first thought was, *Is this dog still this side of the dirt?* Then it was, *I've got to do something.*'

The first thing Karen did was go to her calendar and count how many days it had been since the accident that cost Kabang her snout: seventy-two. She knew the chances of the plucky pooch still being alive were remote, but she tracked down the author of the article she'd read and sent off an email.

She didn't have to wait long for a response. The journalist replied and confirmed that Kabang was indeed still alive. 'She said, "Her owner is such a nice guy. He's dirt poor but he just loves this dog."'

Reading about Kabang's veterinary care to date, Karen realised two things. First, the quality of care had obviously been excellent – the sheer fact of her survival was testament to that. But second, she inferred that Kabang's treatment had now hit a wall of sorts. She knew enough about medicine to know that if there were more that Kabang's vets could be doing for her where she was, they would be doing it.

'The moment of impact, the clock starts ticking,' Karen says. 'They didn't know what (more) to do for her. I thought, *If they don't get those gaping wounds closed, if she gets a fungal infection, it's game over.*'

She also suspected that money was an issue. Karen had immediately wanted to make a donation to Kabang's care fund, only to find there was nowhere to donate. Based on what the reporter had told her about Rudy, she figured he couldn't simply 'float himself a line of credit on plastic'.

'I could see that he didn't have a snowball's chance in hell of helping her. He was relying on the vets and they didn't know what more to do,' she says. 'The problem as I saw it was that Kabang needed to get to the United States.'

And somehow she thought she might just be the person who could make it happen.

'When I first had notions of doing something, it wasn't that extensive at all,' says Karen. 'I didn't go out one day and say, "Let me find a gravely injured dog in a remote place and figure out how I can twist people's arms to get her to one of the best vet hospitals in the world and make her a star." It was gut instinct.'

There was another reason Kabang's story resonated so strongly with Karen. Five years earlier, in 2007, she had learned about the illegal dog-meat trade for the first time. She still remembers how 'viscerally disturbed' she'd felt one evening after reading about dogs being tortured before being slaughtered for their meat.

'I couldn't wrap my head around the fact that human beings could intentionally be that cruel. I thought, *Every minute of every day there are dogs living in pens that never get to feel grass beneath their feet*,' she says.

As she went to bed that night, she uttered a prayer of sorts. 'There are times in your life when you say something aloud and it's almost as if it goes out into the universe: "This is my stand on this." I remember the moment almost as if someone else was telling me what to say. I said, "This is so vile that, so help me God, if there's ever a day that I can do something about it then I damn well will."'

What the world needed, she thought at the time, was a sort of poster child: a dog whose story would convey simply and effectively why torturing dogs for meat was wrong. When she later learned that Rudy Bunggal had initially intended Kabang to be food for his family, Karen says it was like a light switched on in her head.

'I thought, *Is this my dog?* Everything fell into place at that point. I was one hundred per cent committed.'

She had fire in her belly, but Karen knew that getting Kabang to the US would not be easy. Before she even considered the logistics of bringing a seriously injured street dog across the Pacific Ocean, she needed to find an American veterinary hospital willing to perform the necessary dental work and facial surgery.

Having worked in three of New York City's leading hospitals, including Cornell University Medical Center, Karen decided to start there. She called veterinarians at Cornell University, who had previously treated one of her cats for lymphoma, and asked for contacts at the University of California, Davis, which was their equivalent on the US west coast. They put Karen in touch with UC Davis's William R. Pritchard Veterinary Medical Teaching Hospital, located near Sacramento in northern California.

'I called UC Davis and said, "This dog needs facial surgery – can you help?" And they bit,' she says. 'They said, "We have the ability, we think we can help her. We can't restore her to normal, but we can make her nose and mouth functional and make her life as normal as possible." So then I had to figure out how to get her to jump the pond.'

Arranging to get Kabang to California was – relatively speaking – the easy part. As well as working closely with Dr Lim and Dr Unson, Karen collaborated with Mona Consunji from the Animal Welfare Coalition (AWC), a network of animal welfare groups in the Philippines. In the end, Mona handled virtually the entire Philippines side of the operation.

'This girl makes it happen. Mona was ferocious – she never let up getting all the ducks in a row from a technical and administrative standpoint,' says Karen.

Meanwhile, back in Buffalo, Karen started working the phones and sent a flurry of emails. 'I've got fifteen hundred emails just getting this dog to this country. I don't even count the ones after that,' she laughs.

One of the first items on her to-do list was transport. She had to work out how to get Kabang from the Philippines to Los Angeles International Airport (LAX), and then 630 kilometres from LAX up to Davis – ideally for free. She googled 'animal transport LA' and one of the first companies on the list was Global Animal Transport.

'I thought, *That's got a ring to it*. A lot of it was intuitive: what is my gut telling me about what I'm doing?' says Karen.

She called and spoke to Susan Foley, who owns the company with her husband, Mike. When Karen explained the situation, Susan was excited. Not only were they happy to help at the American end, it turned out they also had transport contacts in the Philippines.

'Mike made a call and the woman at the company in the Philippines said, "Yes, the dog is considered a national hero – we'll transport her to the States and back for free,"' she says.

Karen could scarcely believe it. Just like that, Kabang, Rudy, Dr Lim and an assistant had passage to the US.

Next, she turned her laser focus to finding a dog-friendly hotel in Davis. She needed a home-away-from-home that could accommodate Kabang and her growing team of supporters for an indeterminate period of time. There was no way of knowing how long Kabang would need to recover from her surgery.

'Sometimes when they do skin grafts like they were planning for Kabang, they don't "take" and you can run into trouble. That was my main concern,' she explains. 'This is an animal, not a person: you can't say, "Don't scratch that, don't pull at your stitches." You can't explain things in a way they'll understand.'

Karen pulled up a map of Davis and looked for hotels that were both close to the veterinary medical teaching hospital and seemed to offer reasonable local amenities. She hit the jackpot with the first call she made.

'The first phone call I made was to the Hallmark Inn, because it seemed like it was conveniently located for lots of reasons. I talked with the general manager, Marisa Schaffer, for about an hour. That girl is a magician. She's got such a big heart. Every time someone needed to come in she said, "You can stay here,"' Karen says.

She also persuaded the dog-loving manager of the local Hertz rental car franchise to heavily discount the team's car hire. Karen couldn't quite believe how quickly the pieces of the puzzle were coming together, but she thought she knew why.

'Kabang was an underdog and everybody feels for the underdog because in some shape or form we all feel that way in our lives,' she says.

All that was left to do was raise the money to pay for the surgery itself.

And that's where Karen's golden run ground to an abrupt halt.

For all the incredible help they were offering, one thing the team at UC Davis wasn't able to do was operate on Kabang for free. Karen tried her hardest to persuade them, but it was no use.

'They used to have a program with funding that would help animals in need, but it was taken advantage of so they stopped it,' she says. 'I twisted their arm pretty hard, but they would not do this pro bono.'

The Philippines team was trying to secure funding through the International Fund for Animal Welfare (IFAW) and for a while it looked like Kabang would make the trip to California in the northern spring of 2012.

Then Dr Lim dropped a bombshell: Kabang was pregnant.

With her wounds being kept clean and free of infection, Kabang was happily back at home with her beloved Bunggals. But being a street dog, she still liked to wander, even with her injuries. It seemed that Kabang had had a romantic interlude during one of her sojourns.

The pregnancy put additional pressure on Kabang's still-healing body. It wasn't safe for her to make such a long journey by air, and she certainly couldn't have surgery before she delivered her puppies. There was discussion of terminating the pregnancy for Kabang's safety, but the reaction from the Philippines' predominantly Catholic community quickly put paid to that idea.

On 13 April 2012, Kabang gave birth to six puppies, five boys and a girl. Like any doting canine mum, she licked her brood clean despite her shattered mouth.

Once she had recovered from the birth, it was full steam ahead for the mission. Kabang finally had a departure date, and in June Karen flew from New York to LA, ready to welcome the hero dog.

But disaster struck once again. 'The day before they were coming out I got this email saying, *We can't come – the funding fell through*,' she says.

It was like a punch to the gut. After the tireless hard work of so many people, both in the US and the Philippines, it seemed they had fallen at the last hurdle. Karen stayed in California for two-and-a-half weeks trying every avenue she could think of to raise the thousands of dollars needed for Kabang's surgery.

'I thought maybe there was someone here who would come up with the funding. I tried Lions Club, Kiwanis, every Filipino-American group I could think of,' she says. 'I lost track of time. I was using two computers and working in five time zones – I was calling people in Missouri, New York, California.'

Devastatingly, all her efforts came to nothing. Karen returned to Buffalo feeling thoroughly discouraged by the operation's financial predicament. When the going got really tough, she would think about Kabang's owner, Rudy.

'Every day that I felt like I had failed I would say, "Come on, Karen, you've got to think of something because this poor guy is hoping that someone, somewhere, is going to help his dog,"' she says.

She was determined not to give up – they were so close to getting Kabang the help she needed – but for the moment she was all out of ideas.

'Move forward to August and I was still kind of in a "bah humbug" mood, so when I got a phone call from Rob Warren at UC Davis I was like, "Yeah? So?"' says Karen.

Rob explained that he was the newly appointed communications and marketing officer for the veterinary hospital.

'He had just started the job and wanted to know more about Kabang. He asked me, "Where are you on this?" and I kind of pulled the phone away and rolled my eyes,' she recalls. 'I said, "Well, in a word, frustrated," and told him why.'

Karen walked Rob through everything she had tried to do to raise the money for Kabang's operations. He was sympathetic to her frustration, and shared Karen's belief that UC Davis couldn't *not* save this dog.

'He saw that this was an opportunity not just for veterinary medicine, but for the human side. He said, "To let this dog die without trying to save her would be an utter waste of opportunity, let alone the dog's life – as I see it, we owe Kabang reciprocation." He just got it,' she says.

In 2018, it seems like public appeals are the go-to method for raising money to support people (and pets) in need, but in 2012 the concept of online crowd funding was in its infancy. Rob gave Karen a crash course in running a fundraising campaign via Facebook.

With his help – and some media coverage, including a front-page story in the *San Francisco Chronicle* – Karen set up the Care for Kabang campaign. In less than a month, dog-loving people from forty-five different countries had donated more than US$27 000 for Kabang's surgery.

For Rob, helping Karen bring Kabang to UC Davis was a no-brainer. The vets were sure they could improve her quality of life, so there was simply no reason not to try.

'There are very few veterinary hospitals in the world that could have performed the surgery needed to close the wounds to Kabang's face – probably less than a handful,' Rob says. 'Our maxillofacial surgeons are considered the best in the world and felt confident that a surgical plan for Kabang's wounds could be formulated and achieved.'

But Kabang still had one more obstacle to overcome. She had been diagnosed with an infectious cancer, and it looked like she would once again be prevented from travelling to the US.

In the end, it was decided that the cancer would be treated at UC Davis before Kabang's surgery. By October, ten months after her heroism almost cost Kabang her life, she was finally cleared to fly.

Karen got to pick the departure date.

Karen describes the moment she finally laid eyes on Kabang for the first time as 'just surreal'. It was two-thirty on a chilly October morning when Global Animal Transport's Mike Foley delivered Kabang and Dr Lim to Davis.

'I felt a myriad of things. They got out of the car and Kabang was so much smaller than I expected. She was alert, happy, wagging her tail. She was so well behaved. I was like, *I can't believe she's here and she's real*,' she recalls. 'She pranced around like she owned the place. I knew this dog was super intelligent.'

Seeing Kabang's wounds for the first time was also overwhelming. 'Her face looked like it must have hurt her. It was painful to look at,' she says.

There was no time to waste. Kabang had waited so long to be repaid for her life-saving deed; her treatment began immediately.

As well as a golf ball–sized transmissible venereal tumour, which was treated with chemotherapy, vets discovered that Kabang also had heartworm disease. The disease is reasonably common in America, but it is endemic in the Philippines. Without treatment, it is always fatal.

A team of UC Davis vets specialising in oncology; infectious diseases; dental, oral and soft-tissue surgery; internal medicine; and outpatient care was quickly formed to coordinate Kabang's multi-treatment care. Because of the nature of Kabang's health problems, each treatment had to be successfully completed before the next began.

Her treatments were successfully completed in February 2013 and Kabang was deemed ready for the dental and facial surgeries that would hopefully change her life for the better.

On 5 March, surgeons Frank Verstraete and Boaz Arzi performed oral surgery to remove two of Kabang's's upper teeth and reconstruct one eyelid that had been damaged by the motorcycle.

Then, in a nearly five-hour surgery on 27 March, they closed Kabang's facial wound with skin flaps that were brought forward from the top and sides of her head. Following that procedure, Dr Verstraete and Dr Arzi collaborated with William Culp, a veterinary soft-tissue surgeon at UC Davis, to reconstruct nasal openings and insert stents in those passages, which would allow two new permanent nostrils to form.

It was gruelling and invasive surgery but, as she had demonstrated every single day since the accident, Kabang was more than up to the challenge.

'Kabang responded well to all the treatments she received at UC Davis. There was never a time we felt her life was in danger,' says Rob Warren.

Because it wasn't possible to reconstruct Kabang's snout and a functional upper jaw, she will never look like she did before her accident. But with her facial wound repaired, she will be better protected against infection and able to live the active life she deserves.

Karen also marvelled at Kabang's incredible strength and resilience. 'She's a very adaptable dog. I think she coped as well as anyone could have hoped for, because she was young and she had been so well looked after before she got here,' she says.

She was thoroughly spoiled as she recovered from her various treatments. Kabang had a whole area in the veterinary ICU sectioned off as her 'territory' and a steady stream of visitors from across the university.

'The director sent an email to everyone saying, *We have a celebrity client, don't start congregating around the ICU door wanting to know how she's going*,' says Karen. 'But everybody did.'

Dr Lim had to return to the Philippines ten days after delivering Kabang to California. Karen stayed in Davis for a month after Kabang's arrival, made another trip for her surgery in March and then returned again when Kabang was discharged. She was listed on the official importation documents as Kabang's owner for the duration of her stay in the US, and it was a responsibility she took very seriously.

Sadly, Kabang's owner, Rudy, wasn't able to come with her after all; he was unable to produce the identification documents he needed in order to be issued a passport. He had put tremendous faith in Dr Lim in allowing Kabang to travel to the US without him, not to mention Karen and a team of strangers on the other side of the world. Karen wasn't about to disappoint him.

'Anton had to do a lot of one-on-one time with Rudy to convince him to let Kabang come, because he was sure that someone would put her down here in the US. I had to sign a piece of paper saying that under no circumstances would I let anybody put the dog down,' she says. 'Rudy had worked since he was nine years old. He'd never been able to go to school. He was a very underprivileged individual who was extremely caring. He really had a kind heart.'

True to her word, Karen doted on Kabang. Every day she was in California, she would bring in Kabang's favourite rotisserie chicken and Hawaiian dinner rolls from the nearby grocery store, and take her for short walks around the university grounds (with a cone around her head to stop her worrying at her stitches).

She believes Rudy was grateful for her dedication to his little dog. 'I was never able to speak to him, but I know he was deeply touched. I know from a comment on the

Facebook page that somebody translated that he thanked Rob and me for helping her,' Karen says.

'Her transformation was incredible to watch and it was phenomenal to help her through it. I thought, *She deserves somebody to do something for her and I guess I've been chosen.*'

After her initial recovery period at UC Davis, Kabang continued convalescing with Dawn Gillette, a vet nurse and the owner of All Species Animal Care, a boarding facility housed on a 20-acre farm at Woodland, 15 kilometres from Davis.

Kabang's treatment and surgery in the US had gone better than anyone involved in her rescue mission could have imagined, and soon it was time to start preparing for her return to the Philippines.

As the date of her departure from America drew nearer, Karen received countless messages from people begging her not to send Kabang home. She admits to feeling frustrated by the misperception that Kabang would not get the love and care she deserved if she lived in a country less prosperous than the US. She knew from experience that the only reason Kabang had survived long enough to make it to the States at all was the excellent care she'd had in the Philippines.

'Rudy went to great lengths and a lot of personal pain to make sure he gave Kabang the best life he possibly could. This dog needed to go home to somebody who had the support to give her the best life,' she says. 'This is a story that has a happy ending, not just for Kabang but for her owner.'

After a final examination and vaccinations, Kabang was discharged from UC Davis on 28 May. On 8 June she returned to the Philippines. She was greeted by crowds of well-wishers at Manila International Airport. In ZC, neighbours of the Bunggal family helped them improve their home in preparation for Kabang's return. There was also a parade in her honour, culminating at Municipal Hall where Mayor Celso Lobregat named Kabang the 'Pride of Zamboanga'.

Farewelling the dog she had worked so hard to meet was bittersweet for Karen.

'I was elated but also sad because I thought I may never see this dog again. It was probably the most personally satisfying thing I've ever done and it makes me want to do more of it,' she says. 'Kabang has a mission. Somebody else decided the mission and we helped her achieve it. She got us to come together for her so that we could do something right for animal welfare.

'My goal now is to get an animal shelter started in her name so that people see it and think, *This is how we take care of animals.*'

Today, Kabang is around ten years old and still thriving in ZC. 'Except for the frequent sneezing, especially when she's excited, and the dry eyes that need maintenance, she is as normal as can be,' says Dr Lim. 'She can eat and drink water by herself. She will have a long, fruitful life.'

He still can't quite believe the extent to which Kabang

captured global attention and won the hearts of so many in the Philippines.

'I was surprised by the generosity of pet lovers worldwide who contributed their lunch money. A lot of the donations were one or two dollars if I remember it right,' he says. 'Kabang was already a sensation in the Philippines, but I did not expect her to be a celebrity in other countries. I was really surprised by the reception when she arrived home – and boy, did she relish it!'

Kabang's heroism and the global effort to help her recover has also had another, equally heartwarming legacy: responsible pet ownership is now considered much more important in the Philippines and life has improved for aspin street dogs.

'She is the face of animal rights and responsible pet ownership. Because of her, a lot of stray aspin dogs were adopted, and abused dogs were saved through the Kabang funds,' Dr Lim says.

Several months after Kabang's return to ZC, Rudy's own sense of responsible pet ownership led him to put his much-loved dog's needs ahead of his own.

'I became Kabang's pet parent six or eight months after her surgery,' Dr Lim explains. 'Rudy asked that I take her in because he was afraid she would be dognapped. He knew Kabang had a lot of followers and since he was always out of the house, he would always worry about her.'

Sadly, Rudy died in April 2018 after a long illness. Though they never met, Karen was devastated by the passing of the man who had done so much for Kabang. 'It was very saddening to learn. I had always hoped to meet him,' she says. 'I would dearly like to see Kabang again and meet her human family.'

Kabang's life has been full of change, but Karen feels the courageous little dog 'is in the right place for all the right reasons'. Five years after spearheading the mammoth effort to rescue the rescue dog, she still marvels at what everyone involved in the Care for Kabang campaign achieved.

'None of us was looking for this. Everybody felt as if they'd been hand-picked,' she says. 'It was quite serendipitous. The planets aligned for this dog.'

It was perhaps Dina Bunggal who best summed up what Kabang means to her, and to the Philippines. 'I am very thankful to her, because without her, maybe I will not be alive today,' she told the *Inquirer*. 'She is not just my friend, she is like a part of our family.'

A global family forever bonded by their love of the rescue dog turned rescuer.

GRACE

RESCUED HUMAN: RACHEL JACOBS

You would have liked Laurence Jacobs. Everybody did.

New York City, a metropolis with a population of eight-and-a-half million, can often feel chaotic, impersonal, even hostile – but long-time New Yorker Laurence made friends wherever he went. In the Chelsea neighbourhood where he lived with his wife, Rachel, he couldn't walk down the street without bumping into a pal.

'My husband was so popular. Everybody knew him, but he was so humble. He talked to everyone, from homeless people to wealthy people. He walked into a room and people just loved him,' Rachel says. 'He's very hard to describe. He was incredibly handsome, but his personality was zany in an almost devilish way. He had the most glowing eyes and such a warm heart. He was very special.'

Laurence had once owned a bar and restaurant in the city, which allowed him to indulge his love of people and conversation. In his fifties he worked in finance and was a keen investor in real estate and the health and wellness sector; yoga and meditation were among his personal passions.

But the greatest joy in his life – aside from Rachel, whom he adored – was animals.

'He loved animals and they loved him. He was so connected to them. He grew up in Connecticut and had many dogs and cats. Later, he had a Rottweiler called Leroy that was famous in New York,' says Rachel. 'People would recognise Laurence years and years later and say, "Did you have that dog that used to push a brick around for fun in Madison Square Park?"'

Rachel, who grew up in Massachusetts, also had a family dog as a child, but when she moved to New York in 1997 and started working in events, fine arts and real estate, she felt her busy career wasn't compatible with dog ownership.

After meeting Laurence in 2005, Rachel soon became a 'cat person', doting on his two rescued felines. Sadly, one of the elderly cats, Lily (named in honour of Laurence's grandmother), passed away soon after the couple met, and in December 2016, her companion, Nike, was also reaching the end of her life. 'Laurence and I were always going to get a dog, but I became a cat lover and I said, "No, we can't get a dog when Nike is close to the end – it would be so mean if we gave all our love to a puppy,"' she recalls.

But when Nike passed away, adding a canine companion to the family was once again on the agenda. 'Getting a dog was the next thing we were going to do. We were going to go to Africa for my birthday in November 2017 and then start going to rescues and shelters, deciding what dog we were going to get,' says Rachel.

Tragically, they wouldn't get the chance.

On Sunday, 2 April, Laurence woke early, as was his custom. Over the years, Rachel had persuaded him not to wake her at 5 a.m. as he readied himself to leave their apartment (though he was also notoriously clumsy and she would sometimes be woken by a *thud* as Laurence bumped into things).

'He was an early riser, so most of the time on Saturday and Sunday he would wake up and, if it was really early, he would go and get a cup of coffee and meet some of his friends, because he knew I wouldn't be up for a few hours,' she says. 'I didn't hear a peep that morning, and I slept so deeply.'

But Rachel was up and about by 9.30 a.m. when Laurence called to say he was on his way home. 'He said, "Hi, are you ready?" I said yes and he said, "Do you need anything before I come upstairs?" I said, "No, I'm all set" and he said, "Okay, I love you, I'm coming home."'

But he didn't come home.

The next call Rachel received was from a hospital four blocks away. Laurence had been admitted, the caller said, and Rachel should get there as soon as she could. 'I didn't think anything was wrong – I thought he'd tripped or something,' she says.

Still, she raced to the hospital on Seventh Avenue. As instructed, Rachel went to the discharge desk and asked for her husband. They had no record of Laurence.

'My phone rang again and it was the same woman who'd called before. She asked how long I would be. When I said I was there, she came out and got me and put me in this private room and I knew then it was something bad,' she says. 'Then the doctor came in and told me.'

Laurence had suffered a massive heart attack on the street, just two blocks from his and Rachel's apartment. Nothing could be done to save him. He was fifty-six; they had celebrated his birthday in February.

In an instant, Rachel's world was blown apart. Laurence had had a full medical check-up just four days earlier and had received a clean bill of health. She simply couldn't make sense of it.

'It was impossible to comprehend. Then I had to go and identify him and it was just shocking,' she says. 'The nurse who took me to see him, I felt like she was so jaded from being in New York City. She was also young, so I think she didn't have much experience. I felt like I was telling her what she needed to do: she needed to get me a chair; she needed to hold me.'

Rachel was then left to find her own way home. 'It wasn't like you see on TV where a priest or somebody would come and walk you out and make sure you got into a taxi,' she says. 'They were just like, "Okay, take a left, walk straight ahead, bye," and just pointed me out onto Seventh Avenue.'

Somehow, something kicked in and Rachel made it back to the apartment that Laurence had left only hours before. She started making calls to share the gut-wrenching news – and within hours, all of Laurence and Rachel's friends and family had rallied around her.

Laurence was Jewish, as is Rachel, so there was a seven-day mourning period called shiva, when family members gather in one home to receive visitors.

'It was so overwhelming, the outpouring of love. My apartment was non-stop people from seven in the morning 'til two in the morning. There were so many people at a time,' Rachel says.

There were also other unique memorials that were testament not only to Laurence's quirky personality, but also to the enormous number of people whose lives he had touched. 'Where we practice yoga, they held a class in his honour and they'd never had so many people in a yoga class – there was 150 people or more,' she says. 'We had a meditation for him. People he had worked with stood up to speak. I didn't even know all of these people.'

Barely a day went by that Rachel didn't encounter someone who wanted to share their memories of Laurence. The owner of the neighbourhood pet store, where Laurence was a regular customer even when he didn't have a pet, simply because he believed in supporting small businesses, told Rachel: 'I remember you, you loved your husband hard.'

The local grocery store where Laurence shopped even gave Rachel CCTV footage captured the night before he died, which showed him good-naturedly ribbing a friend – a few precious seconds of silent video that perfectly summed up his personality.

'I'll be outside and people I don't even know will come over to me and say that the neighbourhood will never be the same. He was a peacemaker; a master, master personality,' she says. 'He came to this earth for a purpose. I'll never, ever meet another person like him.'

But while Rachel was humbled by and grateful for the incredible support she received in the days and weeks following Laurence's death, no amount of love could assuage her deep pain. He was her soul mate, and Rachel was utterly devastated by the shocking loss.

'I was just in such a daze. I feel like I've only just recently come up for air. I'm just fragile,' she says. 'I'm still very sensitive to people and noises and lights, and it was never like this before.'

As spring turned into summer in New York, Rachel felt she might never emerge from the fog of sadness that enveloped her. At the same time, however, she knew Laurence would want her to recapture the love of life they had shared – and which he had embodied in everything he did.

Gradually, Rachel started to think about things that might help her start to heal. Little did she know, a potent balm for the soul was already on the way from South Carolina.

And she had four legs and a tail.

The universe is a mysterious entity. It can be catastrophically random and mercurial, as Rachel sadly discovered on that April morning. But it also appears to be rational, at times even kind: delivering what we need at the precise moment we need it, even if we don't realise it.

By June, Rachel had begun to think about getting a dog. She had read studies that showed a four-legged friend could help people cope with grief and its effects, which in Rachel's case included depression, anxiety and post-traumatic stress disorder (PTSD). Her research suggested that poodles made particularly good 'therapists' – and being small and non-shedding meant the breed would also be well suited to life in a Big Apple apartment.

She hadn't yet made any concrete plans to find a canine companion, though. But that was okay, because on 3 June 2017, the universe made those plans for her.

Rachel woke up that Saturday morning to text messages from three different friends, none of whom knew each other. 'They all said the same thing: *Oh my gosh, there's a rescue event happening on 18th Street – go today!*' she recalls.

Just two blocks away, dozens of rescued poodles, as well as other dog breeds and other species, were awaiting adoption. In the United States, it's common for dogs to be transported across state lines in a bid to find loving homes for them. A small group called Carolina Poodle Rescue had brought these dogs to New York from South Carolina. They were one of hundreds of animal welfare groups participating in the three-day adoption drive.

Rachel's first thought when she and two friends arrived at the event was, *There are no poodles here.* Her second was that the scene was one of total chaos. 'The barking and the screaming and the jumping – there was so much going on,' she says. 'It wasn't just dogs – it was kids, families. It was like a circus. It was so crazy and I had such a hard time. I was in such a fog it was amazing I even stayed.'

But she did stay. Rachel approached a volunteer and said, 'I came to look at your poodles – I heard they're good with grief.'

The woman was incredulous. 'She said, "What are you, crazy, lady? It's the second day – we don't have any poodles left!" Everybody in New York wants poodles because they're hypoallergenic and they don't shed,' says Rachel.

She was crestfallen, but she didn't leave. Deep inside, something told Rachel to take a look around anyway. She and her friends walked up and down the rows of crates, each a makeshift home for a dog that needed a forever family.

And then she stopped. She noticed a black and white dog curled up in the furthest corner of her crate. She was underweight and her eyes were clogged with mucous. The sad canine wouldn't even meet Rachel's gaze.

'She just looked so despondent and so depressed. She was rolled up in such a ball in the back of her cage,' she says. 'She couldn't even look at me.'

An index card taped to the front of the crate gave a brief rundown of the forlorn dog's background. She was ten years old and had been found abandoned in an empty warehouse.

'She had been starved, tied up and left. She had been sitting in diarrhoea and dirt for so long that the rescuers thought she was brown and not black. She had also had many, many puppies – my vet said too many,' Rachel says. 'I felt like she sort of said to me, telepathically, *Nobody's going to want me. I've done this before – everybody's going to want a puppy*. She'd given up. I think we recognised ourselves in each other.'

Never having been to an adoption event before, Rachel didn't know that she could ask to take the dog out of her crate and get to know her a little better, so she simply watched her for a while. Eventually, Rachel's friend gently suggested she go and see some other dogs.

'I walked around some more and of course there were so many gorgeous dogs. One of my friends said, "I could see you with this dog," so I took that dog out and I held it,' she says. 'It was really darling, but I put it back and said, "No, I want to go back and see that first dog."'

This time, Rachel did ask to spend some one-on-one time with the dog. She had a feeling the dog was as uncomfortable in the frenetic environment as she was. 'I asked whether there was anywhere quiet I could sit with her. There really wasn't, but we found a corner somewhere,' she says.

Rachel had wanted a petite, non-shedding poodle; this dog was a big, furry labrador mix. Rachel had wanted a lively dog that would help her process her grief; this dog seemed to feel every bit as hopeless as she did. They were all wrong for each other.

And yet Rachel knew they were meant to be together. She just felt it.

'I said to the woman from the rescue, "How does this work? How do I get her?" She said, "You take an application" – she showed me this lengthy booklet I was supposed to fill out – "then you go in this line and you'll be interviewed." It was this whole thing,' she says.

It was a bridge too far for Rachel. She was too brittle; her brain simply didn't work the way it did before Laurence died. She knew she couldn't sit there in that noisy, chaotic room and methodically complete pages and pages of forms. She just didn't have the strength.

'I had gone there really thinking, *I'm just going to look.* I had no idea what I was going to do. There were thousands of people there. All I had was my cell phone in my pocket, my keys, and for some reason I had my credit card. That was it,' Rachel says. 'I don't know why, but I said to this woman, "Do you know who's going to interview me?" She looked at me like I was nuts, but she pointed and said, "That woman right there."'

Rachel approached the woman tasked with interviewing prospective adopters and briefly explained her situation. Then she handed her the sheaf of papers and said, 'I can't fill this out.'

Fortunately, the woman was sympathetic. She sat down with Rachel and started asking her questions, filling out the form for her as they talked. Stored in her phone, Rachel also had a letter from Laurence's long-time therapist, who had become her therapist since his death. The therapist had already signed paperwork (necessary in New York City, where many apartment buildings don't allow pets) stating that Rachel required an emotional support dog. She showed it to the volunteer.

And then, just like that, Rachel had rescued a dog.

'It was the strangest thing when she said this dog was mine and I could leave with her. I have never, ever, ever in my life felt anything like this before, but where my heart is I felt a deep gash,' she says. 'It wasn't painful, but it was either something unzipping – opening me up to more love – or a wound closing. It was so intense.'

The defeated pooch was called Sally Dog, but Rachel knew that wasn't the right name for her. She decided to call her new friend Grace, because she was sure that divine intervention – or rather, *Laurence* intervention – had played a part in bringing them together.

'Without a doubt I think he brought me and Grace together. He was such an animal lover – that was his passion, absolutely,' says Rachel. 'I think the things that Laurence could do for me after he died, he has done.'

Though she felt she was destined to find Grace, their relationship didn't get off to the most auspicious start.

Rachel left the adoption event with a dog and nothing else. Aside from her family pet in childhood, she'd never owned a dog before. All aspects of dog care, from food to vet visits, were entirely foreign to her. Rachel had to go on a crash canine education course, starting immediately.

'We walked home: me, Grace, and my two friends, Jason and Donna. I was in shock; Grace was in shock,' she recalls. 'This poor dog had come all the way from South Carolina, she'd been sitting in a cage, hadn't been to the bathroom, had never walked the streets of New York. We got back to my apartment and Jason was telling me what I needed to do next: "Okay, now we're going to go to the pet store."'

But before Rachel could run out for supplies, Grace relieved herself on the living room floor. 'I've never seen pee like this. I said, "Oh my gosh, did I just adopt a dog or a dinosaur?!"' she laughs. 'While I was cleaning that up, Grace went into the kitchen and went number two on the tiled floor. It was the size of a rhinoceros.'

Grace cowered when she realised what she'd done and Rachel's heart went out to her. She understood in that instant that this dog needed to heal just as much as she did – and she knew she would do whatever it took to help the frightened dog make peace with her obviously traumatic past.

'I think she thought someone was going to hit her, but I looked at her and said, "I'm scared too – don't worry, you'll never need to go to the bathroom indoors again,"' she says.

Rachel didn't sleep much that night. She had struggled with insomnia ever since Laurence passed away, but that night her midnight thoughts were all about her new friend.

Grace barely slept a wink either. She seemed unable to believe her loving new home was real. 'She would quickly run in every fifteen minutes and put her head on the bed to check to see if I was there and breathing – to make sure she wasn't abandoned,' says Rachel.

Finally, Rachel gave in and got out of bed. 'I wanted to make sure I was up early for Grace, to take her for a walk,' she says.

The pair ventured out onto the street, which was now quieter given the early hour, but far from deserted. They don't call New York 'the city that never sleeps' for nothing. Rachel and Grace had been walking for just a few minutes, when Rachel heard someone calling out to her.

She turned and saw a woman approaching. Rachel didn't know the woman, but the lady certainly knew her dog. Incredibly, she was Grace's original rescuer – she was the one who found her in the warehouse and brought her to Carolina Poodle Rescue. Grace had temporarily lived with the woman and her own dog, a large standard poodle, before she was sent out in search of a forever home.

'It was the last day of the animal fair, and in all of New York City, she had parked her car almost in front of my building,' Rachel says. 'She was crying. She had sat and watched us walk for a while and she said that was why she knew to bring Grace to New York that weekend.'

The woman revealed that the rescue hadn't received a single enquiry about Grace for more than six months. 'Everyone had said to her, "Why are you bringing that dog? Nobody's going to want her – bring another poodle." When I asked to look at her everyone was crying and crossing their fingers.'

The woman had her own dog with her, so Grace also had an opportunity to farewell the friend she had been living with before the fair.

It felt like the last page of the book of Grace's former life (although, to this day, Grace has a special affinity with poodles). There would be no more going back. Now, together, she and Rachel would only go forward.

A couple of weeks after she adopted Grace, Rachel loaded her into the car and they drove north to Massachusetts. On the way, they stopped in Connecticut to see Laurence's father, who was very sick in a hospice.

'We barely even knew each other, me and Grace, but she put her head on his bed, just like she'd done with me that first night. She was so loving,' Rachel says. It wouldn't be the last time she marvelled at Grace's empathy and loving energy.

Next, they made their way to Cape Cod. Rachel and her family have a holiday home on the picturesque peninsula that juts into the Atlantic Ocean, 110 kilometres by road from her hometown of Boston.

'It took her a bit to adjust because she was in a new house – I don't know if she thought I was leaving her there. We stayed with my mother and there were so many people and so much love,' says Rachel.

'Grace loved the beach and she liked walking through the marshes, but she didn't like the water. We'd meditate every morning at the beach then come home and she'd sleep all day. We'd go back at the end of the day, around sunset, and practice yoga. That's how we were for almost four months.'

They stayed on Cape Cod all summer, only returning to New York at the end of September. It was the respite they both desperately needed; a quiet period of time and space that allowed Rachel to begin to make sense of her shattering loss, and Grace to transform into the happy, confident dog she deserved to be.

'I didn't notice at first because I was still in such shock, but my mum and brothers and even neighbours were all saying, "This is not the same dog." She had a bounce in her step,' she says. 'She would run all over the house. She would go in at night and check on everybody.'

Just as everyone Laurence came into contact with was uplifted by his natural playfulness and *joie de vivre*, so too has Grace charmed even complete strangers.

One afternoon, Rachel took Grace to a pretty little park near the house. They noticed a man playing frisbee with a group of young adults with intellectual disabilities.

'Grace walks over and gives every single child one lick. It was like, *Hi, I'm Grace,* and then she'd go on to the next child,' she says.

Once Grace had completed her introductions, she and Rachel sat at a picnic table and enjoyed watching the group play. 'One of the boys threw the frisbee and it was a terrible throw. The teacher, in an extremely loving way, made fun of him,' Rachel says. 'The boy started laughing and I swear my Grace started to laugh. I'd never heard her make a sound before. All the kids heard it and they all started cracking up. They all ran over to her and had this loving moment and I just went, *Wow, she is incredible.*'

From the moment she met Grace, Rachel had felt that Laurence had somehow chosen the dog for her. The more she got to know Grace, the more convinced she was.

'She reminds me so much and in so many ways of my husband, like in her love of babies and people. Laurence drank so much water and seltzer; it was his thing. This dog drinks like my husband,' she says. 'Laurence was always peeing. Grace just walks and pees – she doesn't even stop. It's hysterical.

'My husband had the heart of a puppy dog. He was just a magical being. It's just very funny that they're so alike.'

When they returned to New York, Rachel confided her feelings in a friend. 'I said, "Do you think I'm crazy or do you see what I see with this dog?" She said, "No, you're not crazy."'

Back in the city, Rachel and Grace's bond deepened with every passing day. 'We're just so in love and I bring her with me everywhere. I just feel so blessed that I've had the luxury of being able to be with her twenty-four hours a day. I think that's really the magic of us. I'm just here for her 100 per cent.

'She only has, like, two teeth and she has a snaggletooth, but everybody stops to say hi and say how cute she is,' says Rachel. 'She's pretty and beautiful, but she's been through a lot. She has scars and spots where she's been beat up, but everyone wants to talk to Grace.'

In December 2017, millions of people got to see just how special Grace is. Rachel had been to see a movie and took Grace for a late-night walk afterwards, when fate intervened once more.

'It was a beautiful winter night; not so cold. We saw a cute doggy and went to say hi. We just started talking to this man and his dog for a while, maybe twenty or thirty minutes. The guy then said who he was and that he'd love to photograph us,' Rachel recalls.

The chatty dog owner was Brandon Stanton, the photojournalist behind Facebook phenomenon Humans of New York (HONY). Georgia-born Stanton started a project in 2010 with the goal of photographing 10 000 New Yorkers. Shortly after he started, he began adding captions to his portraits. These grew into full interviews, which are known for being poignant and insightful. HONY now has more than 18 million Facebook fans and has spawned three best-selling books. Stanton has also used his platform to raise money for vital humanitarian projects around the world: in 2015 he crowd-funded US$2.3 million in an effort to help end bonded labour in Pakistan.

Though she still finds it difficult to talk about Laurence's passing, Rachel was excited to tell the world about the profound impact Grace was having on her life.

'We met the next day and just sat and talked. Brandon wanted to know more about my story,' she says. 'He's so nice – he's southern and so likeable. He made it so easy.'

Within days of Rachel and Grace's story appearing on HONY's Facebook page, the post had more than 850 000 likes and 21 000 comments, and it had been shared more than 61 000 times.

Some of the commenters shared stories similar to Rachel's – stories of heartbreaking loss and the healing power of an animal's love. She found many of them enormously comforting and was doubly glad she had shared her own journey. 'There's so much pain, but people's stories are so beautiful,' she says.

In another stroke of serendipity – the kind Rachel has started to get used to since rescuing Grace – Stanton mentioned that his wife, Erin, and her dog were a volunteer therapy dog team, visiting with hospital patients. Rachel and Grace had also just been certified as a therapy team – and they'd had the very same trainer as Erin and her canine companion.

It had been the beautiful encounter with the laughing young adults in the Cape Cod park that had inspired Rachel to sign herself and Grace up for the therapy dog program. She knew Grace had some kind of sixth sense that made her able to comfort people who needed it, and she felt strongly that other people deserved to experience it as she had.

But the training program did not go as smoothly as Rachel had hoped.

'When I first saw the application I thought, *They're never going to pick us because I've only known Grace for a short period of time*. One of the first questions they asked was, "Does she know her commands?"' she says.

Trouble was, Grace didn't know her commands. She can soothe a broken heart, but she wouldn't respond to 'sit' or 'stay'. So Rachel stretched the truth a little and said Grace had her commands down pat.

'I fudged and said yes because I knew if I didn't we'd

never be interviewed, and I knew she had so much more to offer,' she admits.

Of course, when the assessment process began, one of the first things tested was Grace's ability to respond to commands. Her failure to do so was met with consternation.

'I thought they were just going to say thank you and goodbye, but the woman doing the test said, "Give me a minute,"' says Rachel. 'She came back and said, "We like you and Grace very much and we've postponed the next training course, so if you can learn the commands in the meantime, you're in."'

Rachel watched a plethora of YouTube training videos and it wasn't long before Grace was following commands like a pro. 'She learned so easily. It was just a miracle,' she says. 'Every day before class I would whisper in her ear, "Grace, if you want this, go for it. It's up to you. If you don't, I'm cool with it – I want you to be happy." And she would just do it. I never even gave her treats.'

Incredibly, Rachel and Grace were assigned to visit with patients at the same hospital where Laurence was pronounced dead. She couldn't help but feel they had come full circle. When she heard the news, Rachel's sister, Jill, remarked, 'A place that was traumatic for you will now be a place where you can help heal others and provide comfort to others. No one was there for you in the hospital, but you can be that peace for someone in need. Grace is a dog angel.'

Rachel, of course, agrees.

When they're not volunteering or charming their fellow New Yorkers, Rachel and Grace can often be found meditating or practicing yoga. Grace also accompanies Rachel to her counselling sessions with Laurence's trusted therapist.

'I always have uplifting mantras playing in the apartment. I think she has really, honestly benefited from all this. Even when I go to see my therapist, she's getting treated too,' she says. 'She's just my everything. I think dogs are just incredible holy beings and they understand so much more than we realise. They feel the energy.'

Some people, perhaps driven by protective instinct, have cautioned Rachel against getting too attached to Grace, concerned that her senior status may mean their time together is short.

But that doesn't matter to Rachel. Whether she has Grace for ten more years or ten more minutes, every moment they spend together is a gift.

'We'll have the best years of her life together. I always tell Grace, "I'm your forever mama and this is your forever home,"' Rachel says. 'And I tell her, "You don't have to worry, you'll never be alone."'

More than a year after Laurence's death, the loss of her beloved husband is still raw for Rachel. She knows the pain will never fully leave her, but having Grace by her side has helped her rediscover the joy of living.

'I'm so in love with her and I never realised that the reason Grace is getting so much better is that I'm giving her so much of myself and so much love. I think that's the reason *I'm* getting better. She has saved me,' she says.

'Her heart and soul are just so pure. She's just so darling. Whenever people stop me and ask, "What is she?" I say, "She's labrador and angel."'

A four-legged angel sent by a man with the heart of a puppy.

DUKE

RESCUED HUMAN: HARPER BROUSSEAU

'Of all the creatures ever made [man] is the most detestable. Of the entire brood, he is the only one . . . that possesses malice. He is the only creature that inflicts pain for sport, knowing it to be pain.'

So wrote the celebrated American author Mark Twain, called 'the father of American literature' by fellow scribe William Faulkner. But Twain, a passionate animal lover, should perhaps also be remembered as one of the most high-profile early proponents of animal welfare.

Fans of his work may have noticed the prevalence of feathered, furred and finned supporting characters in Twain's books and stories, but arguably fewer would be aware that, in real life, he was an outspoken advocate for animal rights. He was staunchly opposed to vivisection (using live animals for scientific experiments) and bullfighting, for example, while a childhood incident in which he killed a bird would foster in him a lifelong loathing of hunting and hunters.

In his 1896 book, *Man's Place in the Animal World,* Twain penned a blistering account of an English earl who killed seventy-two buffalo on a hunting expedition, leaving all but one to rot:

> [T]he difference between an earl and an anaconda is that the earl is cruel and the anaconda isn't; and that the earl wantonly destroys what he has no use for, but the anaconda doesn't.

Jenna Brousseau is well versed in Twain's writings about animals. As a high school English teacher in Glastonbury, Connecticut, she relishes the opportunity to introduce new students to his wonderful words. But his work also resonates on a personal level – particularly the passage about man's capricious brutality and penchant for inflicting 'pain for sport' – because Jenna is a lifelong animal lover, with a special affinity for those less fortunate.

'I love that piece by Mark Twain and I teach it to my students every year. It's all about how we're the worst animals because we rationalise brutality and mistreatment of animals that just want to help us,' she says. 'I really feel that. That's why my family will always, always have rescue animals. They are these gifts from god and they deserve to have beautiful lives.'

But Jenna didn't anticipate the extent to which a scared, abused rescue dog would make *her* life more beautiful, let alone that he would stage a rescue of his own.

Her earliest experience of the profound impact dogs can have on their humans was a formative one. 'As a child I had a dog, a German shepherd named Jax. He was bred to be a show dog but was "not worthy" because his tail had too much of a curl,' she says. 'He died when I was in first grade and after that we never had another family dog. It was just too painful for my father, Larry. He couldn't stand the loss.'

While it was an impression that stayed with her, it didn't dampen Jenna's desire for a pet of her own. Great grief comes from great love, after all – and she knew she had plenty of love to give a four-legged friend or two . . . or three.

At the time she met Eric, the man who would become her husband, Jenna and her mother shared a much-loved cat. When she and Eric moved in together the cat stayed behind, and Jenna missed her feline friend deeply.

Fortunately, Eric was more than happy to open their home to a rescued animal companion. 'I became depressed at not having an animal and Eric encouraged me to get a cat. I had never rescued before, but decided to go that route,' says Jenna. 'Mijo was about eight when I got him and he had been at the shelter for three years. No one wanted him because he was all black and didn't like people. He was VERY afraid of men. He was declawed as an adult and whoever did it botched the job.'

After they married in 2004, the couple were keen to add a dog to their fledgling family. 'We're both from families that love animals – Eric had a golden retriever, Rocky, growing up – so it was just a matter of time,' she says.

Having welcomed Mijo into the fold, there was never any doubt in Jenna's mind that the first official Brousseau family dog would be a rescue. She also knew she wanted a German shepherd or shepherd mix, in honour of her beloved first pet.

Her first port of call was Petfinder.com, the largest pet adoption website in North America. An estimated 25 million dogs, cats and other pets have found new homes via the site since its inception in 1996.

She read about a dog that seemed like it could be a good fit for the household and got in touch with the shelter that was caring for him, the Danbury Animal Welfare Society in nearby Bethel, Connecticut.

Sadly, when she and Eric went to meet the pooch, he wasn't quite what they were looking for. 'We saw about three dogs that were just too hyper. They were running around all crazy and jumping on me,' she recalls. 'We were thinking we were going to start a family at some point, so we were looking for a dog that was a little quieter.'

Disappointed but not deterred, the couple resolved to continue their search. They were just about to leave, dog-less, when a staff member mentioned another dog that had just come in. He was so new the rescue's volunteers hadn't yet had a chance to assess his temperament or write up a profile for the website – but he was a shepherd mix. Did Jenna want to meet him?

Jenna did – very much. 'They said, "We just got a dog yesterday from a shelter down south. We have no idea about his personality yet – we just know he's got shepherd in him,"' she says. 'So he comes outside, leaps around the yard like all the others did, then comes to a screeching halt at my feet.'

She was instantly smitten. 'When he came to that halt, in my heart and soul I thought, *He'll be perfect*. I was like, "That's it – he's the one,"' she says. 'It was the fact that he practiced the most control. There was no doubt we were going to go with him.'

It was 20 August 2006. The dog's name was Duke, he was about a year old and he'd just found his forever family.

Jenna and Eric weren't able to find out much about Duke's background, beyond the fact that he'd wound up in a high-kill shelter in the southern US. 'I don't know exactly where down south he came from, but he was set to be euthanised. Dogs last about ten days in this shelter and if they don't get adopted they're killed,' she says. 'The mentality with animals is that they're almost objectified. They're like objects instead of beings.'

With a population of more than 350 million people, America has a huge problem with stray and unwanted pets, as well as backyard breeding. Up to eight million companion animals enter US shelters every year. The American Society for the Prevention of Cruelty to Animals estimates that around 1.5 million of these are euthanised annually, while the American Humane Association puts the figure at closer to 3.7 million.

The problem is worse in the southern states, where shelters are constantly at capacity and are often forced to euthanise healthy animals because they simply don't have space to house them for longer than a few days. Those quick to euthanise are known as 'high-kill' shelters.

It's not unusual for rescue groups 'up north' to charter enormous transport trucks and ship dogs and cats from southern shelters to local facilities that have more room. That's what happened to Duke – he got a ticket on a transporter to Connecticut in the nick of time.

But while he had escaped death, Duke still bore the scars of his early life. It quickly became apparent to Jenna and Eric that their sweet dog had endured terrible cruelty.

'We knew he had a history of abuse because of his demeanour. It took about three or four months before Duke would even bark,' says Jenna. 'Even when he did start barking he would be so scared that he'd bark with his tail between his legs. He would pee all the time, just out of fear. We don't know anything specific about his past, but the foster carer talked to us and told us about those tendencies.'

Duke's vet echoed those thoughts when Jenna took him for his first post-adoption check-up. 'The vet told us that the first three months of a dog's life is imprinted in their brain. So even though Duke is safe now, that time shaped him the way it does everybody.'

Even now, more than a decade later, reminders of Duke's difficult early days are still apparent. 'If I'm changing the paper towel roll in the kitchen and I have the cardboard tube and I go to throw it in the trash, he'll cower. He definitely had a tough start,' Jenna says.

Despite his sad past, Duke remained eager to please his humans. From day one, Jenna and Eric were blown away by their new four-legged friend's calmness and good behaviour.

'You snap your fingers and Duke's head perks up and he does exactly what you want him to do. He loves us so much that he wants to do nothing but please us,' she says. 'He would have fun leaping around the yard and he could get very playful, but the minute we wanted him to calm down or sit he could sense what we wanted.'

Indeed, Duke seemed to have a sixth sense when it came to tuning in to Jenna and Eric's moods. 'I saw right away that he was a sensitive dog. He was very intuitive,' she says. 'My mum used to say all the time, "He knows he was saved and he's so thankful." It's just this pure, unadulterated love. It's too bad not everyone can experience that.'

In addition to being closely attuned to his owners, Duke also proved to be 'almost excessively obedient'. He slept at the bottom of the couple's bed, never daring to sneak so much as a toenail outside his allotted area. He could be walked without a leash and never stray from Jenna's side.

'I could take this dog anywhere off a leash and know that he will stay by me and listen to me. We do put him on a leash, but it's really for other people, not us. I have zero fear of him running off anywhere,' she says.

Though Duke is a family dog, he shares a particularly close bond with Jenna. 'He's a Mummy's boy. I say to him, "You were born in Mummy's heart,"' she laughs. 'Eric and I, we kind of joke – in the town where we live there's a bridge and I say to Eric, "The day anything happens to Duke you're going to have to talk me off the bridge."'

Duke was right by her side when her beloved grandmother passed away in April 2007, while Jenna was pregnant with her first child.

'I was her only grandchild, so she was like another mother. I got the call early in the morning to go to the hospital and be with her,' she says. 'Duke was the one comforting me. I was kneeling on the floor with my head down and he was just right there next to me.'

And when that child – a son, Matteo – was born a year after Duke's adoption, the gentle dog loved him just as fiercely as he loved Jenna and Eric. 'A lot of people worry that their dogs are going to be jealous of the baby or that there'll be some issues – never, ever did it cross my mind,' says Jenna.

'When we brought Matteo home and he was in the car seat, we just put him on the floor so Duke could walk right up to him. He just sniffed him and kissed him like, *This is my boy*. In hindsight maybe that was a little naïve, but we'd had a year to get to know Duke and love him, day in and day out, and we knew he was living his life for us. It's a beautiful thing.'

Matteo and Duke have been partners-in-crime since the beginning. 'When he started kindergarten, Matteo had to fill out this "getting to know you" sheet and for brothers and sisters he wrote Duke,' she says.

In August 2012, five years after Matteo was born, Duke was just as relaxed about the arrival of another human 'sibling' – this time a sister, Harper. But Jenna didn't fully appreciate just how valuable Duke's calm, collected nature could be until one autumn night later that year.

That night, Duke wasn't calm at all – and the drastic change in his behaviour saved a little girl's life.

Sunday, 7 October 2012 was a big day for the Brousseau family. Baby Harper was just nine weeks old and Matteo was still on a high from his all-important fifth birthday a month earlier. The family had attended a christening earlier in the day, then spent the afternoon celebrating with family and friends at a local restaurant.

By the time night fell, the whole clan was exhausted. Jenna, Eric and Matteo all fell asleep together, with Harper swaddled in her bassinet next to Jenna's side of the bed. Duke, as always, was in the same spot at the end of the bed where he'd slept for the past six years.

'He sleeps at the bottom of the bed unless we call him up to us. He respects boundaries,' Jenna says.

But on this night, the faithful dog seemed determined to push those boundaries. Jenna was just drifting off to sleep when she felt the bed moving. Duke, stealthy yet steady, had crept up the bed and wedged himself between Jenna and Eric.

Desperately tired, in that way that anyone who's ever had a newborn baby will appreciate, Jenna just wasn't in the mood for her dog's uncharacteristically cheeky antics. With a sharp reprimand, Duke was dispatched back to his approved position.

But seconds later, he was back again.

'He kept creeping up between me and Eric or Eric and Matteo. I would snap, and he would want to go back to the end of the bed, but then he'd crawl back up,' she recalls. 'Finally, Eric stood up and snapped at him. He grabbed his collar and dragged him back to the end of the bed. It was a forceful gesture, but in Duke's eyes it was scary. That sent him back to the end of the bed, but then he came up *again*.'

It was completely unlike Duke to be so disobedient but, teetering on the edge of much-needed slumber, Jenna wasn't fully processing the unusual behaviour. Then Eric noticed that Duke was trembling.

'He was shaking like a storm was coming, tail between his legs. Eric is a bit of a hypochondriac at times. We balance each other well – I tend to downplay things, but he's always worst-case scenario,' she says. 'He said, "Jenna, just check on the baby." I remember thinking, *This is ridiculous. I'll check on her, but come on.*'

Jenna turned on the light and leant over to peer into Harper's bassinet – and what she saw chilled her to the core.

'I looked at her and right away I knew something was wrong. Her colour was off. I started screaming, 'The baby, the baby – oh my god, what's wrong?!" she says. 'She was grey. She looked like a doll. It was bizarre.'

Harper wasn't breathing. Jenna plucked her tiny daughter from her bed as chaos broke loose.

'I sort of threw her on the bed and did everything you should not do. I did everything wrong: slapping, thumping her back. I had just been CPR certified but it never even occurred to me to do CPR,' she says. 'Matteo was crying in the corner. Eric was dialing 911.'

After what seemed like hours, Harper took a breath. 'It was probably less than a minute, but the way I remember it, it seems much longer,' says Jenna. 'A lot of the memory I have is from people telling me what happened, because I swear I've blocked it out.'

When paramedics arrived minutes later, Harper was breathing on her own. 'She sort of came to. She was stoic. She hadn't cried yet. I'm not sure if she was in shock or what, but her colour had started to come back by the time the ambulance arrived.'

Harper was rushed to the local hospital regardless, and later transferred to the larger Connecticut Children's Medical Center in Hartford, 30 kilometres from the Brousseaus' home in Portland. There, doctors tried to identify why the little girl had come so close to losing her life.

Their best guess, says Jenna, was that Harper had choked on vomit caused by acid reflux, a common complaint in babies. 'The doctors said that they think a lot of children who die from Sudden Infant Death Syndrome (SIDS), it's actually acid reflux – they choke in their sleep,' she says. 'They did all kinds of tests on her and told us it was reflux and it got caught in time. They ended up calling it an ALTE: apparent life-threatening event. It was an out-of-the-blue, freak occurrence.'

The diagnosis was a shock to Jenna, as Harper hadn't made a sound throughout the entire ordeal. 'I didn't hear choking or anything like that. Needless to say, she slept in her car capsule for three months after that,' she says. 'We ended up moving in with Eric's parents for a while afterwards and we would all take shifts watching her. It was awful.'

If it hadn't been for Duke, Jenna realised, she and Eric would have slept soundly that night, tragically unaware of the danger Harper was in. Her sweet, obedient rescue dog – the one her mother was convinced knew he'd been given a second chance – had returned the favour by saving her daughter's life.

'Duke's behaviour that night was counter to what we had been used to for six years. He is grossly obedient. If he hadn't been behaving so bizarrely, I hate to think about what might have happened,' she says.

She's not sure exactly how Duke knew Harper's life was in jeopardy that night, but she suspects he heard changes in the baby's breathing that she and Eric could not. Dogs can hear noises at a much higher frequency than humans, with an average hearing range of 67–45 000 Hz compared to Homo sapiens' relatively paltry 64–23 000 Hz. Dogs can also hear sounds from four times the distance of a person with average hearing.

A dog's sense of smell is even more powerful. Depending on the breed, canines have up to 300 million scent receptors in their noses, compared to just six million in the human snout. Plus, the part of a dog's brain that analyses smells is forty times larger than a human's. Doctors said Duke may actually have smelled the milky reflux obstructing Harper's airway.

Harper's doctors were as certain as her mother that Duke played a critical role in saving her life. 'When we were telling the doctors what had happened, giving them a rundown of events, they said they were not surprised, because our dogs are so in tune with our breathing patterns,' Jenna says. 'Duke must have been so connected with her breathing pattern that the change set him off.'

The mechanics of scent and hearing aside, Jenna believes there was another, deeper connection at play that night as well: Duke's love for his people, plain and simple.

'It totally makes sense to me. He's so sensitive to begin with. He could sense my pain when my grandmother was dying. It is incredible, but it's understandable,' she says.

And the funny thing is, this amazing thing that *her* dog did served to further cement Jenna's belief that *all* dogs are amazing.

'I want it to be this extra amazing thing because Duke is our dog, but if you think about it, we have dogs in the police force, dogs that sniff out bombs,' she says. 'We have dogs that are leaping out of helicopters! They are brilliant, brilliant animals.'

Harper spent two days in hospital after her ordeal, with Jenna and Eric constantly by her side. While they were busy in Hartford, Matteo and Duke went to stay with Eric's parents, Kevin and Maria.

Duke's 'grandparents' were equally moved by his determination to alert Jenna and Eric to Harper's plight that night. 'I was telling them the story and Kevin put something on Facebook like, "This is Duke, our hero dog – he's the one that saved Harper." If you really want to put it in plain terms, that is what happened,' Jenna says. 'It just blew up after that.'

Local news outlets jumped on the story of the rescued-dog-turned-rescuer, and national and international media swiftly followed. Jenna admits the interest in their beloved dog was at times difficult to cope with.

'The reaction surprised me, and at times it bothered me. People were taking liberties with my story and Harper's story and sensationalising it,' says Jenna of the global response to Duke's life-saving feat. 'I wanted this happy, feel-good story out there, but we'd come home and people's cards would be stuffed in our door. At one point the TV show *The Doctors* wanted me to fly out to California. I was like, "My child almost died. I'm not flying across the country, I'm staying with my family."'

Ultimately, however, the possibility that Duke's story might encourage other families to adopt rescue dogs helped Jenna feel more at ease with the intense scrutiny.

'I was very conflicted at times, but overall I think it's phenomenal. It needs to be out there because there are thousands of displaced animals that need rescuing,' she says.

Frustrated by the widely held misconception that rescue animals are somehow irrevocably damaged by their past, she has used every interview and media appearance to stress her belief that people need to afford second-chance pets the same degree of patience and empathy they would give a child.

'When you have a baby you don't know what you're getting. You can't choose or design your child to make it into some perfect being, yet you deal with the imperfections because somehow your love trumps that,' she says. 'It should be that way with our rescue pets, too. You know you're going to be putting some work into making that animal feel better.'

Harper, now five, of course has no memory of her brush with death – but that hasn't stopped her proudly telling anyone she meets about her devoted dog.

'If someone asks about it she'll say, "My Dukey saved my life." They've been very close since the beginning,' says Jenna. 'Harper will lick an ice cream cone and then give it to Duke and he'll lick it. She shares her French fries with him. I think they would have been close anyway, because it's just how they are.'

Matteo, now eleven, does remember that night – and it forged an even deeper bond between the boy and his dog.

'Harper tells the story, but she was just a baby. Matteo remembers more of it than I do because he was witness to all of it. He's a very sensitive boy anyway. He adores his sister, who's a sassy little thing, but he really loves Duke,' she says. 'He started school and it was a big deal: "He saved my sister, that's my dog, he's my brother."

'I remember sending my dad a picture of Matteo and Duke and my dad text back, "There's nothing like the relationship between a boy and his dog." It's what storybooks are made of.'

In his later years, Duke has also been responsible for saving another life, though not in quite such a dramatic fashion. Jenna's father, Larry, who was so devastated by the loss of her childhood dog, Jax, is now the proud dog parent of a rescue named Ellie. 'My dad says to this day that the only reason they have Ellie is because they fell in love with Duke,' says Jenna.

As for the man himself, Duke is fourteen now and has 'all sorts of grey on his face and his feet'.

'He's still energetic, but it's a little harder for him to get up on or jump of the bed. He'll still leap around the yard, though. God forbid a squirrel should run across our yard. He's very happy. He thinks he's a lap dog and he weighs 22 kilos,' she laughs.

She puts Duke's enduring youthful energy down in part to the arrival of a new young playmate. The Brousseaus rescued Brooks, a pug–beagle mix (known as a puggle), in 2015. Now a spritely four-year-old, he is Duke's polar opposite – every bit as rebellious and impetuous as Duke is compliant and reliable.

'Brooks is definitely *not* obedient. He's such a pain in the butt, but we love him,' says Jenna. 'I think Brooks helps keep Duke a little more youthful. We let them play when we get home and they jump on each other and growl and bark and run around.'

The story of how Brooks came to be rescued by Jenna and Eric is eerily similar to Duke's adoption tale. 'Brooks was literally found on the streets of Hartford and was at the pound and set to be euthanised the next day when another, private rescue came in and got him,' she says.

That rescue was Westley's Wish K9 Rescue, based just over an hour's drive away in Colebrook, Connecticut.

Like many small rescues, Westley's Wish doesn't have its own shelter facility; instead, dogs and cats are looked after by a network of private foster carers while they wait to find new homes. 'They explained to me that when the pound has a dog that they think has really good family potential they'll call the private rescues to see if they have room to foster, and that's what happened with Brooks. He was just hours away from death when Westley's took him.'

Boisterous and attention-seeking he may be, but Brooks is under no illusions about his place in the canine hierarchy. 'He and Duke love each other, but Duke is still number one in this house. He eats first and gets more rides in the car,' Jenna says.

As his 'live and let live' approach to life would suggest, Duke, of course, didn't bat an eye when Brooks arrived.

'Something that I love and appreciate about Duke, and wish I could be more like, is that he's not jealous. Brooks is super jealous – Duke, never,' says Jenna. 'He's just so accepting. He is heaven. He's the love of my life.'

And that brings to mind another Mark Twain pearl of wisdom: '*Heaven is by favour; if it were by merit your dog would go in and you would stay out.*'

Duke is an elderly gentleman now, though he 'still has a lot of life left in him', says Jenna. But when his work on earth is done, there's no question that devoted Duke is heaven bound – for his life-saving deed, certainly, but more importantly for his beautiful, love-filled life.

CLOVE

RESCUED HUMAN: P.J. REGAN

Addiction has been a part of P.j. Regan's life almost as long as dogs have. And it was a very special rescue dog that helped him swap his potentially deadly habits for a natural high – in the most literal sense of the word.

Growing up in Long Island, New York, the Regan family was never without at least one four-legged member. 'Right from the start I was a dog person. We always had one or sometimes two dogs, but they weren't adopted dogs – they were always labradors that we got from breeders,' P.j. says.

'Every single one of them was an amazing dog. I always felt some kind of connection with dogs, right from when I was a young boy.'

But by the time he reached his teens, P.j.'s deep love of dogs had a dangerous rival: a growing dependency on alcohol and hard drugs. 'I've always had a problem with addiction, going back to my teenage years. I've always had an addictive personality,' he says. 'As soon as I was introduced to alcohol and all the drugs it became not just a habit but a lifestyle, and it progressed very quickly.'

His first attempt to get clean and sober came at just seventeen, when he voluntarily spent twenty-eight days in a rehabilitation facility. It worked for a while – and then it didn't. He was back in rehab at eighteen and again at twenty-one.

'I got mixed up with a lot of heroin, crack cocaine, a lot of pills and opiates. It really took me to a very dark place in my life. The way I describe it to people was like a constant sense of doom that I couldn't overcome,' says P.j. 'Addiction is kind of like a cycle: you have a feeling of hopelessness or you're sick when you're not on a drug, and then when you're on the drug it's like you're constantly feeding this thing.

'Unless you start making huge changes in your life, you're doomed.'

After his stint in rehab at twenty-one, P.j. did manage to make those changes – and for five years, it seemed they had stuck. But in 2007, when he was twenty-six, he relapsed.

'Every single relapse I had was worse and worse, but my relapse in 2007 actually put me out on the street. I was homeless for quite some time,' he says. 'Unfortunately with addicts, if you're not constantly doing something for your recovery, if you're not moving forward, you're sliding backwards.'

He went into rehab again, and when he emerged after the twenty-eight days, P.j. felt good. He was in a relationship and got a job as a veterinary technician, which he loved. The work was interesting and fulfilling, but more importantly it meant he got to spend his days with dogs.

'At the vet hospital we worked very closely with some local shelters, doing low-cost spaying and neutering. Some of those dogs would be brought in because of neglect and abuse,' he says. 'We would give them whatever medicine they needed to help them get adopted.

'I grew up with dogs that were well taken care of and I saw the other side – I guess the dark side – of what dogs go through. Kind of immediately I felt a connection with these dogs that were coming in, because of my own history.'

He wished he could adopt a dog in need, but P.j. didn't think it was a good idea – he needed to focus all his energy on his newfound sobriety, after all. He had to be sensible.

Then, at the end of 2008, he met Princess – and sensible went right out the window.

Princess was a pit bull, about eight years old, and she had arrived at the shelter in a terrible state, with a laundry list of ailments that meant she didn't have long to live. When he met her, P.j. knew he couldn't let her spend her remaining days alone and unloved, without a family to call her own.

'Princess was the name she came with, but she really *was* a princess. She was a great dog. All of her health problems were because of abuse and neglect, but she was my first taste of the resilience that dogs can have,' he says. 'Even when they've been through so much, they can bounce back – maybe not physically, but definitely in an emotional or trust sense.'

Princess moved in with P.j. and his then-girlfriend just before Christmas, and the couple made sure she was thoroughly spoiled. 'She got a ton of presents and a warm home to live in. It was a great Christmas that year. It was all about her.'

Sadly, Princess was very sick and passed away in January 2009. P.j. commemorated their 'short but beautiful journey' together by having her paw print tattooed on his arm. 'She ended up living only three more months after I adopted her because of all the diseases, but they were an amazing three months,' he says.

Their time together also shattered the prejudices P.j. held about pit bulls.

'Honestly, I had some preconceptions about the breed, with the media hype and all the stories that circulate,' he says. 'Princess was with me for a very short period of time, but she showed me a lot about the breed. She gave me a different experience of pit bulls and opened my eyes up. I really fell in love with the breed.'

Still, P.j. and his partner decided not to adopt another dog right away. Their time with Princess has been wonderful but intense, and her death – while expected – had hit them harder than they had anticipated.

But then, in February 2009, a pit bull called Emmalene appeared at the vet hospital – and once again the sensible path didn't seem so sensible after all.

'It was the same scenario: Emmalene came into the hospital via the local shelter, but unlike Princess she was a puppy. She had this crazy leg. We didn't know whether it was caused by neglect or malnutrition, but it turned out like a duck leg, almost like a flipper,' says P.j. 'She was just going to go back to the shelter after we checked her out in the hospital, but I fell in love with her. I thought, *She's going to have a lot of trouble getting adopted.* We were just going to take her home for the weekend, but she ended up being a permanent resident.'

Just as he had with Princess, P.j. doted on Emmalene. Unfortunately, after two years of sobriety, in late 2010 P.j's demons started to get the better of him once more. But while his 2007 relapse had left him homeless, this time he was determined to get the help he needed before he lost everything.

'Having been through a handful of rehabs, nothing changed. I did the twelve-step programs, I took all the suggestions that were given to me, but nothing ever worked,' he says. 'Doing a 28-day rehab is great, but you've got to really follow through. I knew I needed something different.'

P.j. made a big decision: he would enter rehab for eighteen months.

'I went into a long-term facility for addiction of my own accord. With addiction, it's constant vigilance every day to stay on top of it. It was about trying to break a cycle of repeated behaviour,' he explains. 'You think of eighteen months as a long time in your life, and it is a pretty decent chunk, but I looked at it like an investment: the time and energy that I'm putting in now is going to result in some kind of sustained recovery.'

But while he knew it was his best shot at conquering his addictions, the choice to spend a year and a half in rehab was by no means an easy one. For one thing, it meant the end of his relationship. It also meant P.j. had to say goodbye to his beloved Emmalene.

'It was incredibly hard,' he says. 'I left that situation not knowing if I was ever going to come back or see Emmalene again.'

Life in rehab was no picnic either. For the sake of his own recovery, P.j. was completely cut off from everyone he loved for the duration of his stay at the facility.

'It was almost like a boot camp. You go in there and they kind of take away all your adult privileges. They told us, "You can't have any contact with family or friends, we're going to tell you what to do and when to do it, you'll go to these certain things every day, these are the only people you can talk to, this is the only free time you're going to have,"' he says.

He had the option of throwing in the towel and leaving any time he wanted. But he didn't. 'They break you down to begin with and then give things back to you little by little.'

It was in rehab that P.j. had his first taste of the healing power of nature. 'There was a large field in the backyard of the facility and I would go there and just sit. I'd kind of tune in but also tune out a little bit and really immerse myself in where I was,' he recalls. 'I would sit with my thoughts and the birds chirping and the geese coming up on the lawn. That was the first time I really experienced total presence in where I was.'

The only thing missing, he felt, was a canine companion by his side.

But that was okay. She would be there soon enough.

P.j. left rehab in October 2012 after completing the full eighteen months. His return to 'real life' was both a homecoming and a clean slate.

'The rehab was on Long Island, not far from where I lived, but I more or less returned to society anew. I really started fresh in every sense,' he says.

The same month, Hurricane Sandy slammed into America's eastern seaboard; at the time, it was the second-costliest hurricane on record in the United States. The storm caused particularly severe damage in New Jersey and New York State, destroying countless homes and buildings and leading to a long period of rebuilding.

The metaphor was not lost on P.j. as he faced the daunting prospect of rebuilding his life from the ground up.

'It wasn't like the rehab facility kicked me out the door and said, "Good luck." They introduce you back into the real world gradually,' he says. 'There was a point towards the end of the stint where you could get a job. If you had availability of a vehicle you could start driving again. You could go out for one day on the weekend.'

Nonetheless, when he first left the facility he felt a little bit like a toddler learning to walk. 'In a lot of ways I was prepared, but in a lot of ways I wasn't – like being back in those social settings and trying to learn how to support myself and live in an apartment.'

He got a job – actually, he got a few – and moved in with his best friend. But it was a relatively short-lived period of stability. In June 2013, his friend decided to move in with his girlfriend. P.j. couldn't afford to remain in the apartment on his meagre earnings, so he began hunting for a new place to live.

He was in a relatively precarious situation, and the last thing on P.j's mind was adopting a dog – but as Princess and Emmalene had proved, that didn't mean much.

'I was in this mad scramble to find an apartment. I was working odd jobs, including walking dogs for a local rescue group, making cash here and there,' he says. 'I was spending a lot of time on the internet looking for jobs and I was on Facebook one day. I'd started following a lot of rescue groups over the years, just by being involved in rescue and with dogs. I was scrolling through and I saw this face pop up on my screen.'

The face belonged to a blue brindle pit bull – and she looked terrified. 'She was very timid looking, with cropped ears, and she was very skinny. She had this look in her eyes that just looked right at me,' he says.

'I used to see a million dogs every day between working for this rescue group and running an internet support group for dogs looking for homes, but for some reason this dog stuck out.'

Against his better judgement, and in spite of the fact that he didn't know where he'd be living the following week, P.j. felt the hand of fate reach out, just as it had when Princess and Emmalene had barrelled into his life. 'I had to meet this dog,' he says.

Some quick sleuthing revealed that the dog was being evicted from the apartment where she was currently in foster care because the homeowners' association had discovered she was a pit bull – and unlike P.j, they apparently weren't interested in challenging their perceptions of the breed.

In short, the dog needed another foster care placement immediately.

Frightened, unsure what the future held and about to become homeless himself, P.j. could relate. He got in touch with Diane Indelicato from Ruff House Rescue, the private rescue group that was looking after the forlorn pooch. He was upfront about his situation.

'I said, "I don't have an apartment right now that allows dogs, but I'm going to find one and I want to foster this dog." Diane said, "Okay, we're in such a jam right now that if you can find an apartment we'll work with you,"' P.j. says.

The dog's name was Clove and the rescue thought she was about two years old. Still not at all sure how he was going to provide a home for a rescue dog, P.j. nevertheless jumped in his car and drove to meet her at the apartment she was about to be turfed out of.

Unfortunately, their first encounter did not go well. 'Clove hid in the other room the entire time. She was eventually coaxed into where I was, but she definitely wasn't happy to see me,' he says. 'She lay on the ground with her belly up and looked in the other direction. She wouldn't even look at me.' The belly-up position was a submissive posture that signified Clove's fear.

Though P.j. left the meeting feeling 'a little disenchanted', he also hoped he'd get the chance to spend more time with Clove. But as the days passed, he didn't hear from anyone at Ruff House Rescue.

In the meantime, he found an apartment in the Long Island village of Port Jefferson. 'It was somebody's back porch in the house they were renting. It was six hundred dollars a month and there was no heat,' he says. 'It was pretty terrible.'

But it was his and, importantly, it was pet friendly. As P.j. moved his belongings into his new abode, his parents gave him one of the large crates they had used for their beloved labradors – just in case.

'I didn't think I was going to hear back about Clove. I thought maybe the foster carer would report back to Diane that the meeting didn't go so well,' he says. 'A week or two had lapsed and I thought maybe somebody else took her and they didn't need my help anymore.'

He tried not to feel too disappointed. Perhaps Clove just wasn't the four-legged friend for him. Besides, it probably wasn't the best time to rescue a dog anyway. P.j., still fresh out of rehab, was taking his sobriety one day at a time.

Then, the day after he moved in to his new place, P.j's phone rang at 10.30 p.m. It was Diane.

'She said, "Do you have an apartment that you can keep dogs at?" I said I did and she said, "Can you pick up Clove right now? She's in Oyster Bay."'

Oyster Bay was about an hour from P.j.'s apartment and it was late at night, but there wasn't time to worry about that.

'The other dog at the foster home is attacking her, so she needs to be picked up immediately,' Diane explained.

Once again, P.j. got in his car and raced to meet Clove. He arrived to find a scared dog and an emotional foster family. 'The family had only had her a few days but they were very emotional to see her go, and I think they had their doubts about who Clove was going to. It was late and I looked dishevelled. I've got tattoos. I'd bought a car for about six hundred bucks and I rolled up in this well-to-do neighbourhood in this car that's falling apart.'

For her part, Clove seemed equally dubious about the stranger who had come to rescue her. 'It looked like she was having a tough night. She got into the car and she wouldn't even look at me,' says P.j.

Despite Clove's apparent trepidation, P.j. sensed somehow that something important had begun. 'I remember looking back at her and saying, "This is it,"' he says. 'I had no idea why I said that or what it meant – what "it" was going to be or where it was going to take us.'

Because if P.j. had any inkling that night of where he and Clove were going to go together – and the ways in which she was going to rescue him – he would never have believed it.

*

In his soul, P.j. knew he and Clove were in it for the long haul. Clove, however, took a little more convincing.

'I took Clove home, let her walk around the backyard a little bit. She went inside and lay on the floor,' he recalls. 'She jumped up on the bed for a short period of time and let me pet her, but right after she jumped off. It was a rough night, but I knew she was home.'

He may not have recognised it on a conscious level to begin with, but P.j. also knew that Clove would be an important part of his recovery. Though he felt confident in his ability to stay away from drugs and alcohol after eighteen months in rehab, every weapon in his recovery arsenal was crucial.

'It had been nine months since I left rehab, but I still considered myself to be in early recovery,' P.j. says. 'This was the first time I had my own dog to myself; the first time I was taking in an animal on my own accountability. She was something that was going to keep me accountable with my recovery.'

He had rescued Clove, sure – but P.j. also knew that he was in debt to her. He was asking a lot of his new four-legged friend and he knew he owed her the good life, the patience and understanding, she had been denied so far. He was determined to fulfil his obligation to this creature that had been an afterthought all her life, starting immediately.

'My first idea was to bring her somewhere where she could meet other dogs and see other people, and maybe she would come out of her shell a little bit,' he says. 'The next day I woke up bright and early and took her to the dog park.'

As P.j. had expected, Clove was indeed hesitant at first. As the dog park regulars cruised over to check out the newcomer, Clove cowered. She growled and barked, with her tail clamped firmly between her legs. After a little while, however, she started to loosen up.

'She would run off with the other dogs, then she'd run back near me. She'd had a lot of different homes, so maybe she was worried about permanence,' says P.j.

He decided to see what would happen if they ventured a little further afield. They were in the fenced 2-acre off-leash area in Blydenburgh County Park, but dogs are permitted on leash throughout the 627-acre park.

Located at the head of the Nissequogue River, the thickly forested park offers hills, valleys and a manmade lake fed by the river's headwaters. It's perfect exploration territory for a man and his dog.

'I'd never done any kind of nature walks, never hiked before, but I decided we'd do a little walk through the park. What I recognised was that Clove loved it. She got so excited. She was rolling around in the grass. It was like she felt a sense of freedom,' he says. 'For the first time she was wagging her tail and looking back to me with her tongue hanging out and that pit bull smile. That kind of set the tone for what we'd be doing for the next year or so.'

From that day on, P.j. and Clove set out to 'hike everything that possibly could be hiked or walked on Long Island, which isn't a lot,' he says. 'It's very flat and there isn't much to it, which is fine – there's beauty to walking in the woods.'

And every time they went walking, their connection deepened. 'Every single time we'd go on a walk we'd do a little exploring and I noticed that our bond became stronger and stronger. She went from not even looking at me to being attached to my hip twenty-four-seven,' says P.j.

He could see that she trusted him more every day. 'She always kept me within eyesight. She would run up 50 yards, but then stop and look back and wait for me. I think that says a lot about letting me into her circle.'

At the same time, P.j's recovery went from strength to strength. He swapped odd jobs for a permanent position as a laboratory courier. He upgraded his car and moved to a nicer apartment, where he and Clove still live.

They were rescuing each other.

Though she had blossomed in his care, P.j. was aware that Clove still bore the painful scars of her past. The closer they got, the more he found himself wishing he had a greater understanding of her background.

'I really wanted to learn what she went through because it obviously affected her a lot,' he says. 'To this day she has a real fear of men. She'll walk up to any woman and say hello, but when it comes to men she'll hide between my legs. Sometimes she'll even growl.'

P.j. decided to do a little digging. He got back in touch with Ruff House Rescue, which in turn put him in touch with the pound in Clayton County, Georgia, that Clove had initially been brought to. He learned that she had been removed from a property in Georgia along with several other dogs.

'There were two theories as to what actually happened,' he explains. 'Some were saying it was a property that was used for dog fighting. Others were saying the person who owned the property was abusing these dogs and ended up being arrested and taken off the property, and the dogs were left there.'

Whatever the true story, Clove's early life was clearly marked by violence and cruelty. 'She's got a lot of scars on her, especially around her ears and neck – they're definitely bite wounds. She's also got a few slashes on her legs. I'm not sure what they are, but to this day they still stand out,' says P.j.

Clove was taken to Clayton County Animal Control, a county-run pound in Jonesboro, Georgia, with a high rate of euthanasia. As with many local government-run shelters, the facility advertises impounded animals on its Facebook page in the hope that either their owners will reclaim them or rescue groups will take them into foster care with a view to adoption. Dog-loving members of the public are also able to pledge donations to contribute to rescue groups' transport and veterinary care costs. If animals aren't claimed one way or another within a designated time period – usually a week, but it differs from county to county – they are put to sleep.

So it was for Clove. The other dogs she had arrived with were quickly taken out of the shelter by rescue groups, but Clove and her sister, Effie, were left behind. Clove was scheduled for euthanasia on 12 January 2013.

As he read through the Facebook posts about Clove, P.j. was shocked to realise how close she had come to dying in that shelter.

'All these people were pledging money to take Clove off the euthanasia list and then she was being put back on it,' he says. 'She was pledged to be taken off, then put back on, then pledged again.'

Finally, Ruff House Rescue stepped in and offered to take both Clove and Effie (who, P.j. later discovered, were named after characters in *The Hunger Games* novels). Based in Freeport, New York, Ruff House Rescue has saved more than 6000 homeless pets since its inception in 2009.

'It's amazing, Clove's journey and all the people who've played a part in where she is today. It's like a cast of hundreds,' says P.j.

Learning about Clove's past further strengthened the bond P.j. felt with his resilient rescue dog. It was almost as if she was his canine counterpart: working hard every single day to make peace with the past and forge a brighter future.

'I've never had any history of abuse or anything like that, but both Clove and I came from a rough start in life. I held on to a lot of resentments, not only for things that I did myself, but things that involved other people,' he says. 'I realised we were on this journey together to put aside those resentments and find forgiveness for whatever happened in the past. For Clove to put that aside and trust after everything she's been through . . . it's become almost like a spiritual journey together.'

And nature, P.j. now understood, was a key part of that journey for both of them. In their walks in the parks and woods of Long Island, they had both begun to heal.

Now it was time to take that healing to the next level.

P.j. woke up on Wednesday, 17 February 2016, feeling antsy. It was his thirty-fourth birthday, he'd been out of rehab now for longer than he'd been in and he wanted to push himself out of his comfort zone.

'I think in a lot of ways I was stagnating in my recovery and I needed a little push, something new to keep me on this journey that really never ends,' he says. 'I was going through a breakup and it was an emotional period of my life. I woke up and said, "We need to do something different."'

As part of his job, P.j. frequently drove to the northeastern reaches of New York State, home to stunning wilderness including the Adirondack, Appalachian and Taconic Mountains. He was fascinated by the spectacular mountain vistas. 'I would see these mountains and have a sense of awe, but it was like, *Oh, I'll probably never go there*,' he says.

That day, however, he would. 'I said to Clove, "Let's just drive north. Let's see what there is up there."'

The pair drove four hours to the Bash Bish Falls State Park in the Taconic Mountains, tucked into the corner where New York State, Massachusetts and Connecticut meet. Then they simply started walking.

'I didn't follow any trail, but it was that sense of being in the mountains that really caught me. We just started exploring. It was an eye-opening experience,' says P.j. 'I might as well have been dressed for climbing Everest with the amount of clothes I had on, though. Within two minutes I was sweating and trying to catch my breath.'

Attire issues aside, P.j. knew immediately that this was something he and Clove were going to continue.

'Clove loved it. She was running around like crazy, sprinting up on these boulders. I was like, "You know what? This is our new thing. This is what we're going to do,"' he recalls. 'We were expanding the little bubble we'd been living in for the past two years. I think a new addiction started, really.'

That weekend, they went to the Hudson Valley and climbed Schunemunk Mountain. At 507 metres, it is the highest peak in Orange County, New York – and P.j. felt every last step.

'The entire time I was sweating and heaving, trying to catch my breath. My legs were killing me. My knees were screaming. Clove was in the same boat with me,' he says. 'But when we got to the top of that mountain, the view was jaw-dropping. I couldn't believe what was in front of me.

'I had told myself I didn't have the time to drive for six hours to make day trips to the mountains – that all went out the window.'

Before long, P.j. and Clove had thoroughly explored the Hudson Valley, the Catskills, the Adirondacks and the White Mountains of New Hampshire. They hiked come rain or shine, in soaring heat, biting wind and bone-chilling cold. They even braved snow and sleet, with P.j. ensuring Clove was always happy and well protected against the elements.

He quickly became passionate about researching and planning every aspect of their hikes.

'Planning is half the excitement. Every single time we do these hikes it's a learning experience, and a lot of research goes into where we're going,' P.j. laughs. 'I went into this whole lifestyle with no experience whatsoever and I kind of dived right into it. I wanted to learn everything about it, getting all this special gear for Clove, different treats, making sure her paws are protected.'

In the summer of 2017 they made it across the country to hike the trails and mountains of the western states, culminating with an ascent of Colorado's Mount Elbert that August. At 4401 metres, it is the tallest summit in the Rocky Mountains and the second highest in the contiguous US – quite literally an enormous step up from the comparatively small peaks the pair started out hiking a little over a year earlier.

Their Mount Elbert excursion was a little bit terrifying, P.j. admits.

'We got some of the scariest weather I've ever experienced in my life on top of Mount Elbert. We got caught in an electrical storm. There was such an electrical charge that Clove's hair was standing straight up,' he says. 'I've had some frightening moments on hikes, being concerned for her, but this was like, *Wow*. I was like, *Hit the decks!*

'It is the highest point in America that a dog is permitted to stand [the others are in national parks, where dogs aren't allowed]. Clove was the tallest dog in the country that day.'

There is no doubt in his mind that Clove loves their wild adventures every bit as much as he does.

'Clove always turns and looks back at me and I see joy on her face when she's running down a trail or climbing up a tough section of a mountain,' says P.j. 'She has a sense of pride like, *I did this!* I think she is experiencing life to the fullest.'

At the same time as P.j. and Clove were pushing themselves and testing their limits, the wider world was also taking notice. P.j. had an Instagram account that he used mostly to share pictures of Clove and their walks in the woods, as well as posts about breed awareness.

But as their hikes grew ever more ambitious – and the photographic evidence became ever more spectacular – P.j.'s Insta-audience grew. When pit bull mythbusting account @spreadtherumer shared a post about Clove, it caught the eye of animal lovers' website The Dodo. The site, which boasts more than 20 million page views per month, made a short video about P.j. and Clove's mutual rescue that promptly went viral.

P.j.'s Instagram account, @thebullhikes, now has more than 60 000 followers. He has been able to use his growing profile to raise money for animal welfare causes, including a $25 000 corporate grant for Ruff House Rescue.

'When we first started hiking mountains, Instagram was just a collection of our pictures. You know: "We hiked this mountain and took this trail." Not too much detail about the feelings that went along with it,' says P.j. 'At that point I wasn't really comfortable sharing too much about the emotions that came out of the hikes. It was "Here's a picture of a pretty sunset" and that's it.'

Over time, however, P.j. has become more comfortable sharing details about his past struggles with addiction, his ongoing recovery and the healing power of nature. He often posts about the many ways his rescue dog helped to rescue him.

'It's turned more into the emotional side of things that comes with hiking. A lot of the time when I'm hiking I'm thinking; they call it walking meditation. My main focus is really to stay present in what I'm doing. I've learned to share that with the world.'

And it really is the world – people have reached out to P.j. via Instagram from every corner of the globe. 'I think people see a lot of hope and positive affirmation from the things that I share. It's become something so much bigger,' he says.

'It's not about the followers or any kind of fame. I realised this could do a lot of good for rescue and the breed, but also maybe people who are struggling with addiction or mental illness. Part of recovery is giving back and if this can help somebody, that's the most important thing to me.'

Instagram even led to love for P.j. He met his girlfriend, Rachael, via the platform in 2017. Now he and Clove are often joined on their hikes by Rachael and her rescued pit bulls, Dahli and Terzo.

P.j. has now been sober for more than seven years. It is his longest period of recovery since his first stint in rehab in 1998 and he has no doubt that his four-legged fellow adventurer has been integral in keeping him on the right path. He celebrates Clove's birthday on his sober date, 10 April.

'It's been a slow process. I'm not going to say it's been a smooth road: there have been a lot of bumps, but it's been a steady journey of improvement,' P.j. says. 'I think Clove has been probably the most important influence on my recovery to date. I don't know if I would have ever gotten into the outdoors and started using nature as an outlet without her.'

P.j. has, of course, considered what a life without Clove would mean for his recovery. She's about seven years old now, fit and healthy and showing no signs of slowing down. In 2017, she had surgery to remove mast cell tumours. Her prognosis is excellent, but they will likely return at some point. There will inevitably come a day when P.j. has to take to the trails without his best friend. What then?

'My best friend is a realist. We're the only two who went to rehab who are still sober of the hundreds that went through it during the time we were there. He came to me with a question. He said, "What happens if something happens to Clove? Are you going to be okay?"' says P.j.

'As much as I have to consider that, I'm a man of the present. I'll cross that bridge when I come to it. I want to show Clove so much of the world and the time that we share together, we live to the fullest. That's what matters most to me.'

Today, P.j. is thinking only of his tenacious rescue dog and their next mountain adventure. It's a life he never could have imagined for himself when he was in the depths of his addiction.

'Seven years ago, when I was battling addiction, I was locking myself in a basement apartment for days on end.

The only time I would leave the apartment would be to get a fix or meet my dealer or walk up to the gas station to buy beer,' he says. 'I lived such a sheltered existence for so long, almost like a prison. Clove also lived a life of uncertainty.

'If you had told me then that I'd be hiking mountains with an amazing rescue dog, I would have laughed in your face to think that my life would've got to this point. It's wild if you think about it.'

And now P.j. and Clove are wild and free – together.

BRIAN

RESCUED HUMANS: DEBBIE AND GEORGE PATEK

The life of Brian is the stuff of a Hollywood blockbuster. It's a rollercoaster of emotion, a tale of humble beginnings, triumph over extreme adversity, high-octane heroism, and indomitable pit bull smiles. Above all, Brian's is a story about the redemptive power of unconditional love. You'll laugh! You'll cry! You'll definitely need tissues.

And if Brian's life story is the main attraction, the prequel is Debbie Patek's unwavering love of animals. Debbie, who lives in Wollongong, a seaside city 90 kilometres south of Sydney, has never been able to turn her back on an animal in need – not even when her own safety has been at risk.

Without Debbie and her husband George's shared drive to be a voice for the voiceless, without their refusal to turn a blind eye to the mistreatment of pets, there would be no Brian.

And without Brian, there would almost certainly be no Debbie.

Animals have been a part of Debbie's life for as long as she can remember. Growing up, the family pets were a succession of dachshunds – her German-born mother's way of maintaining her connection to her homeland after immigrating to Australia in 1952.

As an adult, Debbie has had several much-loved dogs and cats; she still keeps the ashes of those that have passed away on her mantelpiece. All of her canine and feline companions have been rescues. Often Debbie has adopted them from pounds and shelters, but sometimes they simply turn up. It's as if they know she's an ally: a safe haven from whatever awful circumstances they're leaving behind.

Max the poodle was a pound pooch. Debbie and George rescued him from Liverpool Animal Shelter, the animal holding facility for Liverpool City Council in Sydney's western suburbs. He was in a pitiful state when the couple brought him home.

'He was all matted. He sort of had Bob Marley hair, but I cleaned him up and he turned out to be the best dog. I could walk him up Parramatta Road (Sydney's major east–west arterial road) without a leash,' she says. 'God, he was a good dog.'

Max lived life on his own terms. He tolerated the other dogs Debbie and George rescued during his lifetime, but he let the interlopers know in no uncertain terms that he was in charge. When an elderly Dobermann moved in, for example, Max set firm boundaries.

'She used to live next door to us at our previous house, but she kept escaping her house and coming over to our place,' says George. 'Debbie started walking her and once she started that, the owner could never keep the dog in. He changed the locking mechanism that many times, but she'd still find her way over to us. The guy was going to put her down, but we said no and ended up having her for another three years.'

The dog, Tequila, was unwell and nearing the end of her life when Debbie and George took her in – but Max was unsympathetic. 'She was skinny and really old and had one tooth. Her arthritis was that bad that I'd have to stand her up and warm her joints so that she'd unstiffen and could go to the toilet,' George says. 'She'd bark in the middle of the night, wanting to come inside, but Max wouldn't let her in the house.'

Even when Max became blind and deaf, he remained the king of his castle. 'We had to move house when he was blind, which we didn't really want to do. We thought it was going to be hard on him but he did a grid search – he'd go sideways and longways, mapping the new house.'

Max was about eighteen when he died at home in 2005. 'He was looking up at the sky like he could see something, then he just took a big, deep breath and put his head down and that was it,' George recalls. 'His tail was still wagging right up until his last day.'

Though devastated by his loss, Debbie and George were heartened to see that Max's passing allowed their other rescue dog, Brian, to blossom. Though they had lived

Traumatic brain injury survivor Janaye Kearns wanted a dog she could train to carry out mobility assistance tasks. She never imagined that Colt would also instinctively alert her to imminent seizures, regularly saving her life. *(Janaye Kearns)*

Rachel Jacobs was devastated when her adored husband, Laurence, died suddenly. Senior dog Grace had all but given up on life after being abandoned. Together, they are rediscovering joy. *(Rachel Jacobs)*

Clove the pit bull trusted no one after a lifetime of abuse and neglect. Newly sober, P.j. Regan wasn't sure he could trust himself to build a life without drugs and alcohol. So they put their faith in each other – and in the healing power of nature. *(P.j. Regan)*

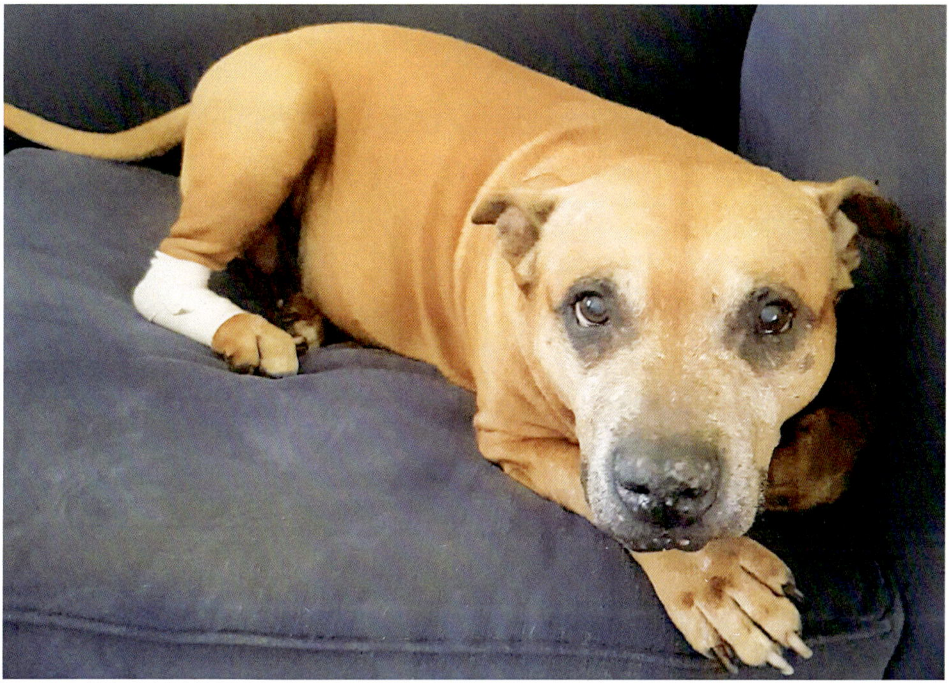

Plucked from cruelty by Debbie Patek and her husband, George, Brian the Staffy didn't think twice about putting his own life on the line to save Debbie's. *(Debbie and George Patek)*

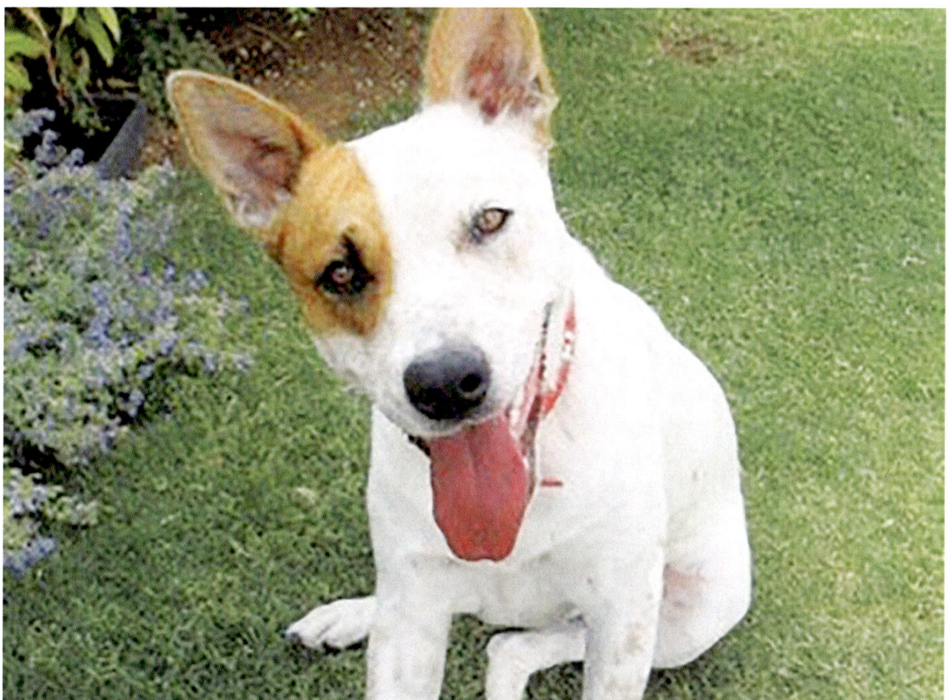

When Sue Pethick fell and became stranded on a cliff face, it was loyal rescue dog Abby that raised the alarm. *(Sue and Mike Pethick)*

Nobody knows for sure how two-year-old Alexander Kenney tumbled into a dam on a rural property – but what is certain is that his beloved canine companion, Leala, saved his life.
(Jodie Grevengoed, Leeboo Photography)

TRG

Tiny Teddy helped nurse his doting owner, Andy Szasz, back to health after a battle with cancer – and when Andy clung to life in a coma, Teddy was there to save the day a second time. *(Andy Szasz)*

Her childhood rescue dog, Tammy, taught Debra Tranter a powerful lesson in loyalty. Decades later, a rescued poodle named Oscar helped Debra save thousands of dogs from appalling mistreatment.
(Debra Tranter)

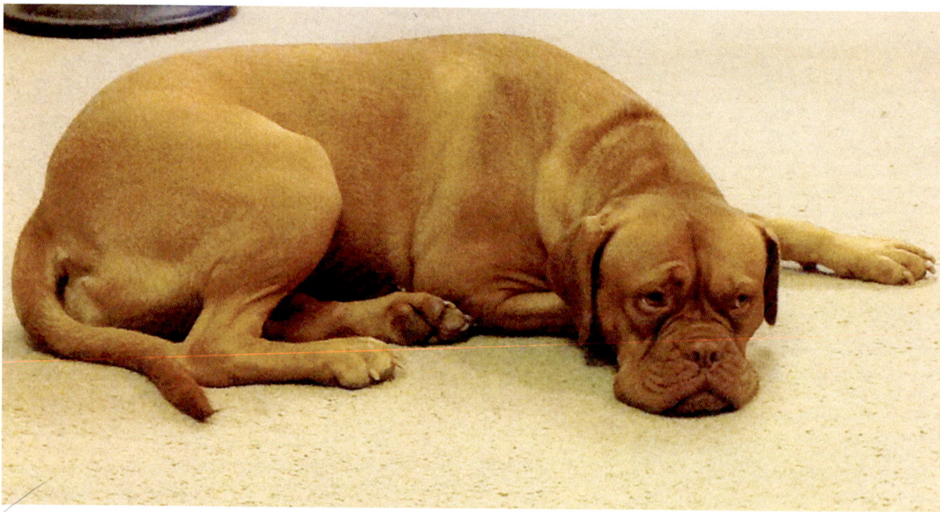

Trish Borg's life has been saved by rescue dogs not once, but twice. Just days after being adopted by the Borg family, devoted mastiff Rhianna fought off two dangerous assailants. *(Trish Borg)*

Sick and frail when saved from a backyard breeder by Judy Scrivener, Buddy the labrador saved Judy and her disabled son from a terrifying blaze. *(Judy Scrivener)*

Caesar the tracking dog wasn't trained to sniff out mines on the battlefields of Vietnam, but he did just that – saving the lives of his Australian handler, Peter Haran (right), and a dozen other soldiers. *(Peter Haran)*

A shocking motorcycle accident left Mike Turner with debilitating injuries and crippling depression. It took an exuberant rescue dog called Caoimhe to help him smile again.
(Mike Turner)

Battling severe PTSD and thoughts of ending his life, Steve Warwick couldn't see how getting a dog would make any difference to how he felt. But he didn't get just any dog. He got Sarge Kester. *(Steve Warwick)*

under the same roof for about six months, Brian had always been deferential to Max – the ageing poodle insisted on it.

'Max wasn't very tolerant of Brian and he would try to bite him. He actually bit Debbie once, thinking she was Brian,' says George. 'Until the end of Max's life, Brian never tried to be dominant. He knew that Max was an old dog and that Max and Tara, the cat, were the bosses and so he just left them alone.'

Brian's live-and-let-live approach to his cantankerous housemate is testament to his relaxed nature. Perhaps he forgave Max's grouchiness because he was simply grateful to have a loving family and a safe place to call home – after all, Brian had endured far worse in his young life than a snappy older sibling.

Brian was just fourteen months old when the Pateks rescued him in 2005, but he had already had two homes. Debbie doesn't know much about the first home – just that Brian's owner was a single mum with two young children who found the needs of a puppy too tough to manage – but she knows plenty about the second.

The boisterous young pit bull lived nearby in a small apartment with a family that she believes neglected and abused him.

'The owner was apparently trying to get Brian to mate with his female pit bull, but she wasn't on heat so Brian couldn't do it – and the guy belted him. He used to hit him with a two-by-four [length of wood] and throw him off a second-storey balcony,' Debbie says. 'Another time they left him by himself in the flat for two weeks – I assume he drank water from the toilet.'

The playful, happy-go-lucky pit bull is a naturally rambunctious, high-energy breed that thrives on human company. It's why many people love them so much, but it's also why they are among the dog breeds most commonly surrendered to pounds and rescue groups: people take them on without properly researching their temperament. Debbie suspects Brian's abusive former owner had absolutely no idea how to meet the needs of his exuberant young dog – and what's worse, he evidently had no interest in learning.

'People take on pit bull puppies and say, "Oh, aren't they beautiful" but they don't realise they can be quite hard to look after both as puppies and when they're young dogs. They don't settle down until they're about four or five,' she says. 'There were so many people in that block of flats. People must have known what he was doing to this dog, but nobody did anything.'

Debbie and George, however, *did* do something. When they heard about what was happening to the poor dog, they quickly swung into action.

'In the end the owner said he was going to take Brian and put him down if nobody paid fifty dollars for him. George went over and said, 'Here, take the fifty,' and walked off with him,' she says.

Brian wasn't called Brian then. He had the sort of aggressive name* typically given by people who choose a dog in

---

* Name withheld for privacy.

the hope it will make them appear tough and intimidating. It didn't suit the chunky little pit bull at all. He was a sweet, friendly boy despite everything he'd been through. Debbie and George knew he deserved a new name to mark his new start.

When George heard the dog's name he thought, *I can't call you that*. 'These dogs have got a bad enough name as it is, let alone having an *actual* bad name,' he explains. 'I was going, "Jeff! Harry! Bill!" I went through about twenty or thirty names and as soon as I said "Brian" he jumped up in the air like he was trying to kiss me. I said, "It's Brian, is it?" and he answered to it from that second on.'

He has well and truly moved on from his terrible start in life, but Brian still remembers where he came from. Dogs may forgive, but they don't forget. 'Two years after we rescued him, a member of his former family came around and Brian just growled at her,' says Debbie. 'It surprised me that he remembered her, but he wanted nothing to do with them. When he came to me he was happy.'

Since day one, Brian has been as devoted to Debbie and George as they are to him. As rescue dogs often do, Brian shows in myriad ways every day that he's genuinely grateful to have been given a second chance – or third, in his case – at a happy life.

But if ever they needed unequivocal proof that Brian would do anything for his owners, they got it on Wednesday, 16 October 2013.

*

Next door's dogs were barking again. As Debbie stepped into the backyard, she tried to remember the last time she had been able to enjoy pottering around in her garden without her neighbour's three dogs hurling themselves at the rickety fence that separated the two properties.

She couldn't recall – it had been that long.

Debbie could hear the dogs snarling, snapping and fighting with each other. She wondered if they were battling over food again. Debbie and George treated their rescue pets to the best home-cooked meals, including chicken necks and chuck steak for Brian, but she knew her neighbour didn't have the same attitude towards her dogs' respective diets.

'These dogs were always hungry. We used to throw food over the fence to them until the woman told her son to tell us not to feed them because "they only get enough food to sustain life". They only got one bowl of biscuits between them a day,' Debbie says.

The meagre rations weren't nearly enough to satisfy the pack: an enormous female mixed breed, an extremely intelligent and energetic male kelpie and a Staffordshire bull terrier. The dogs' social skills left a lot to be desired, too.

'The owner never took them for a walk, never socialised them. The kelpie used to jump the fence and take himself for a walk,' she says. 'He would always be running around loose – he wasn't hurting anyone, he just wanted some attention.'

But the big female, Zelda*, who appeared to be a combination of several breeds including Bull Arab and bull terrier,

---

* Name has been changed.

was particularly antisocial. She had already bitten Debbie twice. And Debbie knew she had bitten others. She says Zelda had tried to attack an elderly couple walking past the house, too – two teenagers who lived there witnessed that frightening incident and laughed about it.

Zelda's bites weren't bad enough to seriously injure Debbie, but they definitely caused serious alarm. 'I'd tried to be nice to her. She was young and had no attention. I'd given her food. She would come up to you and pretend to be nice and then bite you on the hand,' Debbie says.

She had called the local council multiple times to report the out-of-control animals and the flimsy fencing. And she wasn't the only one in the neighbourhood lodging complaints. The local council had issued the dogs' owner with a non-registration infringement notice relating to Zelda six months earlier, but no other action was taken. Debbie says her neighbour was determined to keep all three dogs, despite having no apparent interest in their welfare.

By October 2013, it felt like the tension between between the dogs' owner and her neighbours was at flashpoint.

'The fence wasn't up properly. The dogs could push through the palings easily,' says Debbie. 'There were three properties that shared this fence. The girl that lived behind the dogs was too scared to put her clothes on the line because Zelda would go off her head.'

Even Brian, who loves all dogs and seems to have a particular affinity for those with 'issues', was no fan of the rowdy trio next door. George recalls a visit to the local vet clinic when Brian appointed himself protector of a sick

German shepherd. 'This dog was really skinny and sick. He came over and looked at Brian and gave him a big lick, and Brian gave him a big lick back and sat down next to him,' he says.

'Every time another dog came into the vet, Brian would go over to the German shepherd and stand over him and put his paw on him. He was saying, *I'm looking after my friend.*'

But the sympathetic pit bull seemed to sense his canine neighbours were trouble. 'Brian kept patrolling, walking up and down that fence. Any time they were trying to get through the fence he'd be there,' says George. 'They were trying to dig their way under and he'd just whack them on the nose and push them back through.'

On 16 October, the dogs were performing their usual ferocious act on the other side of the back fence. Debbie knew the owner's son was at home but, as she'd come to expect, he made no attempt to calm the animals. George was inside the house as Debbie stepped out of her back door and made her way down the side of the house to get to the driveway. She was going to ask whoever was at home next door to do something about the dogs.

Debbie didn't know that Zelda also had access to the area behind the shared side fence. She hadn't seen her there before. But she was about to discover that a neglected 60-kilogram dog will go pretty much wherever it wants.

Before Debbie could register what was happening, Zelda barrelled through the fence like a missile and attacked her.

'She just came straight through – smashed the palings out – and grabbed hold of my leg,' she says.

The dog knocked her to the ground and pinned her there, trying to sink her teeth into Debbie's throat. Then Zelda used her full weight to headbutt Debbie in the chest, causing severe bruising that would last for weeks.

The attack dragged on for what felt like days, but was probably a matter of seconds. Debbie fought with all her strength to free herself from Zelda's jaws, but the force of the frenzied dog was too great. 'I was holding her back, but she weighed sixty kilograms. It was a lot. In the end I don't think I could have held her any longer,' she says. 'I really believe she did it because she was hungry and she wanted to eat me.'

Terrified, Debbie opened her mouth and screamed for help.

'Brian!'

Debbie still doesn't know what made her call for her twelve-year-old dog in that moment. She doesn't know why she thought Brian could possibly be a match for the crazed Zelda. She didn't even know if Brian could hear her – he was probably snoozing inside the house with George.

Whatever the reason, clearly some instinct kicked in that told her she needed Brian by her side.

'BRIAN!' she screamed again.

And then there he was. Just as rapidly as Zelda had lunged through the fence, Brian appeared and launched at the attacker.

'He came running and put his whole right leg inside Zelda's mouth, then he latched onto her face as well,' Debbie says.

Zelda had released Debbie from her potentially deadly grip, but now she wouldn't let Brian go. Her two packmates had kept their distance when she attacked Debbie, but when Zelda turned her attention to Brian they joined the fray. He was now desperately trying to fight off three dogs while Debbie lay on the concrete driveway, bleeding and so stunned she didn't even feel the pain of the multiple bites that had punctured her left leg.

Fortunately, the commotion – not to mention the speed with which Brian had propelled himself from the house – had caught George's attention. 'He just bolted and I thought, *What's he running at?*' George told Wollongong's *Illawarra Mercury*. 'As I stepped backwards, I realised Debbie was on the ground screaming.'

Racing to his stricken wife's aid along with two neighbours who'd heard Debbie's screams, George was forced to hit Zelda with a shovel to make her release Brian. She ran into the street. It took around twenty minutes to contain the other two dogs in their own backyard.

Debbie's memory of what happened next is hazy; she was in such deep shock she couldn't properly process what had occurred. She knows the police were called, and Wollongong City Council's animal control wardens arrived on the scene. She vaguely recalls being helped into a vehicle, swathed in towels to staunch the blood gushing from her leg. Brian's leg was bleeding so profusely that neighbours initially placed him in the bath to contain the flow while they tended to Debbie. He was rushed to the vet shortly after.

Debbie later learned that the police had been forced to use pepper spray to try to subdue Zelda; it didn't work. The animal control officers were no luckier in trying to contain her. 'They couldn't get near the dog. The animal control guy said he hadn't seen a more vicious attack in over twenty years,' she says.

Amid the flurry of activity in and around Debbie's home, one person who was conspicuously absent was Zelda's owner. When contacted by police, she reportedly seemed unconcerned about the terrible attack.

'When the attack happened the owner was at work. The police rang her, because they couldn't catch Zelda, and she said she wasn't going to come home until she'd finished her shift,' says Debbie. 'The police waited for two hours for her. As soon as she came home, Zelda ran back inside, probably because she knew she was going to get belted.'

Debbie's first clear memory after the attack was waking up in Wollongong Hospital. She'd had surgery to repair the deep gash in her leg. 'I stayed overnight, but I was in such shock that I don't remember a thing until I woke up from the operation,' she says.

That was when the full horror of the attack started to sink in – and when Debbie realised how close she had come to being mauled to death.

'I realised straight after the attack that Brian had saved my life, but I couldn't think straight. It was later that I really understood that if it wasn't for Brian I would be dead, because George wouldn't have got there in time. Zelda would have ripped my throat out, I've got no doubt,' she says.

'There's no doubt in the world that Brian saved my life. He's my hero dog.'

It was an incredibly selfless and heroic act on Brian's part: he literally offered up his own life in a bid to save his owner's. Everyone who hears the story is astonished. 'I tell as many people as I can because I'm so proud of him. He saved my life and he deserves every good thing he gets,' says Debbie.

On reflection though, Debbie says Brian's actions that day weren't entirely surprising. 'Brian has always been protective of me. People will go near me and he'll growl if he feels like he doesn't know them. I think he feels my energy: if I like the person he's fine, but if he feels like I'm not comfortable he's on alert,' she says. 'Dogs are just such good animals.'

They sure are.

For both Debbie and Brian, recovery from the attack is an ongoing process. Debbie's leg was in bandages for five months, surgical mesh knitting her torn skin back together. Five years later, she still suffers from nerve damage and has a livid scar.

Vets initially thought Brian's right leg was broken, but scans revealed he had severe ligament and cartilage damage. To this day, one of Brian's wounds has yet to completely heal; it periodically re-opens and at times has to be freshly dressed and bandaged twice a day.

'They had to fill him up with stitches,' says George. 'One of the scars never grew hair back.'

But even as her physical injuries slowly mended, Debbie's ordeal wasn't over. She says the dog's owners made life incredibly difficult for her in the wake of the attack.

The council declared Zelda a dangerous dog, a label that automatically imposed a raft of strict requirements on her owners. Among other conditions, owners of a declared dangerous dog must ensure the animal is contained in a secure enclosure that meets council requirements.

'The council said if they wanted to keep Zelda they'd have to keep her in a four-metre by three-metre cage for the rest of her life,' Debbie says. 'They tried to build this cage, but it wasn't even bolted down.'

Debbie believes Zelda was ultimately seized and euthanised by the council. She says the attention-starved kelpie was then kept in the enclosure for months on end instead.

It was incredibly frustrating for eternal animal-lover Debbie who, even after almost losing her life, only wanted her neighbour to take proper care of her pets.

'It was just horrible. I try to help out; try to get people to desex their dogs; to not leave their dogs in the backyard their whole lives,' she says. 'Dogs are not meant to be by themselves. I can't think about it. It just makes me cry.'

When Debbie tried to mount a civil case against Zelda's owner, she says the woman lied about the circumstance of the attack. 'She tried to tell everyone that I was in her backyard, but the police and everyone could see what had happened. They could see the palings were off the fence,' says Debbie.

'I had to live next door to them for two more years with all this going on. They finally moved out and I was so glad I wouldn't have to see them anymore.'

Despite the stressful situation, devoted Brian was a constant comfort to Debbie and George. His reassuring presence made Debbie feel extra glad they had saved Brian from a similarly loveless fate.

Sadly, it wouldn't be long before Brian would play the rescuer again, this time for George. In 2016, George started feeling tired after his and Brian's daily walks. Their strolls were often long and vigorous, so it wasn't entirely unusual for George to feel a little weary in the evenings – but this constant, all-consuming exhaustion definitely wasn't normal. He also had a lump in his neck, but when he queried it with his doctor he was told it was probably just a cyst.

George might have put the tiredness down to middle age and left it at that if not for his loyal little dog. Brian's and his daily walking regimen was a relatively recent thing. For eight years, George had struggled with post-traumatic stress disorder (PTSD) so severe that he rarely left the house.

'I went to the local shopping centre four times in eight years and even that was at ten o'clock at night. We were just starting walking again and we were doing really well,' he says.

Their outings were hard won and George wasn't prepared to lose them to whatever was making him feel so terrible. By the autumn of 2017, when he became so fatigued that he struggled to walk Brian at all, he went back to his GP again.

'I kept trying to go on, but it kept getting worse and worse. I thought I might need a vitamin injection or something, so I went back a couple of weeks later and said, "Usually I can walk miles and miles and miles, no problem,"' he says. He insisted the doctor investigate further. 'I knew before them. It had been seven months that I'd been complaining about it. They couldn't find it, but I knew it was really bad.'

George was right. Doctors eventually discovered that he had stage 4 lymphoma. It had originated in his tonsil, which is very rare.

George had emergency surgery to remove the lymph nodes in his neck. The cancer had fused his subclavian artery to his collarbone. He felt constantly nauseated because of the toxic fluid dripping from his tonsils into his stomach. He endured nine gruelling weeks of chemotherapy as well as radiation five days a week. In a matter of weeks, his weight plummeted from 130 kilograms to 60 kilograms and he lost all his hair.

'When I was in hospital I was within hours of not being here and I remember thinking, *I'm going to fight for every day and every minute*,' he says.

George survived. 'I still have problems with pain but there's no sign of cancer. I'm back to walking Brian,' he says. 'Brian saved me as well. He looks after everyone.'

Not long afterwards, Brian was involved in yet another life-saving situation. George was finally strong enough to resume his walks with his faithful dog, and one afternoon they were ambling around Coomaditchie Lagoon at Port Kembla, Wollongong's key seaport. It wasn't part of their usual walking route, but George's mother had recently moved to the area so he decided to explore.

When Brian followed his nose to a densely wooded area adjacent to the lagoon, George trailed after him. What he found there still haunts him.

'I looked to the right and saw this girl sort of sitting against a tree. I thought she was in a funny position and then I realised she was hanging out of the tree,' says George.

The young woman had tried to take her own life. She was just eighteen and George later realised that he knew her. That he was able to remove her from the tree and call emergency services, saving her life, was partly fortuitous and partly thanks once again to Brian's uncanny ability to be there for the people who need it most.

Brian is fifteen now and 'still in good nick', according to George. He suffered a suspected stroke in March 2018, but soon recovered. 'Physically and mentally he's pretty good. He's still strong. He enjoys his walks,' he says. 'I think getting walking again has helped. I reckon he's got a fair while in him yet.'

But the sweet pit bull has seen an awful lot in his life and he hasn't been left entirely unscathed. Aside from his ongoing wound issues, Brian also has fairly severe anxiety.

'After Debbie's attack and my cancer, Brian got separation anxiety, so we can't leave him alone ever,' says George. 'Either I'm here with him or Debbie's here with him. But we don't mind. Brian has done a lot for a lot of people.'

All dogs deserve to be spoiled, but if any pooch has earned a bit of extra indulgence, it's Brian. For the rest of his days, he will continue to enjoy the good life.

'He just loves getting out and about. He's got his own car – he's not allowed in the 'good' car. He's chewed out all the seat belts and everyone knows that's Brian's car,' George laughs. 'He gets fed twice a day, once by me and then by my mum. He's a really funny dog. Our next-door neighbour is a Vietnam veteran whose wife died a few years ago. Brian goes in there every day and checks him out and checks out the whole house, and he gives Brian something to eat. It's the same with another neighbour who's alone – Brian does the same for him.'

For Debbie and George, Brian's incredible life is testament to the thing that all dog lovers know to be true: dogs are angels in disguise.

'He's got that soul. He just notices everything. He's got that look in his eyes,' says George. 'I say to Debbie, "He's coming back as a human."'

Maybe he will. Or maybe humans will get really lucky and Brian will come back as another wonderful dog.

Lifeline: 13 11 14, lifeline.org.au
Suicide Call Back Service: 1300 659 467, suicidecallbackservice.org.au
Beyond Blue: 1300 22 46 36, beyondblue.org.au

LEALA

RESCUED HUMAN: ALEXANDER KENNEY

As anyone who knows their way around a search engine will attest, there are a lot of rumours about a lot of things on the internet. Some are patently ridiculous: remember the viral video that purportedly demonstrated how to charge an iPhone with an onion and a glass of Gatorade? Others – like the one about billionaire philanthropist Bill Gates handing out wads of cash to strangers via his charitable foundation – crop up again and again, because they somehow seem plausible (even when they're bunkum).

The dog world isn't immune to online myth and legend. One such supposed truth holds that all dogs are colour-blind (they can actually see shades of blue, yellow, green and grey), while another old chestnut claims that one year of a dog's life is equivalent to seven human years (in fact a dog is already a 'teenager' by the time it's a year old). But perhaps one of the weirdest canine rumours on the information superhighway is the one that says Staffies can't swim.

That's right, the personality-packed Staffordshire bull terrier – the second-most popular breed in Australia, according to Dogs NSW and the Australian National Kennel Council – will apparently sink like a stone if placed in water. Hogwash, surely? Well, maybe not.

While it may sound absurd, this is a rumour that does have some truth to it. As a general rule, stocky breeds like the Staffy can't swim – at least, they can't swim *well* – because their short legs and dense musculature make it hard to stay afloat. Plus, the size and weight of their head in proportion to their body means they struggle to keep their nose above the water, making breathing understandably tricky.

There are, of course, exceptions to the rule. Some Staffies will throw themselves into creeks, rivers, oceans and backyard pools with joyful abandon and swim like dolphins. But on the whole, the Staffy is a dog that prefers to keep his paws dry.

Leala the Staffy definitely got the 'no swimming' memo. Growing up on the far north coast of NSW, she had plenty of options for taking a dip should the mood take her. Most of the rural properties in her neck of the woods had dams; some also had their own creek or a river – or both. And, of course, the mighty Pacific Ocean was on her doorstep. But while she could sometimes be cajoled into paddling alongside her humans, she would never swim by herself. Generally speaking, Leala was happy to remain firmly in the landlubbers' camp.

Her take-it-or-leave-it attitude to water was typical of Leala's laid-back approach to life, says Lisa Brockbank, who rescued the lovable pooch with her then partner David Kenney in 2008.

'David and I had decided the time was right for a family pet and we both really wanted a Staffy. They're the best dogs – I just love their personalities,' she says. 'Ever since I was a kid I've had a dog in my life, but I don't know if I really am a "dog person". I was definitely a Leala person, though.'

Then aged around four, Leala was given away by breeders after she had produced several litters, none of which contained the 'right' type of puppy.

'I was just googling and she came up on a website, "free to good home". She came from a breeder who had bred a lot of puppies out of her and that was that – they didn't want her anymore,' Lisa recalls. 'We went and met her and that was it: she was ours.'

Well, technically she was theirs – but really she was David's. 'We were both in love with her, but she instantly bonded with him. He just looked at her and said we were taking her home. She was always David's dog.'

It wasn't long before everyone in the rural hamlet of Nana Glen, about 25 kilometres northwest of Coffs Harbour, was similarly enamoured of the friendly, chilled out little Staffy. 'From the moment she walked in our door she was just an awesome dog. She was really, really laid-back. She was such a calm dog. She never went off anywhere – she was always by our side. She went everywhere with us, and everyone loved her. We got her before we had children, so she was our constant companion,' says Lisa.

'She was just a cool dog. It wasn't just David and me who felt that way. It was a universal feeling. She was a very special girl.'

Leala didn't even take it too personally when David and Lisa welcomed their daughter, Alanah, in 2011. Two years later, Alexander arrived, and Leala again proved to be a devoted big sister. 'She was a bit put out at first, like, *What is this noise?* But she was always by their side. They loved her,' she says.

In fact, the arrival of the kids brought out Leala's maternal side and she quickly earned a reputation locally as something of a 'nanny dog'.

'She was very motherly, maybe because she'd had her own puppies. She'd had three litters and I think about fifteen puppies. She was a bit of a protector of the children,' says Lisa. 'We'd see her following other people's kids. If there was a kid being a little bit left behind, you'd always see Leala with that kid. There was one little girl in particular – she wasn't bullied or anything, but she enjoyed her own company – and Leala would always be sitting with her.'

Staffies have garnered an unfair share of bad press over the years, but Lisa never had any qualms about allowing Leala to spend time in close contact with kids – her own and others. 'I trusted her 100 per cent,' she says. And she knew no amount of boisterous play would faze her patient dog. 'She was robust. She was a tough dog, a true Staffy.'

Leala not only had the typical Staffy good looks – including the adorable wide grin – she also had the typical Staffy character. The breed's a unique mix of fearlessness and toughness, coupled with a relaxed and affectionate nature and an affinity for children, means these nuggety little dogs make ideal family pets.

On one occasion, Leala was instrumental in saving a little boy from potential disaster. 'My friend had her son over at our property and he was heading out to the road. Leala got between him and the road and was barking and carrying on while we were running over to him,' Lisa says.

At the time, the incident seemed like a simple case of fortunate circumstances: it was just lucky that Leala happened to be there to raise the alarm. But in retrospect, perhaps it was more than that. Perhaps it was merely the first time Leala demonstrated her inner warrior; the first time she showed that she would never allow a child to be harmed on her watch.

It wouldn't be the last.

September 5, 2015, was a typical spring Saturday for the Kenney-Brockbank clan. Lisa was enjoying a day out with girlfriends not far from the couple's home, while David took Alanah, then four, and two-year-old Alexander to his friend Jason Cluff's house for a casual get-together. Leala, of course, went along as well.

Alanah and Alex were among 'a whole heap of kids' tearing around the Cluffs' property as the afternoon stretched into evening. Leala was eleven or maybe even twelve by then, but she could more than hold her own in the company of a pack of rowdy youngsters. 'She did slow down in later life – she was always a bit of a lazy bum, definitely a lounge lizard – but she'd get excited about a few things, like little kids with a ball or on a trampoline,' Lisa says.

It was one of those idyllic days that was reminiscent of a simpler time when children and their four-legged friends could go out to play in the morning and wander home, exhausted, when the street lights came on. The kids and the dogs all looked out for each other that afternoon, though of course the parents at the gathering kept a close eye on their offspring, too. Lisa, who works in change management and frequently travels internationally for her job, could have pursued her career in any major city, but knowing her children had the space to play and the freedom to explore was one of the things she and David liked best about raising their family on the north coast of Australia.

Suddenly, Leala appeared by David's side, panting, barking and carrying on. At first glance, there didn't seem to be any immediate reason to worry – she was his little shadow, after all, and she was probably just worked up after running around with the children.

But then he noticed that Leala was dripping wet.

'She enjoyed playing in rivers and stuff, but only if we went in with her – especially cold water,' says Lisa. 'There are waterways everywhere where we live, but she'd never hop in by herself.'

If Leala was wet, it meant *someone else* had been in the water, too. And nobody, as far as he knew, was supposed to be swimming that day. 'David just looked at her and went, *Oh, shit.* He went bolting down towards the dam,' Lisa says.

David was met with a truly horrific sight. Tiny Alexander was floating face down in the dam.

David plunged into the icy water and retrieved his unconscious son. He couldn't wrap his head around how the little boy had made his way to the dam. David had seen Alex playing with Leala only minutes earlier; he must have scurried away in the blink of an eye.

He dragged Alex to the bank and – along with Jason Cluff and his son, Josh, who had recently completed a CPR course – immediately began life-saving measures. Another friend called the emergency services. The men continued CPR for the twenty-seven long minutes it took for a squadron of ambulances and police cars to reach the rural property.

Alex still wasn't breathing when the ambulance arrived, but paramedics were able to restart the little boy's heart using a defibrillator. Still, he was by no means out of the woods. The situation was absolutely critical.

Meanwhile, over at her friend's place, Lisa was oblivious to the desperate scene unfolding not far away. But the Nana Glen district has a population of less than 4000 people, and news travels fast – especially bad news.

It wasn't long before the telephone rang. 'I got wind of it when someone rang up and said there were a whole heap of ambulances and police at the Cluffs' place. We made some phone calls and discovered it was Alex,' Lisa says. 'I wasn't very far away, so my friends took me there.'

When she arrived, Lisa could barely make sense of the picture that confronted her. The Westpac Rescue Helicopter had landed on the property, ready to transport Alex to Lady Cilento Children's Hospital in Brisbane.

'I got there and there was the helicopter and ambulances and police everywhere. Alex was laid out with tubes and stuff hanging out of him. They pulled me aside and said, "Just understand that this is not good,"' she recalls. 'I don't think I processed it correctly at first. I just didn't really believe it, I guess. It took me a while to say, "Wow, this is bad."'

Alex was loaded onto the chopper and Lisa and David accompanied him for the 360-kilometre flight to hospital. Still unable to breathe on his own, the little boy was placed on life support. On arrival, the critical care doctors who treated Alex echoed the paramedics' grave prognosis. Alexander's chances of survival were slim at best. If he did pull through, the prolonged period of oxygen deprivation meant he would likely be profoundly disabled.

'They said, "You probably won't be taking him home and if you do there'll be something majorly wrong with him,"' says Lisa.

Still, he was alive – and that was thanks to Leala. Even as he stared down the barrel of unimaginable tragedy, David knew it was his ever-vigilant Staffy that had given Alex this tiny fighting chance.

'When I got there, David was just an absolute mess. He'd just fished his boy out of the dam. He kept saying, "I'm sorry, I'm sorry, Leala saved him,"' Lisa says. 'There weren't many words exchanged, but that's what he said. He knew it was definitely her. It was also David knowing his dog so well and thinking, *She's wet and she's barking and something is not right.*'

Leala had done her absolute best and now the doctors were doing theirs. All David and Lisa could do was wait.

The following days felt endless as Lisa and David kept vigil by Alexander's bedside. Still on life support, he had yet to regain consciousness. He was in the highest priority critical care bed at Lady Cilento and doctors continued to be pessimistic about his prospects.

'They didn't think he was doing too well, but he did have a couple of responses where his pupils would dilate,' Lisa says. 'The doctors said, "It's either good because it means there's brain activity, or it's just an involuntary reaction, like a muscle spasm."'

The outlook may have been bleak, but the tiniest possibility that her son would recover encouraged Lisa to keep hoping. 'It gave me a teeny-weeny bit of hope and I think that might have been enough for me not to turn into a blubbering mess.'

Thankfully, the worried parents weren't alone through their ordeal. Alanah had gone to stay with her grandparents, but Lisa and David were staying at Ronald McDonald

House, a charity that provides a home away from home for families of seriously ill children being treated at nearby hospitals. Plus, friends and family had rallied around.

'We had an entourage. All of our people just hopped in their cars and were there with us. The service and support we received was just amazing,' she says.

The only other thing that could have helped to ease the pain would have been having Leala there, too. She remained in Nana Glen, where she was being doted on by friends.

'We were in Brisbane for a while so Leala had to go and stay at someone's house. She was very well liked anyway, and after this she was the hero dog. Everyone just wanted to see her and give her a hug,' says Lisa. 'There was a lot of publicity and a bit of a circus that went on for a bit. She was extra spoilt.'

After three long days with little change in Alex's condition, doctors decided to withdraw the life support measures and see whether he could breathe on his own. It was a make-or-break moment.

'They told us there were three things that could happen: he might be able to breathe on his own, but he won't wake up; he might not be able to breathe and he won't wake up; or he'll start breathing and wake up,' she says. 'They said, "We'll try it a few times. It's often not something you get lucky with on the first go."'

As the medical team began the painstaking process of disconnecting the machinery that was keeping Alex alive, David stayed by his side while Lisa stepped out of his room to relay the latest update to supporters. She was on the phone when a nurse came barrelling towards her.

'She came running out to me and said, "You've got to come!"' Lisa's heart leapt into her throat and she immediately assumed the worst.

But the nurse continued: 'He just spoke! He said *no*!'

Racing into her son's hospital room, Lisa found a sight nobody had predicted. Alexander was awake – and he was deeply annoyed.

'They had slowly pulled everything off him and he woke up and said, "I need to go to the toilet." He wasn't happy about being in a nappy.' The proudly toilet-trained two-year-old then proceeded to climb out of the highest-level intensive care bed in the hospital and walk to the toilet.

It might have been funny if it wasn't so astonishing. 'The nurses and attending doctors were like, "What the hell has just happened?" It was a miraculous thing,' Lisa says.

Alexander was soon able to be moved out of the paedeatric intensive care unit and onto a general children's ward. 'The consultants actually came down to the ward and the nurses said, "They do not come down here. What's happened to your son just doesn't happen."'

But it *did* happen. Alex had survived who-knows-how-long face down in a dam, followed by twenty-seven minutes without a heartbeat and three days in a coma. He wasn't expected to make it, and if he did live he was certain to be disabled.

And yet, aside from a blood clot in the main artery in his leg, Alexander was entirely unscathed. 'He had a bit of swelling from the clot, but that was the only thing that was wrong,' says Lisa.

Even the doctors were perplexed by the little boy's apparently miraculous recovery. 'The main doctor who worked on Alex that first night had lost his dad the day before. He said to me, "I knew this wasn't good so I had words to my dad and I think he helped,"' she recalls. 'He was deadset. It must have been a nice feeling for him. It was quite touching.'

Lisa and David had a slightly more pragmatic view of the circumstances that had ensured their son's survival. 'Alex fell into a really clean dam – there were no bugs in there, so there was no infection. It was also freezing. When the paramedics were working on him his core temperature was 27 degrees and they think that helped his brain,' she says. 'The CPR was given immediately and we got a bed at Lady Cilento right away. I think really it came down to good timing. We had a lot of bad fortune followed by a lot of good fortune.'

But the most vital link in the chain was, of course, Leala. Lisa has imagined a million different scenarios to explain how Alex came to be in the dam with his dog. She suspects Alex wasn't in there for very long and that the shock of falling into the frigid water was what knocked him out.

But ultimately it doesn't matter how or why the pair went in the water; what matters is that devoted Leala was by Alexander's side as always. 'Leala had been in somehow – for what reason, who knows?' she says. 'Alex was really familiar with that place – it wasn't like it was somewhere unusual. There's a part of me that wonders if he and Leala went for a bit of a wander together, because they were joined at the hip.'

Whatever happened that afternoon, Lisa will be forever grateful that Leala was with Alexander.

Incredibly, just a week after he narrowly escaped death, Alexander was back home and back at preschool. Leala was naturally overjoyed to have her little pal back where he belonged.

She had never wanted for love and affection before Alex's accident, but Leala was positively smothered with attention after her heroic feat. 'She definitely had a good life. She would go on holidays with David's family,' Lisa says. 'I did some work in New Zealand for a bit, so she came there with us for six months. At one point I was also going to be possibly working in the UK, so we had her all ready to go.'

But while she took everything life threw at her well and truly in her stride, there was never any doubt that Leala was happiest on Lisa's 10-acre country property with the people who took her in at four years of age and gave her the life she'd always deserved.

It was there, on 7 February 2017, that thirteen-year-old Leala performed one final, selfless act for her family.

She had been diagnosed with a brain tumour two months earlier after a period of seizures. The news was devastating for Lisa, David and the kids.

'The vet said, "I can't tell you what's going to happen – it could be a really fast one or it could be a really slow one." We had her on medication, but she was an older dog and there was no point doing anything more invasive,' Lisa recalls.

Leala's fits worsened, and in early February, Lisa and David started to wonder whether euthanasia was the kindest option for their beautiful girl. 'David and I had said, "It's time to take her to the vet. We knew it was hard decision time,' she says.

In the end, though, Leala took the decision out of their hands. She took herself for a walk – and simply never returned.

'She walked off into the bush and just never came back. She was just so unselfish until the end,' says Lisa.

The family, as well as their friends and neighbours, searched the surrounding area, but they found no trace of the strong little Staffy who had meant so much to them all for so long. 'There were major search parties because she was such a local legend, but we live on a river and next to the bush. She could have gone anywhere,' she says.

It is a poetic farewell for a devoted dog like Leala. She seemed to have been sent to watch over a growing family, to keep them safe no matter what, and she left on her own terms when she knew her work was done.

But while Lisa appreciates Leala's selflessness, not a day passes that she doesn't miss her cool little dog. 'I would have liked her to come home. I would have liked her buried on our property. That was her home,' she says. 'She was selfless, but I really struggle with the fact that she's not home.'

In Leala's honour, Lisa rescued another dog a few months later. Nelson is a five-year-old Staffy that has some emotional and behavioural issues as a result of his early life.

'Nelson is a beautiful looking dog, but he's harder work than Leala ever was. He's nothing like her at all,' she laughs.

No dog will ever be just like Leala, of course – because Leala was truly one in a million.

All dogs are.

TEDDY

RESCUED HUMAN: ANDY SZASZ

They say that good things come in small packages. It's an adage that Andy Szasz has long known to be true. Although in Andy's opinion, this well-loved proverb doesn't go quite far enough. 'They' should also say that those packages often come wrapped in fur and adorned with a damp nose and a wagging tail. They should clarify that the best small packages are dog shaped.

Andy, from the southern UK city of Southampton, has always had a penchant for pint-sized dogs. The Jack Russell terrier (JRT) was his breed of choice for many years, and when their four sons, Louis, Josh, Daniel and Charlie, were growing up, Andy and his then wife, Estelle, always had at least one JRT in the house as a playmate.

The family farewelled its last beloved JRT, Boomer, in April 2012.

'He was fourteen years old. My whole family went to

the vet with him and we all cried,' Andy recalls. After such a wrenching loss, the Szasz clan collectively decided it would be best to wait a while before welcoming a new four-legged family member. But what Andy didn't realise at the time was that the decision to get a dog often has nothing to do with the people involved: it's usually the dog itself that decides.

'We weren't going to get another one, but a month later my son Daniel's girlfriend's sister was working at Stubbington Ark RSPCA Animal Shelter and this little ball of black fluff came in, fifteen weeks old,' he recalls.

Andy couldn't help himself. He made the 20-kilometre trip from his home in suburban Sholing to the shelter in Fareham to meet the little dog, a petite schnauzer–poodle mix named Teddy whose original owners simply said they 'didn't get on' with him.

It was love at first sight. 'I had him on the lead and he just wouldn't leave me alone. He fell in love with me,' Andy says. 'He's very clever and very calm. He doesn't moult. I don't know whether his previous owners had allergies or they just couldn't cope with a puppy.'

Whatever their reason for surrendering Teddy to the shelter, their loss was Andy's immense gain. The pair soon became a familiar sight at the local dog park and Teddy even accompanied Andy to his job as a civil engineer.

'Teddy was definitely meant for me. I spent the time with him, took him everywhere with me. I taught him his tricks,' he says. 'He definitely chose me and he's definitely my guardian angel. I believe that, I really do.'

He has good reason to believe it: Teddy saved Andy's life.

Twice.

People who really love animals are easy to spot. They're the ones who'll go to a party and spend the whole evening crouched in a corner, playing with the host's dog; the ones that don't own a single item of clothing not covered in cat hair; and the ones whose chief concern when upgrading their mobile phone is how much storage it has for guinea pig pictures.

It can be easy, when you're passionate about animals, to assume that everyone feels the same way; that the feathered, furred and finned inspire the same degree of delight in all of us. But some people aren't that way inclined at all. Pet keeping is far from a universal pursuit, and plenty of us just don't get why others think animals are such a big deal.

So what's the difference? Why are some people dotty about dogs and cuckoo about cats, while others are decidedly indifferent to the animal kingdom?

Having a rapport with animals was once believed to be entirely a result of 'nurture' – that is, children raised in pet-loving families were thought to be more likely to covet the company of animals as adults and see pet ownership as an important rite of passage for their own offspring.

But while the pet-keeping habit does tend to run in families, recent research suggests it's not all down to having parents who gave in to their kids' requests for a fluffy playmate. It may in fact be a genetic predisposition that has nothing to do with our upbringing.

In a 2015 study that charted the frequency of play with pets among identical and non-identical sets of middle-aged twins, the identical siblings had a higher correlation on frequency of pet play than non-identical twins, regardless of environmental factors such as childhood exposure to pets. Researchers found that genetic factors accounted for as much as 37 per cent of the variance in pet play.

In other words, we may inherit a biological love (or loathing) of animals from our ancestors. Or, to put it another way, how much or how little we like pets could be dictated by our DNA.

According to Dr John Bradshaw, author and the Director of the Anthrozoology Institute at the University of Bristol, human beings' love of animals can be traced back thousands of years and has played an important part in our evolution.

Dr Bradshaw says that, even as many as 15 000 years ago, some of the very earliest farmers would have felt less inclined to kill and eat animals that displayed 'tame' or semi-tame behaviour.

'The very same genes which today predispose some people to take on their first cat or dog would have spread among those early farmers,' he told news website *The Conversation*. 'Groups [that] included people with empathy for animals and an understanding of animal husbandry would have flourished at the expense of those without, who would have had to continue to rely on hunting to obtain meat.'

Andy definitely has the animal-loving gene, says his sister, Mary-Anne Rabenort. 'He's always had a love for animals, and them him. We grew up with cats and he loves all dogs. Animals just seem to like him. He has a special sense about him that animals feel comfortable with.'

Many of her earliest memories of her big brother include animals. 'Our neighbours had pigs and Andy was there when their sow gave birth to about twenty piglets. I remember he was so proud,' she says. 'In fact, one of the piglets turned blue and Andy got it up to our house, gave it a little milk and got it warm, and by lunchtime it was running around our living room. Andy was *not* losing a piglet.'

Even in dark times, the Szasz family has always considered its pets to be family members. Mary-Anne wonders if it was in fact a terrible family tragedy that played a part in fostering their enduring love of animals.

Andy, Mary-Anne and their sister Julia Douglas are of Romanian descent. Soviet soldiers killed their paternal grandmother and aunt when the USSR invaded Romania in 1944. The family's farm and vineyards were seized and their grandfather was taken to a prison camp. Their father, Samu (known as Alex), aged just 14, witnessed the horrific crime; he and his uncle, Andrew – Andy's namesake – were then forced to fight for the Soviets.

'That was the last time our dad ever saw his family. That made us have a strong, loving bond within our family. That is what binds us, not just with the adults and kids, but also with our pets. We are a very loving, caring family,' says Mary-Anne.

It was that loving, caring family that was quick to rally around Andy when in August 2012, just three months after he adopted Teddy, he was diagnosed with bowel cancer.

'We were very worried that we would lose him,' says Mary-Anne, who, along with Julia, has lived in the American state of Minnesota since 1980. 'Being so far away was so very hard for all of us. To lose him would have been devastating for us all. He's such a great guy and we love him so much.'

They needn't have worried. Back in England, though seriously ill, Andy was determined he wouldn't be going anywhere just yet. He couldn't – as well as his wife and sons, he had a little dog to look after. He wasn't about to leave Teddy just as they were getting to know each other.

He had surgery in October and was unable to work for months as he recovered from the gruelling operation. 'I was home for twenty-six weeks with him. When I first came home after being in hospital, he'd come up on the bed with me and give me a little bit of a lick on the nose,' Andy says. 'As I got stronger, I'd walk him two, three, sometimes four times a day. He bonded with me.'

Some days, the sweet little fluff ball's playful presence was the only bright spot amid the pain and anxiety. 'Teddy isn't mischievous, but he loves a bit of play and loves his toys. If I say, "Find the car," he knows exactly where we're going and he'll sit by the door and wait to get in. If he wants something he'll tap me on the leg. He's not backward in coming forward! He's a little character.'

In his darkest moments, when the fear of what lay ahead threatened to overwhelm him, it was Teddy who helped Andy to find the strength to fight on.

'You never know what's going to happen. I was very scared, but Teddy was my little rock. I'd just lay on the lounge with him. I'd look into his eyes and he'd look into my eyes and we'd talk to each other. You can tell this little thing anything,' he says. 'He kept me calm. He'd lick my hand and make me play with him all day so my mind wasn't on the cancer.'

Only when he received the all clear after his cancer surgery did Andy fully appreciate what a lifesaver Teddy had been – he really was a crucial part of Andy's survival. 'It was only afterwards that I realised what a help he'd been. How much they give you back. I rescued him and he rescued me.'

And it wouldn't be the last time.

By November 2016, Andy was back at work and life was virtually back to normal. After slogging his way through cancer treatment three years earlier, he was well and feeling positive. 'We were brought up the old-fashioned way. We don't give in too easily, us old boys,' he laughs.

Best of all, his bond with Teddy was stronger than ever. After what they had been through together during Andy's cancer ordeal, man and dog were virtually inseparable.

'Teddy comes to work with me every single day. I'm a highways engineer and I visit various work sites all day.

I might do twenty or twenty-five different jobs over the year and always people comment on what a lovely, calm little dog he is,' Andy says. 'He walks beside me in his little jacket or sits in the diggers. He has a dog bed on the front seat of the car. In the office, he sits on his couch or runs off and sees the secretary or the managing director for a bit. They're perfectly happy for him to come in. Everyone loves him.'

Winter had well and truly set in – the days were short and the weather was cold and snowy, meaning working outdoors wasn't much fun. By now sixty-two, Andy got himself vaccinated against the flu, just in case. He was looking forward to a quiet Christmas break at home with Teddy and the family.

But then came a call from the United States. Andy's 88-year-old mother, Audrey, who lived in the US along with Mary-Anne and Julia, had suffered a heart attack. Audrey had been struggling with dementia and heart problems for some time; this heart attack was her second. Andy made urgent preparations to fly to her bedside.

Andy had road-tested living in the US earlier in his life. His parents' and siblings' move across the Atlantic was inspired by Audrey's sister, Dorothy, who married an American GI. She settled in Minnesota, and after Alex and Audrey visited her there in the late 1970s, they decided to do the same. Mary-Anne and Julia, who were in their twenties at the time, went with them, but Andy, who was recently married, chose to stay in the UK. He and his wife made the move five years later, but decided American life wasn't for them, and returned to England after nine months.

Now, just as he had during his cancer battle, Andy felt acutely aware of every one of the 6500 kilometres between him and his beloved family.

He stayed in Minnesota for two weeks, long enough to satisfy himself that Audrey was on the road to recovery, and to spend some quality time with his sisters – much of which was spent regaling them with stories about his best mate, Teddy, who evidently wasn't happy about being left at home with Estelle during Andy's trip.

'When he got home to the UK, Teddy sat on Andy's suitcase as if to say, *You are not leaving me again*,' says Mary-Anne.

Andy didn't want to leave Teddy either. In fact, he didn't want to do much of anything upon his return from America. He had started to feel unwell on the flight home and hadn't been able to shake it. He felt exhausted and weak, and he knew it wasn't just jet lag. It was as if he had a nasty cold coming on, or perhaps the flu – Andy knew some people still got it despite being vaccinated.

He took a couple of days off work, but when he still wasn't improving, Estelle insisted Andy go to the doctor. When it came to his health, she felt they couldn't be too careful.

Andy dragged himself to see his GP on Friday, 9 December. 'They took one look at me and called an ambulance,' he recalls.

He was rushed to Southampton General Hospital and admitted to the intensive care unit (ICU), where tests revealed he indeed had influenza A – and pneumonia to boot. Though intravenous medication was administered immediately, later that night Andy's condition rapidly deteriorated. 'I crashed and they had to resuscitate me,' he says.

It was touch-and-go all through that long night. Then, the next morning, Andy crashed again. He stopped breathing. He was clinically dead for several minutes before doctors managed to revive him again.

In a bid to stabilise his condition and encourage his body to begin to heal, doctors decided to place Andy in a medically induced coma and on breathing support. They told his family the coma would last for about a week, and then he would be gradually woken to see if he was able to breathe on his own.

Family members on both sides of the Atlantic were terrified. 'He was so ill we thought we'd lost him. We've always been a very close, loving family and we were scared to death. My brother-in-law works for Delta Air Lines and was ready to get us all on a plane,' says Mary-Anne.

Science hasn't yet been able to conclusively prove whether – or to what extent – people in comas are aware of their surroundings, but increasing evidence shows that even people in a vegetative state can respond to external stimuli, suggesting they are at least partially aware of not only the outside world, but also themselves. Anecdotally, people who have emerged from comas often report having heard and understood people around them even when they were unconscious.

For Andy, his time in a coma was like being in a strange shadow world: all the usual reference points, like the time of day, were gone; experiences were both foreign and familiar; people were there but they weren't.

'My eldest son came in one day when I was comatose in the ICU and I heard someone say, "Hi Louis, what are you doing here?"' he recalls. 'I felt that someone had been sitting with me for an hour, but when Louis came in he was gone. He was about six foot tall with grey hair. I wonder if he was my guardian angel. It was a very strange experience.'

One thing there was no ambiguity around, however, was Teddy. Andy's family festooned his room in the ICU with pictures of his adored canine companion. They knew Teddy's presence – even in photographic form – would be a comfort to his devoted 'dad'.

'When I was in my coma I had seven pictures of Teddy stuck on the wall, along with pictures of my sons and my wife. Even the consultant couldn't believe I had seven pictures of my dog there and only one of my wife and children,' he says.

Dogs weren't allowed in the ICU, but they are permitted onto hospital grounds. A garden reunion with a much-missed pooch can be an enormous boost for a long-term patient. With this in mind, Andy's sons would walk Teddy past their ailing father's window and encourage him to 'speak' to Andy.

Even unconscious, Andy says he always knew when Teddy was there. 'I could hear him barking. It was like a shout out,' he says.

But as the days dragged on, Andy's condition was still grave. Pneumonia can be a stubborn infection that is often slow to respond to antibiotics, and doctors warned it was likely the severity of the illness would cause scarring in Andy's lungs. Waking him from the coma too early could have disastrous consequences. They were adamant that only a full week would give him the best shot at making a complete recovery.

But Teddy had other ideas. He missed his human – first Andy had gone off to America without him, and now he was desperately ill in hospital. Standing outside his window was torturous: he could smell Andy in there, but they wouldn't let him go inside. It simply wouldn't do! Teddy wanted Andy to come home.

So he decided to wake him up.

As well as their clandestine walks outside his ICU room, Andy's family had taken to having Teddy call his owner in hospital.

Whoever was at home with Teddy, usually Estelle or one of the boys, would use their iPhone's FaceTime video call function to dial Andy's number. Then his current hospital visitor – there was someone constantly at his bedside – would hold Andy's phone up to him in the hope that some part of his comatose brain would register that Teddy was on the line.

The calls were more for Teddy than Andy, really – he was morose without his human, and his family wanted him to see that Andy was still there. They didn't know whether Andy could even hear the calls, let alone understand that the yelps and barks emanating from the phone were his dog's way of saying, *I love you! Please come back!*

But he could.

After four days in a coma, during a call with Teddy, Andy began to wake up. It was three days before doctors had planned to rouse him from his induced sleep. When his astonished medical team had removed his breathing tubes, one of the first things Andy did was ask to see his dog.

There is no doubt in Andy's mind that it was Teddy's 'voice' that brought him out of his coma. 'He was barking and playing around and that was what woke me up,' he says. 'He's always there for me. Even if I cut myself or bruise myself, he's very concerned. Dogs are just uncanny animals.'

Across the pond in Minnesota, Mary-Anne wasn't at all surprised to hear that it was Teddy that had rescued Andy from his chemical slumber. 'Andy was so sick but that little dog was our brother's miracle,' she says. 'Teddy was all Andy needed. They were meant for each other. Anyone who sees them can feel the bond they have.'

Within days, Andy was well enough to be moved from the ICU to a high-dependency ward. But he wasn't yet strong enough to venture into the hospital's garden, where Teddy would have been welcome. The daily video calls were still helping to fast-track his recovery, but having seen how vital Teddy was in Andy's rapid improvement, Estelle decided to arrange an in-person visit from his little saviour.

Fortunately, the ward's supervising nurse was a dog lover. She agreed to allow Teddy to pay a not-strictly-legal visit, as long as it was brief. Estelle smuggled him in inside a Tesco supermarket carrier bag.

It's difficult to say who was more overjoyed by the reunion, Andy or Teddy. 'He leapt up onto the bed and licked my face,' Andy says. 'As soon as he knew I was all right he gave a big sigh and sat down, and that's where he stayed.'

Seeing the beautiful bond between their patient and his dog, Andy's canny doctors used it to their advantage, dangling Teddy like a carrot to motivate his ongoing recuperation. 'They kept saying that if I used my oxygen I could go home and walk my dog. That's what spurred me on and I was home within five days after that. They were quite amazed – I shouldn't have even been able to walk at that point,' he says.

Andy made it home just in time for Christmas 2016 and, true to his word, Teddy remained the focal point of his gradual return to health.

'I take him round the park at five-thirty every morning. I can't let Teddy down. He's never let me down, so we're always up and we go out no matter the weather,' he says. 'We have plenty of friends we go out and visit. One of Teddy's best friends is a Welsh sheepdog called Buddy that he met down at the park. Buddy's owners can't drive, so we go and pick them up every time we go to the park.'

Word of Teddy's life-saving feat quickly spread. His and Andy's story has been featured in national and international newspapers and the faithful dog has been featured on YouTube, as well as in the UK television documentary series *The Dog Rescuers* and *Inside Edition* in the US.

When the RSPCA got wind of their Stubbington Ark alumnus's devotion to his owner, they honoured Teddy with a special award that recognises animals that have cared for humans and had a significant impact on their lives.

Presenting the award, the RSPCA's Michael Ward said: 'Teddy is a brilliant example of the intense bond between a dog and man. The connection between the two of them is so strong that even in a coma Andy responded to Teddy. It just shows how rewarding – and life changing – giving a home to a rescue animal can be.'

Andy says that bond has deepened even more since Teddy rescued him a second time. 'Teddy's and my bond was always strong, but it's even stronger now. He's always by my side. It's almost like he's stuck to me. Wherever I go, he's there,' he says. 'If I go out without him he doesn't like it at all now. He'll sit on the back of the settee and look out the window for me and when I come back he "talks" to me.

'I only go to certain places where he feels comfortable. I will never leave him at home alone unless I really have to. I shouldn't say this, but he even comes to the pub every now and then.'

As expected, his battle with pneumonia caused scarring in Andy's lungs. He now has chronic obstructive pulmonary disease (COPD), but Teddy continues to be a key factor in Andy's ability to cope with it.

'I still go to work and still walk ten miles a day, but the condition is classed as severe,' he explains. 'Teddy is full of energy and he just loves life. He sleeps on my bed every night. He has salmon once a week. He lives very well and he's worth it.'

Sisters Mary-Anne and Julia have continued to marvel at Teddy's profound influence on their brother's life. They were thrilled to finally meet Teddy in the flesh when they visited the UK in September 2017. Sadly, their beloved mother, Audrey, passed away in July that year, just three days before her eighty-ninth birthday. Their father, Alex, died in 2002.

'We knew that Teddy would be the medicine Andy needed due to the bond they have. Teddy is the most amazing, loving little dog I have ever met. That dog loves our brother so much,' says Mary-Anne. 'Julia and I both fell in love with Teddy right away. He was everything Andy had told us about him and more. He would come in every morning and give us kisses, then go off to find Andy. I hated to leave him, that's how much he grew on me.

'You could just feel the love that little dog has, and the effect he has on people. Teddy has done wonders for Andy, and Andy gives Teddy all the love and care any dog could hope to have. Watching them together just makes you smile all over.'

Andy retired from his job this year, but he won't stop working – and neither will Teddy, now aged six. Andy plans to get their Pets as Therapy certification, which will enable them to visit sick people in hospital. Andy feels strongly that others should have the opportunity to experience 'the power of Teddy' – the same power that saved him from life-threatening illness twice.

'It's a little bit of giving something back. Teddy is calm and he doesn't moult. He's very good with children and he's not fazed by anything,' he says. 'I can't wait.'

Because that's the thing about rescue dogs like Teddy. Though they may be fiercely loyal to one special human, they possess a certain kind of magic that rubs off on everyone they meet.

Andy has seen this firsthand. 'They are so intelligent and so loving, these rescue dogs. They're so loyal. There's definitely something about them,' he says. 'They're here for a purpose. I think these rescue dogs are there to find us.'

We should all be lucky enough to be found by a dog like the small but mighty Teddy.

OSCAR

RESCUED HUMAN: DEBRA TRANTER
RESCUED DOGS: TOO MANY TO COUNT

You never forget your first dog.

Whether she was a longed-for puppy delivered by parents wearied by years of nagging or an ageing mutt that was like a pungent part of the furniture, the four-legged friend that starts it all undeniably leaves paw prints on the human heart.

Debra Tranter is very familiar with the butterfly effect that can be triggered by a beloved first dog. Her relationship with her own childhood canine companion, Tammy, was so formative that it inspired a national movement, which has saved the lives of literally hundreds of dogs.

Tammy was a rescue dog, a middle-aged beagle plucked from Melbourne's Lost Dogs' Home by Debra's father, Jeff, as a surprise for her birthday.

'I think I was around seven years old. I had two rescued kittens that we just sort of found around the house where we lived and adopted them, but I'd always wanted a dog and nagged my parents,' she says. 'I remember going to my grandmother's house and my dad saying he just had to step out for a moment, and then coming back with Tammy.'

It was love at first sight: Debra and Tammy instantly formed a strong bond. When her parents divorced soon after and Debra began to shuttle back and forth between two homes, Tammy was her one constant.

'She became my best friend. She was so gentle and so laid-back. Whatever I was doing, she was doing – going for walks, or if I was sitting down she would always have her head in my lap,' says Debra. 'She was just a calm, confident dog, and she followed me everywhere.'

She means that quite literally. Debra lived at The Patch in Victoria's Dandenong Ranges, 39 kilometres east of downtown Melbourne, and Tammy would accompany her to school most days.

'She would walk to school with me at Kallista Primary and sit under my chair and Mum would have to come and get her,' she laughs. 'She just wanted to be with me.'

The Patch is a picturesque village on the edge of Sherbrooke Forest, a state forest within the Dandenong Ranges National Park. Debra's father's house was bordered by the forest on one side and rural land on the other. Their only neighbour at that stage was Debra's uncle, her father's brother.

'They both built their family homes on a block of land that was given to them by my grandparents. Back then ours were the only two properties in the street,' she says.

Neither property was fenced, but Tammy never wandered. She might meander next door to say hello to Debra's uncle and cousins, but aside from that she was always by her young mistress's side. Debra never once worried about Tammy leaving home.

Until one day she did exactly that.

It was the school holidays, and ten-year-old Debra and her dad had taken a trip to Mallacoota, a seaside township halfway between Melbourne and Sydney. Tammy had been left back in The Patch, 500 kilometres away, in the care of Debra's aunt and uncle.

'Tammy just walked away. Whether she was looking for me I don't know, but she disappeared,' Debra says. 'They went out looking for her, but they just couldn't find her.'

By the time a fretful Debra returned from her trip, Tammy had been missing for several days. Debra's biggest worry was that her best friend had become lost in Sherbrooke Forest. The 35-square-kilometre woodland is known for its dense growth, including the towering *Eucalyptus regnans*, the tallest flowering plant in the world. It was also then – in the mid 1970s – a popular destination for recreational shooters, who would often set steel-jaw traps in a bid to catch the wild deer that populated the forest. (Leghold trapping of all species except rabbits, foxes and wild dogs was banned in Victoria in 2008.)

When nearly a week had passed with no sign of the little dog, Debra grew ever more fearful that Tammy would meet a gruesome end out there, all alone.

Then, late one night, she heard the unmistakable sound of a howl emanating from the dark forest.

Debra and her father each grabbed a torch and plunged

into the tangled thicket. As Tammy continued her mournful keening, they thought they were getting closer to her. But sound travels differently in the bush, especially at night, and Debra simply couldn't locate the little dog.

'We had torches and we were out calling her. There was no barking at all, just this howling,' she recalls. 'The bush can be deceiving and the sound echoes. We'd think we knew where the sound was coming from, but it would end up being a completely different direction.'

As the sun came up, the forest grew eerily silent. There was still no sign of Tammy. Though she didn't want to give up hope, young Debra quietly conceded that she might never see her dog again.

A day or two later, Debra headed home from school feeling sad and defeated. Her mum hadn't needed to come and collect Tammy that day. Debra wondered if she'd ever glance down again to see Tammy's tail give a furtive wag from her favourite spot beneath the chair.

As she arrived home and the rear of the house came into view, Debra thought she was seeing things.

'We drove down the driveway and there was Tammy, just sitting at the back step. I just remember falling up the steps to get to her,' she says. 'Her tail started wagging, but her back leg was mangled; it was almost chopped off. The bones were exposed and there was blood everywhere.'

The scene seemed to confirm Debra's fear that Tammy had stumbled into one of the vile steel-jaw traps in the forest. But, astonishingly, it also seemed that the tenacious beagle had chewed her way out of it.

Most importantly, she had survived – and she was home.

Tammy was rushed to the vet, where there was more good news: 'She was able to keep the leg. There was a whole lot of flesh torn by the trap, but somehow she managed to walk back home,' says Debra. 'It was a relief that she was home, but it was devastating to know she'd been out there alone and in pain.'

It was a shocking awakening to the cruelty that human beings can inflict on animals. 'They give us so much,' she says, 'and it is such a betrayal.'

Tammy made a full recovery from her ordeal and spent another six happy years by Debra's side. Debra was about sixteen when her adored dog slipped peacefully away.

'She just grew old and died in her sleep. I woke up one morning and she had passed away,' Debra says. 'She was getting all grey around the muzzle, so we knew she was getting older, but she wasn't sick. It was devastating and very hard to accept. Losing a dog is so painful and raw.'

She was so grief-stricken that it would be years before she opened her heart to another dog, but Tammy's incredible feat of survival left an indelible impression on Debra. The courageous beagle had been resolute, and that single-minded focus on her goal enabled her to conquer seemingly insurmountable obstacles.

Her dog's determination to get home to her family – particularly to the person she loved and trusted more than any other creature – was a powerful lesson in loyalty for Debra; it represented the profound strength of the canine–human bond.

'The spirit of that dog showed me they will do anything to get back home,' Debra says. 'It really reinforced that dogs are family members and that they want that love, affection and companionship. They want to go back to where they are safe.'

It was a lesson she would not forget – and it would shape the rest of Debra's life.

While it was years before she would again call herself a dog owner, Debra's love of animals – especially dogs – continued to be a big part of her life as she grew up.

By the 1990s, Debra had married and was the mother of two young daughters. She had a flourishing career as an aged care nurse in Melbourne and spent her spare time volunteering for local animal welfare groups.

'I was volunteering for a variety of groups and people, just doing whatever I could. It just felt good to be with "my people",' she says.

It was while manning the phones during a volunteer shift in 1993 that Debra took a call that would irrevocably alter her trajectory.

The unidentified voice at the end of the phone line talked about a situation so horrific that Debra could scarcely believe what she was hearing.

'I was writing madly, taking as many notes as I could as this person described a property hidden within a pine plantation on the outskirts of Ballarat where there were hundreds of dogs in appalling conditions,' she says. 'They said it was owned by a politician who was sending the dogs overseas and selling them in his own pet shop.'

The caller was talking about what would quickly become known to the public as a puppy farm, a large scale commercial breeding facility endlessly producing litters of puppies for supply to retail pet shops.

These privately owned facilities would soon become notorious for the squalid conditions their breeding dogs were forced to endure, as well the cruelty often inflicted on the animals. The dogs were routinely denied veterinary care, were often malnourished and rarely received any affection or socialisation.

When they became sick or were no longer able to breed, the caller told Debra, the dogs would at best be dumped at a shelter. More often than not, however, they were simply killed.

'I was thinking, *This is unbelievable – we have to do something immediately.* I'd never thought about where puppies in pet shops came from and then I couldn't stop thinking about it,' she says.

She showed her notes to her fellow volunteers and the staff of the animal welfare group she was working for. Nobody believed it.

'I took these notes around saying, "This is really bad," and they all thought it was a hoax. They were saying, "We factory-farm pigs and chickens, not dogs – if there were this many dogs on a property, people would know about it,"' says Debra.

Frustrated that none of her colleagues was prepared to investigate further, Debra vented her annoyance to veteran animal activist Laurie Levy. 'I remember sitting down with Laurie, really pissed off, saying, "I can't believe nobody's going to do this," and he said, "Why don't *you* do something?"'

The suggestion was both shocking and enticing. 'I thought, *I guess I could*,' Debra says.

She dug out a street directory – this was well before the days of everyone having a personal GPS in their pocket – and searched for areas near Ballarat, 115 kilometres northwest of Melbourne, that looked like they could be pine plantations.

The following weekend, Debra and a girlfriend made the 90-minute drive to the area.

'Our plan was to go to areas that looked like pine plantations, get out of the car and listen for dogs barking and things like that. I just couldn't let it go. I was saying, "There are dogs out here somewhere,"' she recalls. 'My friend had the idea of getting the maps the Rural Fire Service used, because they have all the fire trails marked through the bush.'

That first weekend mission yielded nothing, but Debra wasn't deterred. For the next three or four months, she and her friend returned to the area every weekend to continue their search.

And finally they hit the jackpot.

'We found it in a pine plantation just out of Ballarat in a place called Learmonth. We walked right through the plantation, which went up a huge mountain,' she says. 'We were sitting in the middle of it, having a rest, and in the distance we could hear dogs. We just sat there for a while going, "Did you hear that?" It was just one of those weird moments.'

When they were certain that, yes, they could indeed hear dogs, they ploughed on through the plantation, eventually emerging on the other side of the mountain.

'It was thick scrub bush with huge boulders everywhere – really rocky terrain. We ended up looking down at the puppy farm on the other side of the mountain. It was an incredible sight,' says Debra.

Incredible and abhorrent.

Laid out at the foot of the mountain was a scene of total horror. Row upon row of makeshift corrugated iron kennels sat baking in the hot afternoon sun. They were arranged within pens, and inside those pens Debra could see dogs pacing back and forth – behaviour consistent with extreme psychological deprivation and stress. (Experts call this pacing 'zoochosis' as it is commonly seen in wild animals driven mad by zoo captivity.)

'We sat down and stared at it for what felt like hours. We didn't even speak to each other and say, "Oh my God, we've found it." We were just in shock, I think,' she says.

They sat there so long it started to get dark, and the setting sun spurred Debra into action. 'We started making our way down towards the dogs. We found a gate with no padlock, opened it up and we were inside.'

As she had expected, it was much worse up close. The property was vast, the stench stomach-churning and the noise deafening. The dogs were in terrible condition, with matted fur, weeping sores and obvious infections.

'As soon as the dogs saw us, they just erupted. There were so many dogs and so many laneways that we ended up getting lost. Every time we turned a corner we'd be confronted with hundreds more dogs,' says Debra. 'It was just incredible.'

She later found out there were a thousand dogs at the site.

The women pointed their unwieldy VHS video camera at anything they thought might be relevant, but Debra knew their footage would not be of great quality. 'We had no idea what we were doing. We were just sort of wandering around in a daze.'

When she finally left, Debra felt that a fundamental shift had occurred inside her. She had no idea what lay ahead, but what she encountered that day made her 100 per cent committed to saving these dogs and others like them.

'I was shocked and outraged and thought, *How can we be doing this?* I had no idea then how nasty the pet industry was or what they would put me through, but the day I saw those dogs was the day I knew I couldn't turn away.'

Debra raced back to Melbourne and told Laurie Levy what she had discovered. He gave her a quick lesson in writing a media release, and before she knew it her grainy video footage was the lead story on the nightly news.

Debra felt elated – she was certain that change would swiftly follow.

'I was so naïve. There were so many dogs on the property that I thought that single farm supplied every pet shop. That's how big it was,' she says. 'I thought it would be easy: *We'll just shut this one down.*'

She was wrong. It was not easy. Far from it.

Debra learned how to submit a Freedom of Information request, which enables public access to government data, and lodged one with Ballarat Council. She received 300 pages of inspection reports on the Learmonth puppy farm alone. 'They revealed that something like ninety-seven puppies had died in one day over summer because of the heat. I started talking to politicians and the media and it became political very quickly.'

It seemed real progress would be made when the incumbent Liberal government announced that a pet industry Code of Practice would be drafted in 1994.

But the Code was toothless, says Debra. 'This puppy farmer was on the writing committee and that's why the Code was so weak.'

That was – and remains – the most uncomfortable truth about puppy farms: they are not illegal. Even today, the RSPCA does not have the power to simply shut down puppy factories; they can only work within existing legislation, which campaigners say is weak and does not adequately protect animals. Dogs can only be seized from an intensive breeding facility if there is evidence of severe cruelty or breaches of the Code of Practice, which didn't exist when Debra located the Learmonth farm.

While the wheels of political change continued their slow grind, Debra focused her energy on raising public awareness of the horrors of puppy farms. She continued to locate and visit more Victorian farms, each worse than the last. She was involved in several raids on farms, where dogs would be removed under the Prevention of Cruelty to Animals Act. Again and again, dogs would be rescued, only to then be euthanised due to disease, injury or psychological trauma. Debra encountered one puppy farmer whose dogs were so malnourished they were brain damaged.

The more she saw, the more Debra was determined to educate people about the ghastly reality of life for the parents of those adorable pet shop puppies. She was angry, and she wanted others to share her outrage. She set up a website and shared the graphic photographs and sickening video footage she took inside the grim breeding facilities.

Years passed, but no matter how hard she tried, Debra felt she wasn't gaining any traction with the general public. Her cries for change seemed to fall on deaf ears. It was as if people simply didn't want to know about the terror that lurked inside the sheds of a puppy farm.

'I thought if I showed people the footage they'd be equally shocked and want to do something about it, but because I was so young and angry and the photos were so confronting, people didn't engage – they were turning away,' she says. 'I was just showing them cruelty and not giving them the tools to act. People want to know "What can I do about it?" When they feel overwhelmed they don't do anything.'

By 2010, seventeen years after she began campaigning to abolish puppy factories, Debra was struggling. She had poured most of her savings into her anti-puppy farm work.

She was exhausted from juggling her campaigning with her full-time job in aged care, not to mention her constant battles with the pet industry. And no matter what she did, Debra kept smashing into roadblocks at every turn.

She didn't understand why her tireless work had yet to achieve any real results, and she wasn't sure she had the strength to carry on. Her marriage ended and she was selling her house to fund her campaigning. At times she truly felt like she was losing her mind.

'I was thinking, *I've given it a go, I've tried my hardest, but I haven't achieved anything – someone else can do a better job than me*,' she says. 'My whole life revolved around the animal world and people that worked in the animal world. My family was concerned. It was like I was walking on the edge of my sanity and I could tip either way.'

Something had to give. Debra needed a lifeline. She needed to be rescued.

And she was about to be – but things were going to get a lot worse before they got better.

In early 2010, Debra received a tip about a puppy farm in a remote part of Victoria. She duly made the drive out from Melbourne, resigned to discovering the standard cruelty she had come to expect.

'It was just a normal tip-off: dogs in terrible condition. I drove up there and knocked on the door, but no one was home,' Debra says. 'I walked to the back of the property to the shed, where I could hear all the dogs barking. I opened the door and started filming and taking photos.'

Halfway into the shed, Debra stopped in her tracks. She saw a male dog cowering in the corner of his pen. At least, she assumed it was a dog. What it *looked* like was a rolled-up rug caked in urine and faeces.

'I couldn't even make out which end of the dog I was looking at. He was the tiniest little dog I had ever seen. He was in a cage with two females that were double his size,' she says. 'My heart broke for this little dog, this quivering mess in this shed with sixty to eighty dogs just barking and barking.'

Barely even registering what she was doing, Debra opened the cage and took the dog out. He was a toy poodle, about four years old, but his fur was matted into one solid lump of felt. His coat was so matted, in fact, that the dog's hind legs were effectively stitched to his stomach. He could neither move nor defecate properly.

It wasn't her intention to remove any dogs from the property that day, but as she clutched the little dog to her chest, Debra knew she couldn't leave him there. He was so terrified he was urinating uncontrollably.

Debra took him straight to the vet, where he had to be sedated before his disgusting mass of fur could be shaved. He was covered in grass-seed abscesses and had rotten teeth, diseased gums and painfully infected ears.

'It was just awful to see this dog so frightened. From that point on I just didn't want to let him go. I wanted to assure myself that he was going to be safe,' she says. 'I wanted to keep him in my sight, so I took him home and went to rehabilitate him.'

To this day, Debra isn't entirely sure what made her pluck Oscar – as she named her little survivor – out of all the dogs in that shed, but it seems they recognised something in each other.

'It was just that he was so shut down and broken. Those are the dogs I'm always drawn to when I go to the sheds. Most of them are standing there barking at me, but it's the ones that don't bark, the ones that hide away and push their faces into the corner so they can't see you,' she says. 'They've got absolutely no will to live. It just kills me.'

She discovered exactly what that felt like five days later, when the police came to her door and physically wrenched Oscar from her arms. Classed as stolen property, he was returned to the puppy farmer and Debra was convicted of theft and fined $1500.

Losing Oscar was, she says, the worst moment of her life. 'It literally broke me. It was the lowest point of my campaign. I was heartbroken,' Debra says.

The puppy farmer later tried to sue her for $15 000 for loss of income, because she'd had Oscar desexed and he could no longer be used for breeding. Anyone else might have been distraught, but Debra welcomed the civil action. She knew that as long as the case was before the courts, as long as Oscar was considered 'evidence', the puppy farmer had to keep him alive. She was in no position to forfeit so much money or pay hefty legal bills, but Debra instructed her legal team to delay proceedings as long as possible while she figured out what to do next.

She was more than familiar with the *Prevention of Cruelty to Animals Act*, but she began poring over the legislation yet again, searching for some loophole that she could use to have Oscar returned to her.

'I was trying to find ways that I could get Oscar back using the law. All I was thinking was, *He needs to come back*. I felt like I had failed this little dog,' she says. 'Then someone said, "You need to think outside the box – don't just look at the Cruelty Act, look at other pieces of legislation that can help what you're doing."'

It was a light bulb moment for Debra. Suddenly she understood that she had been looking at things the wrong way. Yes, of course the government should legislate to abolish puppy farms all together, but failing that, they could ban the sale of live animals in pet shops. If there were no demand, there would be no need for supply. Intensive breeding facilities would go out of business.

And if the puppy farms had no customers, they wouldn't need dogs like Oscar.

In a heartbeat, the entire focus of Debra's activism shifted from the source to the end user. She would lobby for a bill to keep puppies out of pet shops, and she would call it Oscar's Law.

'Everything I was reading was protecting the puppy farmers' commercial interests. There was nothing protecting Oscar or dogs like him,' she says. 'My aim was to teach people that the law is inadequate and show what we needed to do to get it changed. It became more about trying to empower the public.'

A month after Oscar was returned to the puppy farmer, Debra walked into her boss's office and quit her job. While her animal welfare work had been faltering, her career had been going from strength to strength: Debra was now the manager of five aged care homes and the compliance manager for the whole company.

She enjoyed her work and walking away from it felt scary, but she knew it was what she had to do. 'I was absolutely dedicated to that job and I loved it, but rescuing Oscar, the enormity of legislative reform and the fact that I was getting older made me think, *I've got one shot at this*,' Debra says. 'This was what I needed to do and I couldn't do it if I was working full-time.'

For eighteen months, Debra worked around the clock to garner public support for her new-look campaign – and it worked. Thousands of people added their voices to the chorus calling for change, not just in Victoria but across Australia and around the world. (The advent of social media a few years later pushed it even further: Oscar's Law now has 200 000 supporters across Facebook, Twitter and Instagram.)

But in the midst of the groundswell of support in Oscar's name, Debra was still devastated that she was without Oscar himself. She couldn't bear to contemplate what kind of treatment he was enduring at the hands of the puppy farmer, especially now that he was useless in breeding terms.

She kept constant tabs on him via her network in the pet industry. 'I contacted all my sources and asked them to keep an eye out for Oscar: "If you hear anything – if he's alive, if he's been killed – just let me know,"' she says.

Finally, in June 2011, Debra received a call.

'One of the guys who gives me info said he'd seen Oscar. He said, "He's alive and there may be an opportunity in about a month, so keep an eye on the *Trading Post*,"' she says. 'Apparently the puppy farmer had been told she had too many dogs and had to get rid of some.'

Sure enough, about a month later, an ad for adult toy poodles popped up in the classified advertising publication. Debra knew from the phone number that the advertiser was the puppy farmer; one of the dogs *had* to be Oscar.

Debra asked a friend to call the number. The puppy farmer answered and said she was going out of town, but a neighbour could show her the available dogs.

'I immediately knew I had to be there. I bought a wig and glasses and disguised myself,' Debra says.

They went to the farm and the neighbour took them into the shed. There, in the same cage Debra had rescued him from a year and a half earlier, sat Oscar.

'He was sitting up the back, shaking. He walked tentatively up to me and licked my fingers. I just opened the cage and scooped him up and said, "I'm not leaving without this dog,"' she says.

There was just one little problem: the puppy farmer's neighbour had been explicitly instructed not to sell this particular dog.

'The man said, "That one's no good – it's been desexed and it's not for sale." He went out of the shed to ring the owner and I said to my friend, "Whatever we need to do, I am *not* putting him back in that cage,"' says Debra.

The man returned and delivered the puppy farmer's decree: they could have any of the other dogs for a hundred dollars each, but Oscar would cost two hundred.

Debra handed over $400 and left with three dogs.

Over the next ten months, Debra's team negotiated with the puppy farmer to release more dogs to them. They took three each week until the operation was shut down. The civil suit against Debra was eventually dropped.

And while every dog saved from the nightmare of a puppy factory is a victory, there is, of course, one rescue in particular that Debra is most proud of.

That she was able to rescue Oscar the first time around is heartwarming. That Oscar then rescued *her* from despair – and re-energised her entire approach to activism – is wonderful.

That Debra rescued Oscar a second time is amazing.

That Oscar's profound impact on Debra's life and work contributed to the rescue of thousands of dogs from cruelty is nothing short of miraculous.

Because that's exactly what happened next.

On 15 December 2017, Victoria became the first state in Australia to effectively ban puppy farming.

Under a bill championed by the Oscar's Law campaign,

which was passed in Victoria's Upper House in a tight vote, the number of fertile female dogs that a breeder can own and register with their local council will be capped at ten. Only those meeting strict additional requirements will be approved by the Minister for Agriculture to keep an absolute maximum of fifty fertile female dogs.

The bill also banned the sale of puppies in pet shops, with retail outlets only able to sell from shelters, pounds or voluntarily registered foster carers from July 2018.

It's difficult to describe just how much the passing of the legislation means to Debra. 'Twenty years ago I was meeting politicians who owned puppy farms, and now I've stood beside a Ballarat politician [Jaala Pulford, Minister for Agriculture] as she tabled legislation to shut them down,' she says. 'It's been quite an ironic journey.

'A couple of years ago even people in rescue told me, "You're never going to achieve a ban on animals in pet shops – why do you keep persisting?" But I've always been confident it was going to happen.'

The fight, of course, is far from over. Puppy farms can still operate legally in other states, and there is a risk that those shut down in Victoria will simply relocate.

But Debra is nothing if not persistent.

'It's a matter of continuing this political lobbying and meeting with MPs. It can be done,' she says.

Oscar is now a spritely twelve-year-old, and bears little resemblance to the scared waif Debra pulled from the squalid shed in 2010. He still has skin issues and ear problems, as well as luxating patellas (dislocating kneecaps) in his hind legs. Grooming him is still a battle, no doubt because of the terrible pain he endured when he was first freed from his crippling matted coat.

But in every other sense, he is a happy little dog. 'Oscar is really, really happy and confident at home, and when we go out he's fine as long as he can see me,' says Debra. 'The one thing he freaks out about is if he can't see me. I think I probably caused that separation anxiety when I first rescued him, because he was so terrified and it was just me and him in the house for months.

'I think they learn to deal with it, but I don't think they forget.'

As Oscar got better, so did Debra. She wonders sometimes what her life would be like if she hadn't answered the phone that day back in 1993; if she hadn't rescued Oscar and he hadn't rescued her right back; and if she hadn't left her career. She wouldn't be quite so tired, she knows that. She'd have more money too, and she probably wouldn't be so stressed.

But she also knows she wouldn't feel so fulfilled.

'What Oscar has done is changed the course of my life. Before I rescued Oscar I always knew there was something missing. I had a mortgage, life was good – but I wasn't happy,' Debra says. 'It was rescuing Oscar that made me realise I was on the wrong path.'

Which is not to say the work she does now is easy – it definitely is not. 'It's stressful and it's frightening. It's really hard and really hurtful to read some of the stuff detractors write about me. It does bring me down,' she says.

'There's always inner anxiety and turmoil, but I'm doing what I'm meant to be doing. I think that when you connect with what you really want to do, with that comes a sort of inner peace. I can go to bed every night and say, *At least I'm making a difference and doing what I love.*'

She's doing it for Oscar and for the dogs still out there in those sheds.

And she's doing it for Tammy, the brave dog who first taught a little girl that love makes all the difference.

CAESAR

RESCUED HUMAN: PETER HARAN

Peter Haran could be forgiven for being afraid of dogs. It would be entirely understandable if he were not a fan of canines. Should he refuse to walk within fifty paces of a mutt, most people would say, 'And fair enough, too.'

As a young man, Peter was the victim of a dog attack so vicious it left him with permanent facial scarring – and the dog involved was the placid family pet.

It was 1972 and war was raging in Vietnam. Peter, then twenty-three, had recently returned to the family home in Elizabeth, a northern suburb of Adelaide, after his second tour of duty with the Australian Army.

He was about to get married: his wedding was just one week away.

One evening, Peter was in the kitchen with his father's dog, a German shepherd–labrador cross called Rex.

'I was grooming him with a brush. I'd just come out of

the Army, where I'd been a dog handler, so I just handled him very casually. I was bending over him and I opened his mouth and checked his teeth. For half a second I saw his eyes roll back in his head and then he just lunged,' he says. 'He pinned me up against the kitchen sink and ripped my face open. It was a full-on savage attack. He wouldn't stop biting me. He was going for the throat. He didn't relent.'

Peter was eventually able to free himself from Rex's ferocious assault by hitting the dog over the head with the only object he could reach, a sugar bowl. He was rushed to the Royal Adelaide Hospital for surgery on his gaping wounds.

There was, he remembers, a full moon that night. 'The surgeon that operated on me said, "Every time there's a full moon we have a rash of dog attacks,"' says Peter. 'At my wedding I had a big black stripe of stitches down the side of my mouth where the microsurgeon had put my face back together.'

Even before the attack, Peter's formative experiences with dogs hadn't been particularly warm and fuzzy. Born in England, he spent his childhood in Rhodesia, the southern African nation now known as Zimbabwe.

'My father was a builder and we lived there from 1953 until 1961. I went to school there from five through to thirteen years old. It was a beautiful country and a beautiful life in the sun,' he says.

There were always dogs – the indigenous Rhodesian ridgeback – but they weren't really pets. To the young Peter, the large, muscular dogs were majestic, if a little intimidating.

'We had lots of ridgebacks – we went through one after another during the time we were there. There were about five or six of them living on this property that we lived on,' he says. 'They were great, big, powerful dogs and they pretty much did their own thing.'

The Haran family left Rhodesia when civil unrest broke out in the north. They returned to England for eighteen months, where the coldest winter in sixty years swiftly prompted a second emigration.

This time the family would make Australia their home; they arrived in Adelaide in 1964. He still lives there today, with his second wife and their young Weimaraner, Matilda, better known as Tilly. Before Tilly, came Weimaraner siblings Oscar and Emmy – their names a nod to Peter's long career as a newspaper journalist and film reviewer – who were beloved family pets for thirteen years.

Because that's the interesting thing: despite his not-always-pleasant experiences with dogs, Peter still loves them. 'I've always had dogs because I just think your life is not complete without a dog,' he says.

He spent a lot of time thinking about the reason for Rex's attack that day, and concluded that there simply might not have been one. 'I discussed for quite some time with different people why that dog suddenly switched, and I just think the attack was an aberration,' he says.

'I know a lot of people can be badly affected by dog attacks, but it didn't affect me. It was just a lesson in the fact that it doesn't matter how long you've had a dog or how well you think you know it, any dog can snap.'

So, no – Peter is certainly not afraid of dogs.

Not at all. Not even a little bit.

And that's because he owes his life to a rescue dog named Caesar.

Peter was at something of a loose end. He had finished school in Adelaide and didn't have a clear idea of what he wanted to do with his life. His father was adamant that Peter should take an apprenticeship, and ideally follow him into the building trade, but that didn't interest him at all. Nor did becoming a fitter and turner on the assembly line at the northern suburbs' largest employer, General Motors Holden.

Peter needed a job, but felt he had more of a creative bent. He was an avid reader and particularly loved stories of great adventurers and explorers. When three of his close friends announced they intended to enlist in the military, Peter was intrigued: joining the Army could be both a job *and* an adventure.

In late 1965, two months shy of his eighteenth birthday, Peter went to the Army recruiting office in Adelaide and signed on to join for six years. He remembers staring up at a poster of a soldier with the slogan 'A Man with a Mission'. It was precisely what Peter wanted to be.

By 10 January 1966, he was beginning his three-month basic training at Kapooka, the Army recruit training centre in Wagga Wagga, NSW. He was among the youngest of the new recruits – too young to go to Vietnam, where Australia had been involved in the war effort since 1962.

In fact, Peter knew very little about the Vietnam War at that stage. 'I hadn't read anything about it and I had heard no reference to it. Maybe it was on the news – we had a black-and-white TV set – but I didn't see anything on the news that clicked. There was no reference made to the conflict at all during recruit training,' he told the University of NSW's *Australians at War* film archive. 'We weren't being trained to go to war, we were being trained as soldiers to be part of the Australian military.'

At the end of his basic training, Peter relocated to Bardia Barracks at Ingleburn in south-western Sydney. The Australian presence in Vietnam was increasing, but the minimum age for overseas deployment was then nineteen. Still too young to go, Peter was assigned to a demonstration platoon, whose purpose was to show incoming infantrymen how to patrol.

It was, he says, 'really soul destroying stuff' and he was facing another six months of it before he could be deployed overseas, so when he was asked whether he would be interested in joining the experimental Tracking Wing instead, Peter jumped at the chance.

'I went along and did an interview and they said, "Well, we'd like you to be a dog handler." They didn't say, "Do you like dogs?" or "Know anything about dogs?"' he recalls. 'I thought it sounded different and they looked good. So I was posted into the Tracking Wing.'

The purpose of the Tracking Wing, he soon discovered, was to train dogs to track the Viet Cong in Vietnam. The Wing's commanders had used dogs successfully in the

Malayan Emergency and the Indonesian–Malaysian confrontation, and wanted to do the same in this new conflict.

Each Tracker Team would consist of two dogs and their handlers, two visual trackers and two cover men (a machine-gunner and a signaller).

Initially there were fifteen or twenty dogs, all labradors and labrador mixes, and almost all of the dogs were rescues of some description.

'The dogs were being grabbed from anywhere. They were coming from dog homes, they were being picked up from the RSPCA, and some of them were being donated to the Army. There was a real gaggle of dogs down there and they were a mixture, just a strange bunch,' Peter told *Australians at War*. The only real selection criteria were that the dogs had to be black, fit and healthy.

'They were a real wild bunch – they were larrikins. Some of them were fighting all the time, others were just docile labs, failed seeing-eye dogs, some of them were pulled off death row. They cost about three or four dollars, and because of the fact that they were so odd, they were really good.'

For a tracking dog to pass muster, he had to be able to follow a human scent for 5 to 10 kilometres through the bush and then point at the enemy from a distance of 50 to 100 metres.

Generally speaking, a dog 'points' by becoming completely motionless, with his snout towards an object. But perhaps by virtue of their humble beginnings, the dogs of the Tracking Wing had their own unique ways of indicating that trouble lay ahead.

'The handler had to learn his own particular dog's point. It could be the lifting of the ears, it could be the raising of the head, hunching, or just stopping and looking forward. Every dog had a distinctive point, like a gun dog has, and the handler had to know that.'

Each dog was considered a soldier in his own right, and was expected to behave like one.

'The attitude that the Army took and the handlers took was that the dog was a soldier with four legs and had to do every single thing a soldier could do,' Peter says. 'He had to sleep in the bush, eat rations, walk for miles and miles and miles in the rain and the mud, ride in helicopters, be lowered down through trees, hunt the enemy.'

Peter's first canine comrade was simply not cut out for the role. The dog's name was Hadrian and it 'was a nut, an absolute maniac, psycho dog. All it wanted to do was fight. It would fight every other dog.'

Hadrian eventually attacked the chief training instructor and had to be euthanised. The dog's sad end was a real blow to Peter. 'My experience initially with trackers was total failure. I thought I was a man with a mission and I had no mission,' he told *Australians at War*.

At first glance, his next dog didn't look much more promising. Caesar was an excellent tracker, the all-star performer of the Tracking Wing – but he was somebody else's dog. He had been fully trained by another soldier, but that soldier had decided he didn't want to be a dog handler after all and asked to go to Vietnam as an infantryman instead.

So now Peter had a hand-me-down dog and only three months to learn everything about him and get combat-ready himself: it was March, and he and Caesar were scheduled to go to Vietnam with the Queensland-based 2nd Battalion, Royal Australian Regiment (2 RAR), in June.

They would be deployed alongside another dog, Marcus, and his handler, Dennis Ferguson. Marcus was a beautiful dog that had been donated to the Army by the then Governor of NSW, Sir Roden Cutler.

Caesar, by comparison, was something of an oddball. A lab–kelpie cross, he had 'an odd shaped head, kelpie ears – one that hung down because it had piece missing out of it – long legs and a big bushy tail.' But what he may have lacked in the looks department, he more than made up for with his exceptional tracking skills.

Caesar could follow a human scent that was seventy-two hours old in dense bush after heavy rain, pointing by lifting his ears. He had already made headlines in Sydney after police twice called him in to search for missing people. In one of those cases, he found a little girl who had been abducted, following her scent 'up streets, along pavements, across building blocks, past a church congregation of a hundred people' and finally to a playground, where the child had been locked in a toilet block.

It was an impressive effort, and it wasn't the last time Caesar the rescue dog would play rescuer.

*

By August 1967, Peter and Caesar were embedded in Vietnam's Phuoc Tuy province, and had formed not so much a bond as an idiosyncratic marriage of sorts. While the other soldiers in 2RAR developed their own buddy system – pairing off and looking out for each other, especially as the tour dragged on and mental and physical exhaustion set in – the dog handlers each had an added, four-legged responsibility.

'Soldiers in war always pair up with another mate, [but] I couldn't buddy with anybody because I had a dog. In the case of the handler, the dog becomes his soldier mate. Caesar relied on me for everything and I relied on him for everything,' Peter says.

He told *Australians at War:* 'I had to feed him; I had to carry his food and my food. Eventually you probably think you're going mad because you become such good mates with an animal. We actually looked at each other and he'd know what I was thinking and I'd know what he was thinking.'

Which is not to say their partnership wasn't without its frustrations. Just as with a spouse, Peter says there were many times he cursed his furry friend. Caesar never quite mastered the art of helicopter travel, for example. He would leap in the open door of a chopper with such gusto he would often go flying straight out the other side.

Caesar also seemed to have a sixth sense that Peter found more than a little unnerving. 'He would sit up suddenly in the jungle at night and look at things – *left, right, left, right* – like a tennis match. I'd know he was onto something,' he says. 'He could sense something I couldn't and I'd get really cranky with him because I was terrified.'

When the platoon was camped in the jungle, Peter slept with Caesar's leash wrapped around his ankle to ensure the dog didn't wander off during the night – he wasn't always the most obedient of dogs and Peter didn't want to take any chances.

He would always take Caesar just beyond the camp perimeter first thing in the morning so they could both go to the toilet. For their safety, they would leave and re-enter the camp via the exact same route, and they would be watched every step of the way by the two cover men.

One night, Caesar somehow managed to slip his leash. He needed to do his business, but he knew he wasn't supposed to 'go' within the camp. As his master slept, Caesar spied the two cover men. He put two and two together – and unfortunately came up with five.

'He found his way to the other diggers and relieved himself there. It was like he was thinking, *I know this is what I'm supposed to do, I'm just not supposed to do it next to Peter*,' he laughs.

On another occasion, being unleashed nearly had much more serious consequences for Caesar – and indeed for the entire platoon. They had just finished searching a village and had stopped in a dry rice paddy to sit and eat lunch, when Caesar suddenly needed to answer the call of nature.

Peter unclipped the dog's leash – which was a definite no-no – and instructed him to go and do his business just past where the soldiers had gathered in a big circle.

'Then, from the side of the rice paddy, these Vietnamese started screaming at us. We couldn't figure it out,' he says.

The platoon commander and an interpreter walked over to the villagers to find out what the problem was.

'Suddenly they turned around, screaming, "You're having your lunch in the middle of a minefield!" I swallowed hard because I realised the dog wasn't next to me. The guy sitting next to me said, "Can a dog set off a mine?"'

They were about to find out. Peter yelled, 'Stay!' and began crawling towards Caesar with his bayonet extended, prodding the dirt for mines as he inched forward. At the same time, two soldiers with minesweeping equipment swept out to where Caesar dutifully stood motionless. When they determined the area was safe, they grabbed Caesar by his collar and returned him to a sheepish Peter.

They had been incredibly lucky, Peter knew. When it came to tracking humans, Caesar was peerless, but he certainly wasn't a mine detector. He'd had no training to do with mines; none of the tracker teams had.

The deadliest landmine in use in the Vietnam War was the American-made M16, a bouncing mine also known as a Jumping Jack or Bouncing Betty. When detonated these mines launch into the air, spraying high-velocity steel shrapnel 360 degrees around the point of detonation and killing or wounding anyone within 30 metres of the blast.

Consequently, every man in the platoon was terrified of mines. 'The critical thing was, while we were training in Australia before we went there, we were never, ever given any instruction on mines,' he says. 'It was something they didn't want to put inside our heads. I didn't even know what a mine looked like until years later. We were all petrified of mines, because you can't see them. We knew they didn't have to kill us, they only had to maim us.'

On 25 August 1967, just a couple of days after the near miss in the rice paddy, Peter and Caesar were choppered into an area of Phuoc Tuy where Australian soldiers had engaged in a firefight with the Viet Cong. The enemy had fled along a sandy bush trail, and it was up to the tracking team to find them.

There was blood on the trail, so it looked like it would be a fairly straightforward track. Caesar locked onto the scent and off he went, with Peter at the other end of the long tracking leash. He had a cover man by his side, and an infantry platoon following immediately behind.

The infantry soldiers walked in the bush on either side of the dirt track in case of mines. Peter, Caesar and the cover man were on the track itself, but felt they were safe as they were effectively walking in the enemy's footsteps.

After following his nose for several hundred metres, Caesar came to a T-junction. He tracked into the middle of it.

Then he stopped, turned around and came back to Peter.

It was uncharacteristic behaviour to say the least. 'The behaviour was just absolutely bizarre because the dog should never have done that. It was completely contrary to what a tracking dog should have done. He should have continued tracking,' he says.

Peter immediately sensed that something was wrong, but he urged the dog on regardless. Caesar would have none of it. He sat himself on Peter's feet, physically preventing his handler from taking another step forward.

A split second later, an explosion tore through the platoon.

The soldiers moving up the right-hand side of the track had detonated a M16 mine. The platoon commander lost both his legs in the blast, and several other soldiers were seriously injured.

Incredibly, Caesar, Peter, his cover man and the platoon's forward scout had all stepped straight over the mine. The enemy had placed the mines on both sides of the trail, knowing the Australians would not walk on the track itself; the soldiers didn't, but the tracking team did – and it saved their lives.

'The enemy had planted it while we were pursuing them, but they'd put it in the ground slightly sideways,' says Peter. 'When it blew out of the ground all the shrapnel went above my head, but down towards the other men, and they were wounded. All I got was blown up and down.'

The men who were still standing immediately dropped to the ground and rolled off the track into the bush; Peter pulled Caesar with him. It was common in Vietnam for enemy soldiers to ambush a stricken platoon – their biggest worry at that point was being shot at while they waited for help.

Thankfully, the enemy appeared to be long gone. Two medivac helicopters arrived soon after: one airlifted the wounded soldiers to safety, while the second delivered a team of engineers with minesweeping equipment.

'They swept around me and they said, "Where did the dog go?"' Peter told *Australians at War*. He explained to the engineers that Caesar had gone about twenty paces up front and refused to track and came back. 'So they swept up the front, which is normal procedure to see what's under the ground, and then they went down on a spot where they thought was another mine. They looked around and uncovered it and came back and said, "You are the luckiest man alive."'

In the centre of the T-junction, the minesweepers had hit on the same thing Caesar had: a 120-kilogram unexploded American bomb. They later ascertained that it had fallen out of a United States aircraft and the Viet Cong had seized the opportunity, burying it and connecting it to several smaller M16 mines. In a terrible irony, the smaller mines had been stolen from an Australian minefield.

If Caesar, Peter or any of the infantrymen had stepped on one of those connected mines, they all would have been wiped out. By sitting on Peter's foot and preventing the platoon's forward progress, Caesar had saved twenty lives.

'When he got to where the big central bomb was, he baulked at it. He shuddered and came back to me,' says Peter. 'From where the mine went off to where the other big ones were was about 50 to 75 metres. He stopped me so I didn't go any further and step on the explosive that would have killed every one of us.

'After that mine went off Caesar sat in front of me and looked at me as if he was saying, *Well, a fine mess you've got us into this time.*'

But *how* had Caesar known the massive bomb was there, lurking just inches below the dirt? His specialty was tracking humans, not sniffing out deadly explosives. It's certainly possible to train dogs to find landmines – the American military had some 40 000 dogs in Vietnam, many of which did exactly that – but Caesar had no such expertise.

It's a question Peter still ponders more than forty years later. 'This dog was not a trained explosives detection dog. He was just a tracking dog. The other soldiers thought Caesar was alert to big mines, but he was not alert to the one that detonated, which we had stepped straight across,' he says.

'I think he just had a sense of, *Don't come up here, this is really bad*. The dog was looking after me and I was looking after him. Everything came down to that dog walking down the front. The dog was always doing the right thing.

'It was a sense of danger that the dog had for us, but it's not one of our senses; it's not hearing or sight. It was a dog sense that we humans just don't understand.'

Whatever it was, it saved Peter's life.

As he waited for the helicopter that would take him and Caesar back to Nui Dat base, Peter ventured into the T-junction. 'I looked at this tree and saw a red sign and on it was a skull and crossbones and the word *minen* (mines),' he says.

'I couldn't believe it – it was marked as a minefield. The sign had been placed there by friendly troops. The thing was, we came from the other way; that tree was facing the south.'

Nearly two years later, on 21 July 1969, another Australian rifle company came up that same dirt track and stopped about 50 metres from where Peter had spotted the sign on the tree. They didn't see it either. Three men died when another hidden M16 mine was detonated.

That tragic incident was immortalised in Redgum's iconic anti-war song, 'I was Only 19', honouring the men who lost their lives in that minefield on the same day Neil Armstrong became the first man to walk on the moon.

Other soldiers congratulated Peter on Caesar's efforts saving the platoon from disaster, but he found the praise hard to swallow. 'After the explosion they said, "Good job mate – great dog" but all I could think was, *How can they be saying that when I've just led them into a minefield?*'

Peter didn't have much time to process what had happened that day. He and Caesar were choppered out and went straight back to their tracking duties.

'We didn't sit there and think about it. It was too much of a shock and we had to go straight on and immediately do other tracks,' he says. 'My attitude was, *You've got to soldier on and the dog will keep doing what it's doing.*'

And so they did, right up until Peter's tour ended in 1968 and he returned to Australia without Caesar.

According to the Department of Veterans' Affairs, the Australian Army policy was that the dogs would not be brought home at the end of their service. One reason, perhaps not adequately explained at the time, related to an Army veterinary report which noted that large numbers of American tracker dogs in Vietnam had died from a tropical disease, thought (but not confirmed) to be transmitted by ticks.

The report recommended that no tracker dogs be allowed back into Australia 'even under strict quarantine'.

Peter had been shot at and nearly blown up during his time in Vietnam, but leaving Caesar behind was one of the toughest moments he had during his tour.

'I went up and I spoke to him in the cage, sitting in his run, I said, "Sorry I've got to go, you've got to stay, that's the way they run the war. Don't ever forget me, I won't ever forget you." Then I turned and walked straight away,' he told *Australians at War* of the day he farewelled his best friend. 'He had his bowl in his mouth and I heard the bowl hit the concrete floor and I knew that he knew. It was absolutely traumatising. I went back and collapsed and cried in the tent.'

His heartache was eased somewhat by the knowledge that the reinforcement handler coming in to work with Caesar was 'good bloke'. 'I knew the conditions he'd be under, so it was basically a parting of mateship – it was wrenching rather than abandonment.'

When Peter returned to Vietnam for a second tour in 1971, Caesar had been retired. Following a public backlash over its refusal to repatriate the dogs, the Army had done what it thought was the next best thing and given the dogs away to Europeans living in Saigon. Ten of the eleven tracking dogs lived out their days in Vietnam's largest city (one dog, Cassius, sadly died of heat exhaustion after a training run).

'It was people working in banks, people at the Australian and British Embassies and places like that – they were all given the dogs as pets,' he says.

He never saw Caesar again, but the courageous canine's story was far from over.

When he left the Army in 1972, Peter returned to Adelaide and became an advertising copywriter and then a journalist. He married, had two children, divorced and remarried.

He got another dog – an Irish setter called Caesar II.

But as his life went on, he never forgot the original Caesar. He wondered what had become of the brave dog, and was curious about where Caesar's Army-issued identification tag had ended up. He had often thought about it over the years and wished he'd taken it as a souvenir.

In 1987, at the Vietnam Veterans Welcome Home Parade in Sydney, Peter was sitting at a table chatting and reminiscing with his fellow diggers when, apparently out of nowhere, a small silver disc appeared on the table.

It bore an engraved number: *D6N03*.

And a name: *Caesar*.

It was Caesar's tag.

Peter didn't see who left it there. To this day has no idea who it was, but he has a suspicion.

'I think it was an angel from heaven. A deceased digger saying, "Here you are – don't forget us,"' he says.

Peter later donated Caesar's tag to the Australian War Memorial in Canberra, where it is on permanent display.

The more time that passed, the more frustrated Peter became at what he saw as the tracking dogs' exclusion from Australia's war history. 'The dogs did mean a lot to a lot of people, but they were really forgotten by time.'

Peter told *Australians at War*, 'I was sitting at a dinner table and I was telling people, "What did you do in Vietnam?" "I was a dog handler." "We didn't know you had dogs in Vietnam." I was getting that time and time again.'

It was his colleagues at Adelaide's *Sunday Mail* that eventually convinced Peter that Caesar's story needed to be told. In the late 1990s, he sat down and wrote a book about his experiences in Vietnam.

'It took me two or three months and when I finished I gave it to my wife, Denise, to read while I took Caesar II out for a walk,' he says. 'When I got back she'd been flipping through the pages and had thrown them on the floor. She said, "If this gets no better I'll throw the lot on the floor."'

Peter realised his mistake. The book he had written was factual, but it wasn't personal. It didn't shed any light on what life was *really* like in Vietnam for the dog handlers and their tracking dogs.

'I'd tried to write a book about tracking dogs, which was not right,' he says. 'I should have written a book about one dog to tell the story of all the tracking dogs.'

He just wasn't sure how to do that. The answer came to him soon after, during another dog walk – and the way it arrived was every bit as uncanny as the way Caesar had detected that bomb thirty years earlier.

'It was dark, and stretched out in front of me on a long lead in the darkness, Caesar II looked like a black dog tracking – like the original Caesar. This voice came to me: *Tell the story, tell* my *story*,' he says.

So he did. Peter's book, *Trackers: The Untold Story of the Australian Dogs of War*, was published in 2000.

Not long afterwards, he received an astonishing phone call.

'This guy rang me up at work and said, "Peter Haran, sit down – I want to tell you something. I'm the man that got your dog,"' he says.

'Caesar lived in a big villa and ran around on the lawn. They took him to Back Beach at Vung Tau with the kids,' he says. 'The guy said, "He just had a couple of strange behaviours: when he went out to the toilet, he'd come back in and sit down and look at me."'

Caesar had lived with the man and his family in Saigon until they fled when the city fell to the Viet Cong in 1975. The man didn't tell Peter what happened to Caesar after that, and he couldn't bear to ask, although he recently heard a rumour that Caesar was evacuated to the US Embassy and lived the rest of his life in America.

All that mattered to Peter was that Caesar had lived a good life.

Thanks to Peter and his fellow diggers, Australia's Vietnam tracking dogs will never be forgotten. After *Trackers* was published, a group of Vietnam veterans got together and established the Australian Defence Force Trackers and War Dogs Association.

There are now war dog memorials in every Australian state, including a bronze statue of Caesar himself at Sydney's Edmondson Park railway station, just a stone's throw from Bardia Barracks.

'Of all the things I did in journalism, I think writing Caesar's book was the greatest thing I ever did. It will always be there,' Peter says. 'It will just keep going on, and when the book's gone the monuments will be there. You'll always see Caesar in bronze.'

As for Caesar himself, though his final resting place remains uncertain, Peter has a feeling he knows where his faithful dog ultimately ended up.

'The man who had him in Saigon said Caesar liked chasing seagulls on the beach. I keep that picture in my mind of Caesar running along the beach, chasing seagulls,' he says. 'That would have been his heaven.'

He deserved nothing less.

RHIANNA

RESCUED HUMAN: TRISH BORG

If few people can say a rescue dog saved their life, fewer still can say it's happened twice. Trish Borg is one of the lucky ones: fate – and great dogs – seem to have her well and truly in their sights.

Trish hails from the US state of Kentucky, where canines are ubiquitous. From hunting hounds to pampered pets, dogs are as much a part of life for Kentuckians as horse racing and bourbon. And so it was for Trish, who growing up always had dogs and later gave her first husband a boxer puppy called Ginger – so named because of her rich reddish-tan coat.

Ginger may have been a gift for her then husband, but 'she became my girl rather quickly', says Trish. And when Trish underwent gruelling chemotherapy and radiation treatment after she was diagnosed with cancer in 1993, Ginger was her faithful companion.

By the time Ginger passed away in 1999 at the age of eight, Trish had received the all-clear from her doctors and was about to move to a larger farm in a more rural corner of the state. Her husband worked away a lot and she was worried she would feel vulnerable on the new sprawling property all alone. She decided it was time for a new canine companion, and this time she wanted a big dog that would help her to feel a little more secure when she was by herself. It wasn't long before her research led Trish back to the mastiff breeds she had grown up with.

'I've always had dogs and lots of animals. Growing up in the mountains we always had either mastiff breeds or Australian shepherds to help with the animals, and because they were loyal guardians and great family dogs. They're also really sweet and protective. They just made me feel safe,' she says. 'They're very people oriented. They follow you from place to place. It's like having a toddler – you have no privacy.'

Their imposing appearance – mastiffs can grow to a metre tall and weigh more than 100 kilograms – means the various mastiff breeds have been used in guarding and protection roles since the early 19th century. In fact, the greatest weight ever recorded for a dog was that of an English mastiff called Zorba, who tipped the scales at a mind-boggling 155.6 kilograms in 1989. At seven years of age, Zorba was two-and-a-half metres long from the tip of his nose to the tip of his tail, making him the size equivalent of a donkey.

It was with an English mastiff–boxer mix named Roxy by her side that Trish moved to her new property deep in the

Kentucky countryside. Tragically, Roxy was killed soon after. Her loss was so devastating that Trish vowed never to have another dog. 'Someone had shot Roxy and it just broke my heart. I said, "No more, no more,"' she recalls. The perpetrator was never caught.

But Trish's sister, Diana, was concerned about Trish being on her own on the isolated property when her husband travelled for work, and knew the time was right for another four-legged friend. As sisters often do, Diana felt she'd be better off asking for forgiveness than permission.

'My sister said, "I don't like the idea of you out there by yourself,"' Trish says. 'She just came over one day and got out of the car with this dog. I said, "No way – I'm not making eye contact. Take her away right now!"'

But the dog, a female boxer, had other ideas. 'She ran onto the porch and sat in front of me like, *I will not be ignored*. Then she started licking me and loving me.'

It was a done deal.

'I named her Sabrina but it became Bree really quickly because Sabrina was too hard for me to yell,' Trish laughs. 'She was stubborn and very loyal.'

Bree was a rescue of sorts, having found herself facing homelessness when her previous owners moved away and weren't able to take her with them. They didn't want their much-loved dog to end up in a shelter; fortunately, Diana heard they were moving and, knowing her sister loved boxers, stepped in with a solution.

Though she had been reluctant to love a dog again, Trish and Bree became inseparable. She may have weighed more than 60 kilograms, but Bree was as gentle as a lamb, not only acting as a formidable-looking security guard on the property, but also providing much needed support for Trish when her marriage ended. Put simply, 'she was my heart,' says Trish.

In January 2003, Bree's attentive nature suddenly went into overdrive. Boxers are known for their loyalty, docility and loving temperament, but Bree – though always tuned-in to how her mistress might be feeling – wasn't a particularly lovey-dovey dog. Yet without warning, one day she turned into a licker.

'She had never been one of those in-your-face dogs. She was never a licker but all of a sudden, every time she lay down next to me, she kept licking my left side,' Trish says.

She wasn't overly enamoured with the strange behaviour. Trish had been feeling unwell and didn't have the energy to get to the bottom of her dog's out-of-the-blue neurosis – so she went to the doctor. 'I'd lost heaps of weight, felt very lethargic and wanted to sleep all the time, but Bree kept constantly licking me. I'd tell her off: "What's going on with you? Stop it!"'

Devastating news soon followed: Trish's cancer had returned, this time in her left kidney. Immediately, understanding dawned for Trish. 'It didn't click with me until after they found the cancer in my left side – that's where Bree had been licking me. I guess that was her way of trying to tell me,' she says. 'It was like, *Oh my god, she knew!* I'm a firm believer in that. Dogs are so clever.'

This time around, Trish decided not to undergo chemotherapy or radiation. She wanted to try to beat this second bout of cancer without invasive and debilitating treatments. 'I decided I wasn't going down that route again. I went the alternative route and that seemed to pan out for me,' she says.

'I was on a really crazy diet that just supported being really healthy. I got colonics every day to help my body get rid of toxins. It was very full-on, but the cancer is gone and I'm very happy.'

Bree's unwanted tongue baths may have been an irritation, but without them Trish may never have been spurred into visiting the doctor. In her uniquely canine way, Bree had saved Trish's life.

As for most of us in the 21st century, the internet was a handy tool for Trish. But it became something of a lifeline during her second cancer battle. She spent a lot of time online researching treatment options and comparing notes with other cancer patients and their supporters in several internet chat groups.

And it was in one of these groups, not long after her diagnosis, that Trish struck up a conversation with an Australian carpenter by the name of Charlie Borg. 'Charlie's mother had been through cancer and he was more or less browsing the internet and I was there looking for information,' she says.

Though they were more than 15 000 kilometres apart, the pair quickly became firm friends – and it wasn't long before deeper feelings developed.

'We decided that if we were still friends in a year he'd come from Melbourne to the United States to see me, which he did,' Trish says.

That three-month-long visit in 2004 confirmed what both Trish and Charlie had suspected: they had fallen for each other. But being together was never going to be simple. Aside from the not-insignificant fact that they lived on opposite sides of the planet, both had well-established lives in their respective countries. Trish had Bree to look after, as well as a host of other animals on her farm, and she was still a cancer patient. Meanwhile, in Melbourne, Charlie doted on his then seventeen-year-old daughter, Alexandra. For the next year, the couple kept in touch online and by phone, unsure how – or indeed if – their relationship could work in the long term.

In 2005, Trish travelled to Melbourne for a 'make or break' three-month trip. Boarding that flight, she had to admit she was nervous. 'I didn't know much about Australia before my first visit here. I had talked to people online and I had a few good friends in Perth. I just knew it was hot and I probably wouldn't like it,' she laughs.

But just as fate had apparently brought Bree into her life, it was about to intervene once again. This time, however, it wasn't a 'fur baby' but a human baby that shaped her destiny.

'Charlie and I decided we were going to be together and I went home pregnant after my visit to Australia,' Trish says. 'I endured the whole pregnancy, except for the first few weeks, alone. The economy wasn't that good in the US so I decided I'd move to Melbourne after the baby was born. Charlie came over for the birth and we came home in the winter of 2006, when our son, Caleb, was three months old.'

In fact, it was while she was pregnant with Caleb that Trish received the all-clear from her kidney cancer. She believes falling in love played a key part in her recovery.

'The tumours had shrunk, which was why I'd decided to come to Australia that year to see Charlie. I still brought my medication, but I guess just being here and being happy made a difference,' she says. 'We travelled around a bit during that trip – we went to Perth to see our friends there and we also drove the Great Ocean Road. It was the year one of the Twelve Apostles fell and that became our joke: that our son was conceived that day and the earth moved!'

While she was elated to be starting her new life in a new country with her family, her move Down Under meant Trish was forced to make the gut-wrenching decision to leave Bree behind.

'I left Bree in Kentucky with my ex-husband. It broke my heart because she was the dog I had bonded the most with in my life, but she has 116 acres there to run free on and I just thought it would be cruel to take her away from everything she knew,' she says.

Though missing her precious pooch, Trish was surprised at how quickly she settled in to her adopted homeland, moving to the suburb of Wyndham Vale, 30 kilometres southwest of Melbourne's CBD. 'I love the convenience of living in Melbourne and that it's a whole melting pot. At first I kept saying, "I can't wait to get home to Kentucky – I miss the mountains and the change of seasons,"' she says. 'But the last time we went back it was for just over four weeks and as soon as we got on the plane I was thinking, *Gosh, I can't wait to get home to Australia.* Somewhere along the way I started recognising it as home.'

Once she realised she truly felt at home in Australia, Trish began to wonder whether it was time to complete her family with the one thing she hadn't yet felt able to acknowledge was missing: a dog.

'When I first came to Melbourne I was just busy with Caleb and the whole dynamic of being in a new place. I didn't know if I would be able to stay here – if I'd be able to settle in and feel at home – so I didn't think about getting a dog,' she explains.

'In early 2016, Caleb kept asking for a puppy for his tenth birthday. My husband kept saying, "When he keeps his room clean and learns a bit of responsibility he can have a dog." That was never going to happen, so I put my foot down and said, "It's time!"'

Caleb had his heart set on getting a pug and the whole family wanted a puppy, but when Trish started researching online it was a picture of a fourteen-month-old rescue dog that captured her attention – and her heart.

The dog's name was Rhianna and she was a French mastiff. 'I wanted a puppy, but when I started looking I came across Rhianna and fell in love with her. It was just her face – I saw her eyes and that was that,' she recalls. 'I saw her photo on the Homeless Hounds website and clicked to read more about her. She just seemed so well behaved and

I thought, *What a little gem – what's she doing with a rescue?*'

As it turned out, Rhianna had been surrendered by her previous owner because she was something of a canine Houdini. 'She kept escaping and I think he was paying out more and more in [council pound] fees to pick her up. She also had tummy issues and vomited a lot,' says Trish. 'She was tossed around. He was like, "No, I'm not taking her back because she's going to get out again and I can't afford this."'

His loss was to prove the Borg family's gain. 'I asked Caleb, "Would you be disappointed if we didn't get a puppy and instead rescued a dog that needs a home?" He said, "I think that's a good idea, Mum."'

And that was that – except, of course, it wasn't.

Trish contacted the rescue to register her interest in Rhianna, but was told the pretty dog had already had several meet-and-greet appointments with prospective adopters and would likely have a new family soon. 'I was just gutted,' Trish admits.

Nevertheless, she pressed on with her search for a four-legged family member. 'We went to the shelters near us and met a few other dogs and put in papers to adopt one named Buffy, but we didn't get her – they let her go home to another family,' she says. 'Just as we were expecting the call to say we could come and get Buffy, I got an email saying she'd been adopted. I looked further through my emails and there was one saying, "Rhianna wasn't adopted after all – if you want, you can come and meet her."'

She had no idea how she'd missed the email in the first place, but she was determined not to miss her second chance to make Rhianna a part of her family. The very next day – 6 March 2016 – Trish, Charlie and Caleb drove two hours to the Mornington Peninsula, 110 kilometres south of Melbourne, to meet Rhianna at her foster carer's home.

First impressions were overwhelmingly positive. 'She was a bit timid, a bit shy. She would come up straight away, but only if you were sitting down. I just thought she needed love and attention and to feel like she had a home,' says Trish. 'She was a little champion. I thought, *Oh my gosh, how could we be so lucky?*'

The family discovered that Rhianna was actually two years old, not fourteen months as they had initially been told. She was on the small side for the breed, hence the confusion. The Borgs signed on the dotted line and took Rhianna home. On the way they stopped at a pet store to buy supplies and weigh her. She had lost weight when one of the foster siblings she'd bonded with was adopted – she was pining for him and had stopped eating. Rhianna's broken heart only made Trish more determined to show the gentle dog all the love and care she deserved.

It's often said that rescue dogs somehow know they've been given a second chance and will show that they are grateful however they can. Little did Trish know, Rhianna was about to demonstrate her gratitude in the most powerful way.

*

Not even a week had passed since Rhianna became part of the Borg family, but already Trish struggled to remember life without the sweet dog in the house.

'She's so much more than the timid girl we brought home. She's very funny. She owns us, we don't own her,' she laughs. 'Charlie is the primary walker and Rhianna tells him when she's ready to go for a walk and when she's not. She will bark at him and go to the front door and sit down. If he tries to take her out the back gate she's like, *No, I'm going out the front door.*

'She's remarkable, beautiful. Once I had a friend visiting whose daughter was very tiny and fell into the toilet and screamed and Rhianna bolted in to see what was happening. She's like the guardian of the family.'

The family considered changing their new pet's name, but couldn't settle on an alternative. 'I wanted to change her name and asked Caleb, since she was meant to be his gift. He said, "Rhianna is a beautiful name for a beautiful dog – why would we want to change it?"' So Rhianna she would be.

Though she had been offered an inside bed, Rhianna preferred to sleep outdoors, where she could keep an eye on things. 'We kept her inside the first night but the second night she didn't want to be in. We fixed her a nice bed outside and she was happy sleeping by the back door,' Trish says.

The Friday after Rhianna arrived, March 11, was Caleb's tenth birthday. Reaching double digits was a big deal and Trish had planned a special day for her son. 'I had a thousand errands to do and was going to be in and out of the house all day,' she says.

It was around 11.30 a.m. and she had just collected Caleb's birthday cake from a local bakery. She raced home to put it in the fridge and at the same time collect a batch of cupcakes to take straight back to his school for a celebration there at noon. There was also the matter of needing to answer a rather urgent call of nature.

Trish drove into the garage adjacent to the house. Rhianna, as had become her custom, waited calmly in the backyard. In her rush to tick off the many items on her to-do list, Trish dashed inside via a side door. Usually she would have closed it behind her, but today she left it ajar.

'I was bursting to pee so I quickly opened the side door and went in. I was in a hurry and didn't take the time to slide the door closed. I was thinking, *If Rhianna wants to come in, she can come in*,' she says.

While she was using the bathroom, Trish heard the doorbell ring.

And ring.

And ring.

'I just thought, "Who is this? I don't have time for this!"' she says. Irritated, she hurried to the front door.

On her front doorstep stood two men. Trish realised with dismay that the security screen door was open – in their haste to leave the house that morning, none of the family had remembered to lock it – and there was nothing standing between her and the two strangers.

Trish stepped outside, pulling the front door closed but not shutting it entirely. Wearing suits and nametags, and carrying clipboards, the two men looked 'very official'.

'They said they were with the government and needed to measure the roof for solar panels. I said I wasn't interested, but they kept going and going,' Trish recalls. 'I said I was in a hurry and then I made the mistake of saying, "Just leave the paperwork and when my husband gets home he'll give you a call."'

As soon as Trish revealed she was home alone, the men struck.

'The first man pushed past me and ran into the house. I turned around to say, "What do you think you're doing? Get out!" When I had my back turned, the second man started trying to push me into the house,' she says. 'It was like a scene out of a movie.'

Time seemed to slow down as, terrified, Trish began to scream and kick against her assailant. She felt she was fighting for her life. If the man succeeded in forcing her back inside the house, she was convinced she would not survive.

'It seemed like I was fighting the guy forever, but it was probably only seconds. I thought the other guy was checking the house and was going to come back and shut me up. All I had in my mind was, *They're not going to let me live because I've seen their faces*,' she says. 'I was trying to get down the driveway, but I was hemmed up in the door. There was no way I was going back in the house. If they'd got me inside it would have been after I wasn't breathing.'

As she struggled desperately to free herself from the attacker's powerful grip, Trish had another, truly devastating thought. 'I was thinking, *Oh my God, it's Caleb's birthday and they're going to kill me*. I didn't want my son to come home on his birthday and find me [dead].'

She screamed as loudly as she could, hoping to attract the attention of a neighbour or passerby. But nobody heard her. Nobody came.

Well, almost nobody.

Suddenly, over her screams and ragged breathing, Trish heard another sound. A low, rumbling growl came from inside the house. She'd never heard a noise quite so menacing.

Immediately, she knew. *Rhianna*.

'I just heard this growl and I turned and saw the guy who'd come into the house first running. Rhianna was standing up on her back legs, lunging for him, trying to get at his neck. When he started gaining ground, she dropped to all fours in a flash and took off in hot pursuit,' she says. 'The guy that was trying to push me must have seen what was going on before I did, because when I turned around he just ran off.'

The first man also barrelled past Trish and fled down the driveway – but Rhianna wasn't about to give up so easily. She took off after the pair, barking and snarling as she chased them.

'Everything happened so fast. I couldn't get her to stop. She was gone. She just wanted them away from me,' says Trish.

Too shaken to follow, Trish sank down onto the kerb and called Charlie, who was working out of town that day.

'He said, "I'm packing up now, I'll be home soon,"' Trish says. She was frightened that, after less than a week in an unfamiliar place, Rhianna wouldn't be able to find her way back to her new home, but as Trish and Charlie spoke, the brave dog returned – from the opposite direction than the way she had left. Fifteen minutes had passed and the dog was 'all lathered up'.

'I was sitting outside on the phone, just hoping she would come back, scared to death that she'd get lost. She just jumped up on me with her front paws in my lap and sniffed me all over,' she says. 'I was patting her. We both checked each other over really well.' It was the first sign of real affection Rhianna had displayed since her adoption.

Even in her shocked state, Trish understood immediately that Rhianna had saved her life. 'It was just very fortunate that I'd come quickly through the house and left the side door open where she was, because otherwise she wouldn't have had access to the house and to me,' she says. 'I realised right away what she'd done for me. I remember calling Charlie and being barely able to get out, "Thank God for the dog."'

Thank God for the dog indeed. In the five days since adopting Rhianna, Trish hadn't heard a peep from her new four-legged friend. She had even emailed the rescue to ask if she'd had debarking surgery, because she found Rhianna's quiet nature so unusual.

Turns out, 'she'd just had no reason to bark until that point,' says Trish. 'Because she sure barked that day.'

With Rhianna safely back by her side, Trish loaded her into the car. They set out for Caleb's school, still stunned by what had just happened. 'I was so shaken that I just wanted to be away from the house. When Rhianna came back I was like, "That's it, let's get away,"' she says. 'I quickly ran the birthday cupcakes in and my friend took them to Caleb's classroom. My shirt was ripped and I was half sobbing and trying to get it together. My friend came back home with me and that's when I called the police.'

Local police duly investigated attack, but the assailants were never caught. Trish says she later learned that the incident was similar to a spate of home invasions and attempted invasions in surrounding suburbs.

'You wouldn't look at our house and think we were wealthy,' she says. 'To this day I have no idea what they wanted.'

Whatever it was the men wanted, they were never going to get it. Rhianna made sure of that.

More than two years after the terrifying attack, Trish admits she sometimes still wonders, *What if?*

What if the family had been successful in adopting Buffy, the first dog they applied for? What if they'd brought home the pug puppy Caleb had his heart set on instead of rescuing a robust French mastiff? What if she hadn't been in such a hurry that morning and had closed the side door after entering the house?

'Now I quite often think back and it would have been a much different story if it had been a pug,' Trish says. 'I knew I was going to be the one looking after the dog and taking care of her, so I wanted a dog that I had a bond with. I loved Rhianna the moment I saw her and I love her even more now.'

And what if the man Rhianna accosted hadn't managed to get away from her? Trish wonders about that, too. While she's certain her dedicated dog would have done whatever it took to keep her safe that day, she also knows her sweet girl doesn't have an ounce of malice in her.

'I often wonder about that. She's just not a vicious dog. The only time I've ever seen her arc up is when I'll take her to the vet and there'll be an obnoxious dog that will bark at her or lunge at Caleb. She'll put herself in a position to stop that dog,' she says. 'I don't know if she would have grabbed that man, maybe held him. I think she may have stopped them from harming me because she knew they were doing wrong, but I just can't picture her harming anything.'

Trish has largely managed to put the terror of that day behind her, but understandably, there are still moments that make her anxious. 'For the first two or three months afterwards, I would get out of bed at night and check to make sure all the doors were locked. If the doorbell rang during the day and it was just me at home, in my mind there was always that possibility. I would see my hand shaking as I opened the door.'

But if every cloud has a silver lining, in this case it's the fact that their shared trauma has cemented an unbreakable bond between Trish and Rhianna. Rhi – as she's most often called by the Borgs – rarely lets Trish out of her sight these days.

'Those are her rules,' Trish laughs. 'From that day forward she's been inside. She refuses to sleep anywhere but inside. She's my shadow. If I go out to hang out the washing, she's on my heels. If I'm cooking dinner, she's lying on the rug looking at me, hoping I'll drop something that she can snatch up. It's nice to know that when I answer the door she's there by my side.

'It was like she made a decision that I'm her human and no one was going to hurt me. She's been a joy ever since.'

Some experts argue that heroic dogs aren't really trying to save their humans; they're only trying to save themselves. Try telling that to a woman whose life has been saved twice by two different canines; a woman for whom any one of those 'what ifs' could have led to a drastically different outcome.

Then again, maybe Rhianna was also asking herself *What if*? What if her first owner hadn't admitted his shortcomings and given her a chance to find a better home? What if a loving family of three hadn't driven two hours just to meet her? What if they hadn't welcomed her into their home as if it had been hers all along?

What if Rhianna was just returning the favour?

BUDDY

RESCUED HUMANS: JUDY SCRIVENER AND MICHAEL SANDERS

The ancient Greek historian and author Thucydides famously said, 'In generosity we are equally singular, acquiring our friends by conferring, not by receiving, favours.' What he meant, of course, is that it's better to give than to receive – that an act of kindness should be performed selflessly and without thought of reward.

It's a philosophy that dogs seem to live by. Day after day, our canine companions offer love, devotion and, in many cases, specific services and tangible assistance – and they expect nothing in return. The most meagre remuneration – a scratch behind the ears, perhaps, or a few minutes of play with a favourite toy – is like winning the lottery to a big-hearted canine.

Humans, however, have been a little slower to absorb Thucydides' message. Most of us are driven by self-interest, looking out for number one whenever we can. Case in point: according to the Australian Bureau of Statistics, only a quarter of the nation's 25 million inhabitants participate in any sort of volunteer work. It just seems to be in our nature to ask 'What's in it for me?'

It's not in Judy Scrivener's nature, though. And it's definitely not in the nature of her rescued labrador, Buddy.

There aren't many animal lovers in the Northern Tablelands region of New South Wales who don't know Judy. Not only was Judy once a busy local solicitor in the area, she is also an indefatigable campaigner for animal rights, with rescue dogs – especially those saved from untold suffering in large-scale commercial breeding facilities, also known as puppy farms – among her chief concerns.

But while she has always loved animals, Judy's interest in welfare causes was sparked relatively recently. 'As a child I had a dog and in adulthood I've always been interested in animals, not just dogs but also horses. My interest in dogs developed over the last seven or eight years,' she says. 'I was very ignorant of a lot of the horrors with regard to puppy farms and the neglect and mistreatment of dogs, so I started to educate myself.'

The catalyst for that education was Judy's day job. She began working on probation and parole cases in her role as a solicitor and was confronted with shocking evidence of abuse perpetrated by a woman convicted of animal cruelty.

'There was a matter that went before the local court, a puppy farmer. I got hold of the expert evidence that was presented to the court and I ended up crying. I was so shocked and disgusted that I had to go into another room at work,' she recalls. 'There were [reports of] dogs having to be euthanised because of things like compound fractures and bones sticking out of the skin; dogs stuck to the floor with maggots. What started as reading some horror material in my line of work quickly became, *How did I not know these places existed?*'

Incensed and determined to take action, Judy founded the advocacy group Dogs without Borders Australia, which lobbies for better legislation and the closure of the farms. She also started visiting local puppy farms herself to gather evidence, often in disguise, and never fails to be appalled by the conditions she encounters.

'How puppy farmers work is they never allow people to go near their properties. They'll meet prospective buyers in a car park or something instead,' she explains. 'I remember one who was particularly vile. Some of her dogs had things like exploded mammary cysts. Her dogs were kilometres from her house. They were never touched. Some of those dogs were so damaged they still can't leave foster care – and she's still operating.'

Judy has also rescued countless dogs herself. She currently has seven of her own, and has provided a temporary home for numerous down-on-their-luck dogs over the years. More than once, a dog that was supposed to be a temporary resident has become a permanent member of the family.

That's exactly how Buddy joined the household. With six dachshunds at home already – parents Limo and Lexie and their four offspring – Judy certainly wasn't planning to add any more four-legged friends to her menagerie, but given what she now knew about puppy farms and backyard breeding, she was ever on the lookout for opportunities to help spare animals from suffering.

She got into the habit of monitoring local buy, sell and swap websites. In Judy's experience, they were the sales platform of choice for people looking to make a quick buck on puppies or offload unwanted breeding dogs for free.

'I started looking just locally. You'd see on Facebook: "Giveaway, I need this gone" – meaning dogs,' she says. She knew that clandestine dog fighting rings operated in the bush, and she couldn't bear the thought of these apparently 'worthless' dogs being left to the mercy of such unscrupulous people.

'In 2012, I saw a young fellow with labradors wanting to sell all the puppies for $100 each. I thought, *I'll just go and have a look at these little dogs*,' she recalls. When she met the puppies' parents and saw the conditions the dogs were living in, she became gravely concerned about the breeder's ability to care effectively for the animals. 'If you can't afford a vaccination and you can't afford worming, you shouldn't be breeding dogs.'

There were two puppies left and Judy was set to offer to take them both, but she was pipped at the post. 'There was a very young girl there and she said, "That's cute, I'll take that." It was a complete impulse, so I dread to think what happened to that dog,' she says.

That left just one pup. The tiny dog was just seven or eight weeks old, barely big enough to leave his mother. His little belly was round and distended – he was full of worms. Judy left with the bundle of yellow fuzz and set out to deliver him to a friend who ran a dog refuge; she had offered to care for the puppy until he was strong enough to be adopted by a suitable family.

But Judy had forgotten one crucial thing. Her son, Michael Sanders, then 31, was waiting in the car.

Mike, as he's commonly called, was born with monosomy 9p. Also known as Alfi's Syndrome, monosomy 9p is a rare chromosomal disorder in which part of chromosome 9 is missing. Symptoms can include intellectual disabilities, congenital heart defects and dysmorphic features. Mike is completely blind in his left eye and has partial vision in his right.

'Mike is my eternal toddler. He's my shadow. His intellectual function is very much like a young child,' says Judy, who left her job in 2016 to care for Mike full time. 'He's so innocent. Some of what he says goes straight to the bone. When I go to a puppy farm I come up with these huge stories – I never know what I'm going to say or what story I'm going to come up with. Mike says, "Yep, my mum's the best liar!"'

He also has a special affinity with animals. 'Mike has always been exposed to animals through me and he's great, he's wonderful with them. He loves the dogs,' she says. 'His regular comment is, "Which puppy farm are we going to this weekend?" It makes me laugh. Other kids would say, "Are we going bowling?"'

It's hardly surprising, then, that when Judy climbed into the car with a labrador puppy, Mike's eyes lit up. Judy explained that they wouldn't be keeping the little dog, but it was no use.

'The dog was very, very small – a tiny puppy with a huge belly – and he was very affectionate with Mike,' says Judy. 'Mike tends to self-talk. He'll chatter away and he was saying, "You can sleep in my bed, we'll ask Mum, you can be my buddy." By the time we got to the refuge I thought, *Let Mike have him.* So in the 30-odd kilometres it took to drive out there, we managed to acquire another dog.'

Another dog whose name had clearly been decided, too: Buddy.

It didn't take long for the fledgling bond between Mike and Buddy to grow into something truly profound. As the little dog – who was promptly treated for the worms that had swelled his belly – grew bigger and stronger, he seemed to decide it was his mission in life to protect Mike.

'Labradors are exceptionally good and patient with children and in special needs areas. It's like Buddy is an old soul in a young dog's body. I don't really know how to describe it, but he seems to have this knowledge and this patience that you really don't get with most dogs,' says Judy. 'He's almost spiritual in his approach to things. When you look in Buddy's eyes it's exceedingly obvious that there's so much going on.

'There's a depth of understanding. He's wise. Whether that's because of Mike's disability and Buddy's recognition of that, I don't know.'

And it wasn't just the humans in the household who felt the benefits of Buddy's soulful presence – the tolerant lab soon bonded with all of Judy's other animals, from dogs to chickens to the cat.

Yes, Buddy made fast friends with everyone he met – but nobody appreciated just how far he would go for those he loved until 16 December 2016, when the rescue dog turned rescuer.

Judy's house in Red Range was truly her castle. After she purchased it in November 2015, she had spent more than $75 000 on renovations and by December the following year they were complete at last. As her second Christmas in the smart weatherboard property approached, Judy was excited about spending a relaxed festive season with Mike and their menagerie in a home that was no longer a building site.

'I'd had walls knocked out, the kitchen redone by a local cabinetmaker, a brand new bathroom, new floors,' she says. 'I'd done so much work inside and it was just coming together beautifully. It was going to be my dream home.'

The Christmas tree was up, too. Years earlier, Judy had hit on a clever trick to ensure she didn't have to spend hours untangling strings of lights every December. 'What I would do after each Christmas was simply fold the branches up and leave the lights, wrap the tree up in a sheet and put it away,' she says. 'The next year all I'd have to do was open it up and the lights were on it.'

This year, however, she wondered if it might be time to retire the lights. 'The lights had been flickering a little. They'd been on there a number of years and I thought I might have to get some new ones.'

But amid the whirl of more pressing Christmas tasks, ticking that job off her to-do list slipped Judy's mind. There were cards to write and presents to wrap, which is what she was doing on the night of Friday, 16 December.

Mike was already in bed, fast asleep, by the time Judy finished the gift wrapping and decided to turn in herself. Her nighttime ritual isn't a solitary affair, though. She shares her bed with four of her six dachshunds, and their 7.5-centimetre legs mean they can't jump up; they each have to be lifted into position.

'They're smooth-haired dachshunds so they're quite chubby and large. I say to people that I do yoga at night – I never knew my legs could go at that angle!' she laughs.

Two other 'sausage dogs' – Limo and Lexie – have mobility problems, so they sleep in comfy crates in the bedroom. Buddy has his own rug at the foot of Judy's bed.

Finally, with everyone settled, Judy turned off the light and drifted off to sleep.

She wasn't sure how long she had slumbered when, in the dead of night, something roused her. She was disoriented, still teetering on the brink of sleep, but she was sure she had felt the bed move.

This wasn't the subtle sort of movement made by one of the dachshunds stretching or rolling over, though. This was a big shake.

'The dachshunds only have three-inch legs, so they're not tall enough to jump on the bed, but something woke me,' Judy says. 'There was a bounce on the bed and a lick on my face.'

The wet kiss abruptly brought Judy to full consciousness. She opened her bleary eyes, and in the dim light, could just make out Buddy standing over her. It was completely uncharacteristic behaviour: the sweet dog had never jumped on the bed before, let alone in the middle of the night when Judy was sound asleep.

But it wasn't just the sight of Buddy on the bed that worried her – it was what Judy could *smell.*

'When I woke up I could smell smoke, but at first it wasn't overly alarming. In winter, when I have the open fire going and have the window behind my bed open, I'll smell smoke,' she says. 'It didn't hit home straight away, but a few seconds later I thought, *Why am I smelling smoke?* What went through my brain was, *It's December – we don't have the fire going.*'

As horrifying understanding dawned, Judy was on her feet in seconds. With Buddy on her heels, she went to her bedroom door and peered into the hallway, where her worst fear was confirmed. 'I got up and went to the door and my heart went to my throat because I could see smoke,' she says.

The home Judy loved and had meticulously restored was on fire.

'I ran out to the lounge room, which was to the right of my bedroom, and I didn't see flames but I saw this grey, swirling smoke,' she recalls. 'It didn't smell like wood smoke, which has a very distinct smell.'

Immediately, she knew: *The Christmas tree.* The twinkling lights must have sparked the blaze.

Her first thought was for Mike. A notoriously heavy sleeper, Judy knew she was in a race against time to wake him and get him outside.

'It was quite hard – he was dead to the world. At that time he was completely blind in his left eye, so it was very scary waking him from a deep sleep because he can't see, and he takes little steps when he's worried,' she says.

Somehow, she managed to steer Mike through the ever-increasing smoke to safety. She put him in her car, then turned her attention to the beloved pets still inside the burning house.

She raced back in and retrieved the four dachshunds that, just minutes ago, had been sleeping peacefully beside her on the bed. On her next attempt she went in for Limo and Lexie.

'I thought, *How am I going to manage getting these two dogs that can't walk out?* I managed it, but by the third time in the house I was terrified. I couldn't see what was happening then because the smoke was so thick,' Judy says. 'I finally understand now the absolute fear of total disorientation – not knowing where you are even though you know your house so well. Because fear kicks in, and that stops logical thinking, you begin to panic.'

There was one pet Judy couldn't find, a beautiful Burmese cat called Phlop. By now, the smoke was impenetrable and the flames were taking hold. It was a devastating blow, but she knew there was no way she could go back in again.

Only then – once she knew she had saved as many animals as she possibly could – did Judy realise she needed to call the emergency services. But she had lost her mobile phone in the chaos.

'I tried to go back in one last time and just panicked at the door,' she says. 'I didn't have my mobile, which I have beside my bed all the time, so I ran across to my neighbour and banged on the window.'

She tried to make the call herself using her neighbour Margie's phone, but shock was setting in and she couldn't manage it. 'I'm normally a fairly steady, logical person, but I couldn't stop my hand shaking to dial 000. It was bizarre.'

Finally, the call was placed. Now all Judy, Margie and Mike could do was wait for help to arrive.

'Because I was 20 kilometres out of town, it took 30 or 40 minutes for them to get there,' she says. 'Margie and I were standing outside, waiting. I could see flames in the lounge room. I had a big, 2.7-metre window and it exploded. As soon as that happened, the fire went out and up.'

By the time the Red Range Brigade, Fire & Rescue NSW and Glen Innes Rural Fire Service arrived, it was too late. The house had been razed.

'The head firey said to me, "We're really sorry, but with these dwellings, from the moment the fire takes hold it's minutes before it's engulfed,"' says Judy.

It was a horrific experience for Judy, but Mike was particularly terrified. 'It was really, really traumatic for Mike,' she says. 'He was just sitting in the car screaming, "Help! Help!" It's rather surreal when I think back. It was just a shocking sight and sound.'

The next day, as the smoke cleared and she was able to pick through the twisted, charred wreckage of her home, it started to dawn on an exhausted Judy just how close she had come to losing everything; not just her house, but her life – and the lives of her son and their pets.

There was only one reason they had made it out alive: Buddy.

There's a reason that labradors are among the dog breeds most commonly used in detection roles. Whether it's sniffing out drugs, weapons, cash or fire accelerants, a lab's sensitive nose can pinpoint the barest whiff of a scent. To Buddy and his 200 million-plus olfactory receptors, the very first puff of smoke that night would have been a pungent bouquet he simply couldn't ignore.

If he hadn't been there to alert Judy when the fire was still contained – if he hadn't overcome his usually obedient instincts and jumped on the bed – the smoke would have had to fill the house before it was enough to wake her. But by then, she may not have woken up at all: smoke inhalation can cause death by carbon monoxide and cyanide exposure.

And even if she had eventually woken on her own, Judy would likely have been quickly overwhelmed by smoke and unable to find the exit. More people die from the effects of smoke in house fires than from burns.

'The next day a reporter from the local newspaper came and asked to do an interview. I hadn't had a chance to re-live everything because it had only been a few hours. I was desperately tired and I had to re-think everything,' says Judy. 'I really started to think about how close it came. The way that smoke was curling out, it wouldn't have been long before it reached the bedroom. If Buddy had not jumped on the bed I really don't think we'd be here.'

She had long been in awe of the way Buddy selflessly put himself out for those he loved; she just hadn't imagined he would one day become her lifesaver, too.

As often happens in rural areas, the local community immediately rallied around Judy and Mike, donating clothing, household items and pet supplies to help them during the Christmas period.

'I couldn't believe the generosity. I was floored. I didn't know any of the people that donated. It was humbling,' she says. 'That side of human nature is always there and I wish we saw it in everyday life, not just in times of sadness and tragedy. That tiny moment of caring, that helping hand, just means the world.'

But it would be nearly a year before they once again had a home they could call their own.

'We were living in rented accommodation and I'd looked at a number of properties, and even paid for building and pest inspections, but with each of those houses something wasn't right, so I waited,' Judy explains.

It was Judy's younger son, Nick, who spotted the home she now lives in. And just as it felt like fate had brought Buddy into her and Mike's life, the house also seemed destined to be theirs.

'Nick and I had looked and looked through all the houses available in the district, but somehow I'd never seen this one. Then, on the way back from looking at another house, Nick rang me and said, "Pop up and have a look at this one,"' she says.

Judy walked in and immediately felt that she could make the house a home, but she was stunned when the vendors offered to include all their furniture and white goods in the sale at no extra charge. She assumed they must have heard about the fire, but they hadn't.

'I told them about the fire and the man was really quiet. It turned out his sister and brother-in-law had died in a house fire about eighteen months earlier,' she recalls. 'I thought, *This must be so raw for them to have me standing here saying I'd lost everything in a fire.*'

The vendors simply wanted to make a fresh start – and they were happy to help Judy do the same.

'I was stressed because I was thinking I'd have to organise a day to go and buy things like a fridge,' she says. 'I'd only bought tiny secondhand things, because I was determined that I didn't want to buy anything new until we had a home of our own again.'

At last, they did. 'It's lovely. I love the feel of it and the outlook,' says Judy. Mike also adores the property, and the animals wasted no time settling in.

Sadly, however, Judy never found out what happened to her cat, Phlop, on the night of the fire. 'The fireman said she'd probably run away and would come back when things settled, but she never did.'

Two years on from the catastrophic blaze, Judy remains a committed animal activist. 'I spread myself very thin. I can't get to everything, but when I do I push it hard and I generally get some action,' she says. 'One of the most challenging and distressing things is that the owners of these puppy farms, these breeders, they're still operating.'

Buddy's heroism on the night of the fire has further cemented her determination to give a voice to the voiceless.

'Buddy showed his care and intelligence in waking me that night. I think many other dogs would have that in them, but the opportunity just doesn't always present, so people don't get the chance to see what their dogs will do for them,' she says. 'I struggle with the contribution dogs make and what they give. I just wish that we gave much more weight to the recognition of how important they are.'

Buddy's life-saving feat moves everyone who hears about it. He has admirers all over the world because, as Thucydides pointed out in the fifth century BCE, people make friends by way of selfless kindness. Judy wants people in a position to effect real, lasting change to hear about Buddy's act of love, and to know what kind of life he might have had if she hadn't rescued him. It's the same kind of life that hundreds of dogs endure in puppy farms every day.

'So many politicians are so closed down on animal welfare. They're aware of the horror that these dogs live in. These cages are stacked on top of each other. Some are rusted closed because they haven't been opened in years,' she says. 'I really try to put my head where the powers-that-be are. How can people see a puppy farm full of dogs, some with their eyes hanging out, trying to clean little puppies, and allow this in our country?'

Buddy is a special dog, there's no doubt about it. But it's Judy's passionate belief that *all* dogs are special – they just need to be loved and liberated. They need to be respected as individual, sentient beings in order for the beautiful soul inside every dog to flourish.

Ultimately, she wants everyone to have the chance to love a dog like Buddy.

'Buddy is just one example of what a dog will do. Given the opportunity, dogs will lay down their lives for their owners,' Judy says. 'We rescue them, but they give us so much more.'

Indeed they do.

CAOIMHE

RESCUED HUMAN: MIKE TURNER

For all of us, there are moments in our lives that are turning points. They might seem inconsequential at the time, just a tick of the clock that passes without notice. Often it's not until much later – sometimes many years down the track – that we appreciate just what an important part those fleeting instances have played in shaping the person we have become.

Mike Turner has had a few of those transformative moments in his life. The first came when he was just seven years old.

Mike grew up in Belfast, Northern Ireland, in the 1980s. It was the height of The Troubles, the bloody ethnonationalist conflict between loyalists, who wanted Northern Ireland to remain a part of the United Kingdom, and republicans, who wanted Ireland to be a single sovereign state.

The conflict raged for thirty years and claimed more than 3500 lives. There were at least 10 000 bomb attacks during

The Troubles, with many people killed by bombs planted in public places, such as pubs and train stations. The prevalence of car bombs led to security gates being erected around Belfast's main shopping district; cars were banned from the city centre for several years.

By the mid 1980s, Mike's parents, Liz and John, had had enough. They had seen advertisements seeking skilled workers to emigrate to Australia. John was an engineer and decided to apply.

The family had to go to the Australian consulate in Edinburgh, Scotland, to do the paperwork. 'We flew over for the day,' Mike says. 'There's me at the ripe old age of seven in a major capital city, and I pulled on my dad's jacket sleeve and looked up at him and said, "Are you allowed to park cars in the city here?"'

It was an innocent question – one of those seemingly innocuous moments – but it shook John. 'My dad says he teared up. You wouldn't have got a car within kilometres of Belfast city centre at that stage. A kid shouldn't notice that you can't park cars in a city because of bombs.'

John's mind was made up: the family, including Mike, his brother, Chris, and sister, Jude, packed up their lives in Northern Ireland and relocated to Sydney in 1986. Three months after their arrival, the Turners swapped the east coast for the west and settled in Perth.

For young Mike, Australia might as well have been another planet. Everything was unfamiliar and bathed in constant sunshine.

'It really felt like another world. Even the schools – I was used to one big school building with (internal) corridors, and I couldn't believe we got to walk outside between classes,' he says. 'In Ireland we wore full school uniform; in Australia everybody was just in shorts and polo shirts.'

Despite the culture shock, it wasn't long before Mike and his older brother, Chris, had settled in to their new lives Down Under. Mike found his broad Belfast accent was a real icebreaker.

'I was a bit of a novelty to most of the kids. I picked up an Australian accent in Sydney and by the time I came to Perth I had two accents: the one I had at home and the one all my school friends heard,' he laughs. 'Friends would come to my house for the first time and it would be the first time they'd heard my Irish accent.'

When Mike was ten, life in Australia took on an added degree of permanence with the addition of a family pet.

Trixie the Irish setter–kelpie cross was already an elderly lady when she joined the family – and she came as part of a package deal. 'People that my mum worked with, an English couple and their kids, had been out here for fifteen years and they decided they were packing up and going back home,' says Mike. 'Trixie was about twelve by that stage and they also had a rabbit called Thumper. The two of them got on like peas and carrots, so we took them off their hands when they moved back.'

Trixie lived happily with the Turners for three years, passing away at the impressive age of fifteen. Mike is sure she would have kept going even longer if not for the loss of her beloved bunny friend.

Thumper disappeared one day and Trixie went downhill after that. 'She died of a broken heart,' Mike says. 'We think what happened was that the neighbours were doing some construction work and one of the builders brought his dog in a ute. We think the dog got out and got the rabbit.'

He didn't consciously realise it at the time, but it was the first time Mike had seen how much a dog can come to rely on another being for companionship and guidance.

It was a lesson that would change everything for him more than twenty years later.

After Trixie came Buffy, a Staffordshire bull terrier–kelpie mix that joined the family rather by stealth in 1992.

'For my brother's eighteenth birthday he asked my parents if he could have a puppy and they said, "No, you won't look after it,"' says Mike.

Undeterred by his parents' refusal, Chris asked his friends to give him a puppy as a birthday gift anyway, knowing his mum and dad wouldn't be able to resist the wriggling bundle of fluff once she arrived.

He was right. 'My brother moved to Melbourne two or three years later and Buffy grew up as the family dog. She was a gorgeous girl,' Mike says.

She also had a mischievous streak. Buffy was obsessed with rocks: she would dig up 20-kilogram granite paving stones and drag them around the garden. She also infamously destroyed a brick wall that John had cemented in place.

'She was twelve or thirteen when she passed away. Buffy loved swimming and so we spread her ashes on the Swan River,' he says.

Perhaps surprisingly, dog-loving Mike's first pet in adulthood was of the feline variety. He adopted a ten-week-old ginger tabby cat in 2002, the same day his niece was born. The baby was named Elli-Shae, so Mike called his cat Shaemus in her honour.

And that's how it was for the next decade. Just as Trixie and Thumper had gone together like peas and carrots, so too were Mike and Shaemus a contented pair.

Shaemus didn't even mind too much when, in late 2012, Mike started to talk about getting a dog.

It was something he had been pondering for a while – once a dog lover, always a dog lover – but Mike really started to consider the idea when his friend Marielle started fostering dogs through Perth's Staffy and Bully Breed Rescue.

'She's got a Staffy–Shar-pei cross and fostering allowed her to have temporary companions for her dog while she was working,' he explains. 'I was thinking about getting a dog and I thought fostering would be a good way of road testing it.'

Mike's friend, Cathy Prestage, runs CJ Animal Rescue, a small operation dedicated to finding forever homes for pets in need. He knew Cathy was always in need of foster carers, so he got in touch.

'I thought, *There's plenty of people going to these big rescues – I'll try to help out someone with a small one*,' he says. 'I was just looking to foster in the beginning, to get an idea of how well I could look after a dog and train it. I thought I'd do what I could and then move them on.'

Over the next couple of weeks, Mike was sent details of several dogs in need of foster care. He would have been happy to open his home to any one of them, but one after another they fell through.

Then, in early 2013, he received a picture of the most striking puppy he had ever seen.

'It was the eyes that caught my attention. This dog had one crystal blue eye and one brown,' Mike says.

The puppy was about ten weeks old and Cathy had rescued her after seeing her advertised on the buy-sell-swap website Gumtree as 'free to good home'. Though she was born locally, the puppy was quite the global citizen in genetic terms.

She was thought to be predominantly a Catahoula cur, also known as a Catahoula leopard dog or Louisiana Catahoula. Named after Catahoula parish in the American state of Louisiana, the breed is mainly used there for herding cattle and pigs, as well as hunting and tracking. The Catahoula became the state dog of Louisiana in 1970, but it is still relatively rare in the Antipodes; there are fewer than 500 purebred Catahoulas across Australia and New Zealand. The breed's primary function here is hunting feral pigs.

Mike's puppy wasn't just a Catahoula, though. She also had staghound and huntaway in her makeup. The Australian staghound is not so much a breed of dog as a type – a sighthound resembling both the greyhound and Scottish deerhound. It is also used in hunting kanagroos and feral pigs. The huntaway, meanwhile, is a sturdy sheepdog from New Zealand.

For Mike, the puppy's high-energy working-dog lineage and startling blue eye were clues as to why she had been discarded by her breeder.

'The blue-eye gene is very dominant in Catahoulas and it's a pretty good indication that the dog is or will become deaf. I think this puppy was the runt of the litter, and that, plus those eyes, made someone say, "It's not worth my time,"' he says.

But he knew this dog was worth *his* time. Mike agreed to foster her and christened her Caoimhe. The traditional Irish name, pronounced *kwee-vuh*, means beautiful or precious – and Mike's new four-legged friend was both of those things.

He made sure his ward got all her vaccinations and was desexed, then started watching YouTube videos to learn how to teach Caoimhe the necessary obedience skills, plus a few tricks just for fun.

The pair quickly became inseparable and turned heads wherever they went. 'When she was about six months old, this little girl came up in a café and wanted to pat her and asked what breed she was,' he says. 'I said Catahoula leopard dog and the little girl turned around and said, "Mum! It's a leopard caterpillar!" That's kind of stuck with her.'

Caoimhe the leopard caterpillar thrived under Mike's care and before long it was time to think about finding her a forever home.

'Cathy said, "Can you send photos and write a biography for potential adopters?" I started writing that and looking through the hundreds of photos I'd taken and thinking, *I can't give her up*,' says Mike. 'My friend Marielle says she knew from day one that there was no way I would give up the first dog I got, and she was right. I just fell in love with Caoimhe. She was a foster fail.'

And that failure would soon prove to be a life-saving win.

As much as he adored Caoimhe, Mike admittedly wasn't in the greatest shape, physically or mentally, when he decided to take her in.

The notion of becoming a foster carer didn't simply appear from nowhere – there was another reason that he'd started contemplating getting a dog when he did.

In February 2012, Mike had sustained serious injuries in a motorbike accident. He was on his way to work one morning when a car sped through a stop sign and he collided with it.

'I was going down a back street, just around the corner from home. Some woman who was taking her husband to work, and was running late, just ran the stop sign,' he says. 'I'd seen the car coming out of the corner of my eye. It was like, *This car seems to be going a bit too fast coming up to where I know there's a stop sign*. I started slowing down a little, but she was already in the intersection. I went up and over the bonnet, came down and landed on my coccyx bone.'

Incredibly, Mike was able to get up and walk off the road – but he probably shouldn't have. Nor should he have sat on an upturned shopping trolley while he waited for the ambulance. The impact, and the fact that he had landed sitting upright, left Mike with a fractured rib and three compressed discs in his spine.

'There's meant to be at least five millimetres between the discs and the spinal column and mine were actually pushing *into* the spinal column,' he says. 'I actually came away from it fairly well. The way I looked at it was that it could have been a lot worse – I could have been in a wheelchair.'

Nevertheless, his injuries were debilitating – he had back pain and sciatic nerve pain so intense 'it felt like someone was tearing my calf muscle off my leg'.

Mike had private health insurance, but soon discovered it would not cover the surgery he needed to repair his damaged spine. He had met with a private neurosurgeon who recommended operating on all three compressed discs at once, but without the necessary insurance cover he was then forced to wait fifteen excruciatingly painful months for surgery in the public system.

When he finally had surgery in June 2013, 'the public system decided to operate on just one disc and apparently the job wasn't that well done,' Mike says.

The driver of the car that Mike collided with faced criminal charges including reckless driving and failing to stop at a stop sign, and ultimately lost her licence. She did not have comprehensive car insurance, which meant that Mike had to claim for the damage to his motorcycle on his own insurance.

'The bike wasn't completely written off. My insurance company decided they were going to repair the front end of it, so I then had to pay the excess on the policy and get the driver to pay it back. She opted for a payment plan, which took another two years to pay off,' he says.

The woman *did* have compulsory third-party insurance through her vehicle registration, which should have covered all costs relating to Mike's injuries, but battling the state insurer, the Insurance Commission of Western Australia, proved to be every bit as painful as his physical ailments.

'The insurance commission and their lawyers just put me through a living hell. The anxiety and depression I had just dealing with them was extreme. Every time I'd get a letter in the mail with their letterhead on it, my heart would sink,' Mike says. 'I'd be too afraid to open it. They make you feel like the accident was your fault and you just want to give up. I ended up settling for a pittance on the advice of the lawyer who, I later discovered, just wanted to wrap things up before she moved to Melbourne.'

The administrative black hole wasn't the only thing that made Mike want to give up. To manage his pain, he was prescribed pregabalin, which is used to treat both neuropathic pain and epilepsy. The medication had a frightening effect on Mike's mental health.

'These drugs made me want to throw myself out of a window,' he says. 'I had no idea whether I was Arthur or Martha. I was thinking *I can't do this* about the most simple tasks.' He later learned that the reported side effects of pregabalin include mood changes, depression and suicidal ideation.

Even painkillers that didn't directly provoke dark thoughts made day-to-day living incredibly difficult. 'I wasn't able to function at work – I'd face-plant into my keyboard because the painkillers were so strong,' says Mike.

'I'm a business analyst and that's very much "in my head", and to have painkillers fighting me every step of the way was really tough. On the days when I could come to work I had to put in ten- to fifteen-hour days to catch up on everything.'

Frustrated by the painkiller-induced fog, he stopped taking his pain medication all together, choosing instead to manage the pain with the help of an osteopath.

But while his head was clearer and his pain, for the most part, was bearable, there were many days when Mike simply couldn't work at all. The back pain was too intense, mobility too difficult and his depression too consuming. He estimates the value of all the time he took off exceeded $60 000 – the insurance payout he ultimately received was a fraction of that – and the awful irony was he was too unwell even to go to the doctor.

'There were days I just couldn't get out of bed. I definitely couldn't drive myself to a doctor to get the paperwork required by the insurance commission to show I couldn't work, just so they could say, "No, we're not going to pay for this,"' he says.

It was without question the worst time in Mike's life. He couldn't remember ever feeling so low, and he couldn't imagine what he could possibly do to put his life back together.

And in the midst of all this was poor Caoimhe.

Given he was spending so much time at home thanks to his debilitating injuries, fostering a puppy had seemed to Mike like a good way to do something productive and useful. Mike also thought rescuing a dog might motivate him to get back on his feet, to help him put the accident behind him and return to something like a normal life in spite of his ongoing pain.

It worked for a little while, too. He loved Caoimhe and there was no doubt that he doted on her.

'I was really proactive with her training. With a couple of working breeds in her she's very food motivated, but even more than that she's ball motivated,' Mike says. 'She is 150 per cent focused on her ball. When we go to the park she doesn't care about any other dogs. She's even a little protective of her ball.'

The longer he fought the insurance company, however, and the more days he spent bedridden with back pain, the bleaker Mike's outlook became. Meeting the needs of his young, boisterous dog became an increasing struggle.

Caoimhe, too, seemed to be going a little stir crazy. Her and Mike's vigorous daily walks became less frequent, their training sessions dropped off and he never seemed to have the energy to play with her.

Caoimhe's behaviour was growing ever more unruly, and Mike began to wonder whether she'd be better off with a more active owner.

'She would get what I call "crazy eye". Her eyes would glaze over and she would jump all over the couch. It was like she wasn't in her own head,' he says. 'There was a bratty side to her behaviour but it was also a kind of cry for help and I wasn't noticing it. I was like, *What's going on? Is this me doing this to her by not looking after her properly?*'

Mike wasn't the only one to have witnessed the alarming behaviour. Not long after his accident he had gone back to Ireland for two months to see his parents, who had moved back there in 2010. While he was gone Caoimhe was cared for by Cathy Prestage's then husband, Justin.

'He's a big man, very tall and large. I felt confident Caoimhe was in the hands of someone who was very competent with dogs,' Mike says. 'Justin told me later that the first time Caoimhe pulled the crazy-eye treatment with him, she clawed him trying to play and he got genuinely scared. He went and locked himself in the bedroom with a mobile phone in case he needed to call Cathy.'

When he returned from Ireland, Mike consulted an animal behaviourist who told him Caoimhe was submissive by nature. In a pack of 100 dogs, the behaviourist explained, Caoimhe would rank number 99.

'He said, "She's constantly looking to you for direction and when she's not getting that she's making her own decisions,"' he says. 'She was becoming more needy and I was ignoring her and that's when she'd make up her own mind and just go crazy.'

One night, it all became too much. Mike was resting on the sofa when Caoimhe got the by-now-familiar crazed look in her eye. She leapt onto the couch and Mike burst into tears.

'I just started crying, thinking, *I can't do this anymore.* I'd almost given up. I'd just about resolved that I was going to have to give her up,' he says.

Incredibly, Caoimhe seemed to understand exactly how Mike was feeling. She paused her outburst, wrapped her paws around his neck and hugged him.

Mike couldn't believe it. It was one of those transformative moments, just like the day he'd stood in the centre of Edinburgh as a seven-year-old.

'It was a massive turning point for me. That moment on the couch with her really changed my focus,' he says. 'I realised, *This isn't just a pet – I'm her Alpha.* I suddenly understood that I need to be here for her and be actively participating in her life as much as she's a part of mine.'

Mike thought he was rescuing Caoimhe, but clearly she had other ideas. Now, as his dog comforted him, he realised Caoimhe had had a plan all along.

In that moment on the sofa, one thing became crystal clear for Mike: he knew that the way out of the darkness that had enveloped him did not lie with lawyers and insurance companies.

If he wanted to feel well, and above all *happy*, he was going to have to figure it out himself.

Mike's first step was doubling down on Caoimhe's training. He went back to YouTube and boned up on clicker training techniques, word association and tricks.

The effect on Caoimhe's behaviour was instant.

'Her personality completely changed once I realised what she needed. It came down to actively training her, teaching her more tricks. That's all she wanted – just that interaction and leadership,' he says.

'I realised that I'm consciously responsible for her. It's about not just going, "This is a pet that lives in this house and lives by my rules" but understanding that she's someone with her own personality. Stepping up and taking that responsibility brings me happiness. I'm enjoying that positive energy coming back from her.'

For Mike, too, the shift in perspective had enormous benefits. Where once he was largely bedridden, today Mike spends his free time exploring Perth with his best friend by his side.

The eight-kilometre walk that, when he was in the depths of despair, used to take him and Caoimhe 90 minutes is now a brisk 45-minute stroll. And he has introduced Caoimhe – previously afraid of water, despite having the Catahoula's webbed toes – to the joys of frolicking in the Swan River.

'I'll spend two or three hours with her, just chasing a ball in and out of the water. She tires out every other dog there,' says Mike.

Together, they visit Mike's brother in Busselton, 220 kilometres south of Perth, as often as possible. Six months after his surgery, Mike did his first skydive. He has since thrown himself out of a plane a further five times.

Caoimhe, incidentally, doesn't appear to have any hearing difficulties, despite the genetic implications of her striking blue eye. But Mike has taught both the voice cues *and* hand signals for all her commands, just in case.

'Everywhere I can possibly take her, I take her. I'm living a life where my dog is a priority – she's not just a pet that you feed and leave at home when you go out,' he says. 'My life revolves around her – taking her out to fairs and street markets, finding dog-friendly cafés and pubs, going on adventures to find new places for her. It's bringing it back to consciously being in control of being happy.'

Two years ago, Mike bought his first house. Many of the improvements he has made to the property and plans he has for the future have been implemented with Caoimhe's wellbeing in mind.

In 2016, he went back to the private surgeon he'd originally consulted and had his remaining two damaged discs repaired. 'He said most of the work was cutting out the scar tissue from the first operation. The disc had prolapsed and was pushing into the spine again,' he says.

Mike's recovery from his second operation was much quicker than the first time around. 'I was itching to get out and get back to my life. People said, "Aren't you worried about the surgery?" But I was more worried about Caoimhe and Shaemus being without me for the two days I was in hospital. I was way more worried about my dog not getting walked for two weeks afterwards!'

He still lives with pain every day, but he chooses not to let it impinge on his happiness.

'My accident was a reality check. Something like that just really opens your eyes to what is possible and how easily things can go wrong,' he says. 'I have back problems, but I'd rather work in the garden and be in a little bit of pain, but have my swagger, than just give up on life and give up on my dog and my cat and my responsibilities.'

Mike knows how far he's come since the motorbike accident almost robbed him of his love of life. He's celebrating his progress by having a large phoenix tattooed on his back; it rises out of the spinal surgery scars.

'Caoimhe climbing up on the couch that night and giving me a hug was one of those crazy moments. I thought, *These insurance companies aren't going to solve this problem for me – I need to find other ways*,' says Mike. 'I needed to do it for my dog and to bring myself back to the things that make me happy.'

All our lives are a series of moments, a collection of choices that bring us to where we need to be. The moment Mike's father decided to bring his family to Australia. The moment Caoimhe became a foster fail. The moment she leapt onto a couch and rescued a man who hadn't realised how much he needed rescuing.

All of those moments are about one thing: happiness.

'I try not to think about where I'd be without Caoimhe. I wouldn't have had the sort of epiphanies that I've had,' Mike says. 'Life isn't just happy – you really have to look for ways to make yourself happy. Without Caoimhe, I wouldn't have realised that I'm in charge of my happiness.'

ABBY

RESCUED HUMAN: SUE PETHICK

Mike Pethick squinted into the afternoon glare, convinced his eyes were playing tricks on him. Surely he was seeing things. The small blob on top of that distant sand hill, surveying its surroundings, looked uncannily like his red heeler, Abby. But Abby was on the beach below, no doubt engaged in an energetic game of fetch with his wife, Sue. There was no way she'd have run off on her own, not when she had her mum's undivided attention and there was a ball involved. Mike and Sue often joked that Abby was their little shadow.

No, it couldn't be Abby up there. Could it?

Mike kept walking and called out, 'Abby!' At the sound of his voice, the blob on the sand hill turned in his direction. Then, tail wagging, it began bounding towards him.

It *was* Abby. The three-year-old dog barrelled into Mike like a torpedo, smothering him with doggy kisses. But she looked scared. She was overjoyed to have found him, but there was urgency to her demeanour. Who knew how long she'd been up there by herself? They were just metres from the steep cliff face that plunged down to the beach. Mike shuddered to think what might have happened to Abby if he hadn't spotted her when he did.

Mike shared his dog's agitation. If Abby was alone, it meant that, somewhere out there, Sue was, too. She would never leave Abby to fend for herself unless . . .

Unless . . .

He knew immediately that he'd been right to worry when Sue and Abby seemed to be taking an extra-long time on their afternoon walk. He'd been right to pack up his fishing gear and set off to look for them.

Something was very, very wrong. It had to be.

'Abby,' Mike said, cradling the dog's face in his hands. His gaze bored into hers. 'Where's Mummy? You have to take me to Mummy. Good girl.'

Without a second's pause, Abby took off at a trot.

For about ten minutes, she led Mike down a narrow track. She raced off ahead while he trudged through the dunes, and when he next spotted her she was in a cliff-top car park that overlooked the beach. Abby was about 100 metres ahead in a small clearing. She stared intently at him.

He looked quizzically back at Abby. What was she thinking? Sue clearly wasn't in the car park. There was no sign of her there.

Abby edged closer to the cliff edge and glanced over it. Then she looked back at Mike again. It was as though she was saying, *Hurry up!*

Mike's heart sank. He knew what his dog was trying to tell him.

Truth be told, Sue Pethick wasn't really ready for another dog when Abby came into her life.

For as long as she could remember, she'd had four-legged friends. Her favourite childhood dog was Ben, a much-loved dachshund. But he was just one of many formative canine companions.

'In those days you could play in the street. As long as you were home by five o'clock you could do anything – within reason,' says Sue of growing up in the inner southern suburbs of Adelaide, South Australia.

'These dogs would come out and see us kids playing and want to play. We'd go home and, lo and behold, they'd come, too. Some would have puppies, so Mum and Dad never had to buy a dog.'

Once she reached adulthood, Sue was rarely without a dog. During her first marriage the family pet was Katie the black labrador, who lived to a ripe old age before passing away naturally.

Later, there was Charlotte, a little black toy poodle. Tragically, she was struck by a car and Sue, then a single parent, simply couldn't afford the expensive surgery needed to save her. She was forced to make the gut-wrenching decision to let Charlotte go.

In 1995, Sue met Mike, a postal manager. They married in 1997, and completed their blended family with the addition of Jasmine, a Maltese–poodle mix. Sue adored the dainty little dog.

'A few of the children had asthma, so we got a dog that didn't shed hair – but she was no dog at all, really,' she laughs. 'She couldn't catch a ball. She was a princess, but she was just gorgeous.'

With Jasmine in tow, in 2012 Sue and Mike made the move from Adelaide to Mannum, a historic town on the banks of the Murray River, 84 kilometres east of Adelaide. Three years later they relocated again, this time just ten minutes down the road to the tiny riverside hamlet of Caloote. They had fallen in love with the area during frequent visits on the houseboat they once owned and were inspired to buy a historic cottage – believed to have once been the village post office – on a double block with plenty of space for Jasmine and their 'granddogs' to run around.

Jasmine had the run of the property for three wonderful years. She was about thirteen when she suffered multiple organ failure and died on 27 December 2015.

Sue had farewelled a number of canine companions over the years, but Jasmine's passing broke her heart. 'I said, "I'm never going to get another dog again." I think I'm still mourning her,' she says.

But Mike missed the company of a faithful dog. With 57-year-old Sue working nights and weekends at an aged care home in Mannum, he often found himself at a loose end at home alone.

'It can be a little bit boring for Mike – he needed a

friend and some company at home when I was working,' says Sue.

With her blessing – if not quite her enthusiasm – Mike began searching in January 2016 for a dog that needed a home. Sue's one stipulation was that their next dog wasn't a poodle. 'I couldn't bear to have the same breed as Jasmine because I'd always be thinking of her and it wouldn't be fair to the new dog,' she explains.

Fortunately, the dog that caught Mike's eye was about as different from Jasmine as possible.

Abby was a fifteen-month-old red heeler mix – 'She's crossed with I don't know what,' says Sue – that had been bounced around an awful lot in her young life. She had initially been bought as a puppy by an elderly couple. They had been assured she wouldn't grow any larger than a Jack Russell terrier but soon discovered they'd been given a bum steer. Female red heelers can weigh more than 22 kilograms and grow to half a metre tall – not quite the 8-kilogram, 30-centimetre-tall lap dog Abby's original owners were expecting.

The couple devoted hours to training and teaching Abby exemplary manners, but as she grew into a boisterous adolescent they were forced to admit they couldn't cope. 'She outgrew them and outgrew their unit and they sadly had to give her up,' Sue says.

Abby was taken into foster care by another couple who were involved with the Sunraysia Animal Rehousing Group (SARG) in Mildura, 400 kilometres away, across the Victorian border. They hoped to be her forever home, but alas it wasn't to be.

'They looked after her for a year and I'm sure they would have adored to keep her, but one of them fell ill and they weren't able to look after her,' she says.

Which was how she came to be listed on the SARG website that Mike was searching to find his new best friend. Sue doesn't know how they knew Abby was the dog for them; they just did.

In fact, they were so sure of it, they drove four hours to Mildura just to meet her.

'Abby just spoke to us. She seemed like such a good little girl. We went to Mildura to pick her up,' Sue says. 'She's just so different to Jasmine, who was a little lap dog. Abby catches a ball and does "dog" things. She was well trained, but she's got a bit slack with us!'

Abby wasted no time settling in. 'Everything is all about her. People come to visit and Abby thinks they've come to visit *her*. When the granddogs come up she tears around with them,' she says. 'If anybody walks through the back gate, especially a man with a hat on, I wouldn't like their chances, but if you come through the front door she'll lick you to death rather than bail you up.'

Even Sue and Mike's other resident pets didn't mind the exuberant cattle dog. 'We've got chooks – Thelma and Louise – but they just ignore her. We come out in the morning and say, "Let's go feed the chooks." There's a great big dirt pile where Abby skids and sends dirt flying all over them,' Sue says. 'They have got out a couple of times, but she doesn't do nasty things to them because she knows they're part of her world.'

What most surprised Sue, though, was just how quickly *she* fell in love with the sweet-natured dog. 'She was great company for Mike and in the beginning she was probably more his dog because I was still thinking about my baby, Jasmine,' she says. 'But now we both have a little shadow wherever we go. She just wants to please and help all the time.'

But Sue never imagined just how much Abby would help her when she needed it most.

Ask any keen South Australian angler for the top surf fishing spots on the Yorke Peninsula, 150 kilometres west of Adelaide, and Gleesons Landing will almost certainly be on the list.

The four-wheel-drive accessible beach is known for mullet and salmon, and big mulloway in the right conditions (a rising tide that peaks just after sunset is the best bet, according to locals). It's also popular with campers and the west-facing beach, bordered by jagged cliffs, offers spectacular sunset vistas across Spencer Gulf.

In March 2017, Sue and Mike were holidaying at Point Turton, about 30 kilometres from Gleesons Landing. Mike, a keen fisherman, was looking forward to trying his luck at the remote beach during the trip. For Sue, however, the area has a more personal resonance: it shares its name with a woman she deeply admired.

Irene Gleeson was an Australian-born Christian missionary to the children of Kitgum District in war-torn northern Uganda, who suffered as a result of both civil unrest and HIV/AIDS. Over more than two decades of tireless work in the region, she founded five schools, a tertiary training college for young adults, a hospice, a community church with more than 2000 members and even a radio station which reaches more than a million listeners.

'Mama Irene', as she was known, died in July 2013 at the age of sixty-eight, but the Irene Gleeson Foundation (IGF) continues her work. Sue and Irene were friends, and Sue has been actively involved with the foundation for several years, visiting Africa three times.

'There's now almost ten thousand children in the foundation's schools – the first pupils are now running the place,' she says. 'It's just brilliant. I love them all.'

Each year since Irene's passing, the foundation has held a memorial charity walk in her honour. Starting in Kitgum town and passing some of the significant places of Irene's work before finishing at IGF headquarters, the walk raises money and collects book donations for students at forty-eight local primary schools.

Always on the lookout for ways to raise money for IGF, Sue was considering undertaking a charity walk of her own. As a frequent visitor to the Yorke Peninsula, she was impressed with the 500-kilometre continuous Walk the Yorke trail system. She wondered if a section of it might make a suitable route for her walk – particularly if she could incorporate Gleesons Landing.

Sue and Mike's holiday seemed like a perfect opportunity for her to visit the area and check out its suitability for inclusion in her planned walk while Mike spent some time fishing. Abby, of course, would come along for the ride.

Monday 27 March was a hot one. In fact, South Australia had sweltered through most of the month – it was the state's third-warmest March on record. While Mike set up his rods on a cliff, Sue decided to take Abby down to the beach to cool off in the calm gulf waters.

'Mike was worried that Abby was too close to the cliff edge and might fall off. I saw a little bay down below, so Abby and I took the ball and went off for a walk,' she says.

They set off, walking about a kilometre to the south looking for a nice beach where she could let Abby run amok. Engrossed in his fishing, Mike didn't notice which direction they walked in.

Scanning the rocky terrain, at first Sue couldn't see any obvious way to get down to the beach. Then she spied a narrow, twisty path down the cliff face that seemed to promise access to the sand.

She started picking her way carefully down the 'zigzaggy, sandy, very rocky' track. An excited Abby raced past her, having spotted the sea in the distance.

She isn't quite sure what happened next, but her left foot seemed to get stuck somehow. She fell heavily.

Crack! Crack!

'I thought, *I wonder if that's what football players hear when they break a bone*,' Sue says. 'I wasn't actually thinking that *I'd* broken a bone.'

She couldn't have, she reasoned – she wasn't in any pain. Although, come to think of it, her foot did seem to be sticking out in a very unnatural way.

And then there was the troubling fact that she couldn't get up.

'I went to get up and my leg didn't work. I couldn't work out why, so I just sat there. I looked down at my leg and thought, *That's a bit of a weird angle – I don't think that's quite right*,' she says.

At that moment, Abby reappeared, tongue lolling. 'She came bounding back up and started nagging me: *Come on, Mum! Let's go!* I told her, "I can't, my leg's not working," like I was talking to a human being,' says Sue. 'She just stayed there with me and nuzzled under my arm while I sat there and thought about things.'

Sue was stranded about a third of the way down the cliff face. 'Luckily I fell towards the cliff. Probably two steps in the other direction and I would have fallen off.'

She knew she couldn't get up or down without help – but she had no idea how to raise the alarm. She fumbled for her phone, but was dismayed to realise she had left it in the car.

There wasn't a soul on the beach below and she couldn't see Mike from her position. She tried yelling out to him, but he was a good two kilometres away and the wind was blowing in the wrong direction – he'd never hear her.

'I knew Mike was happily fishing and I thought, *You know what? I think I'm going to be here a long time*,' Sue says.

And even if help did arrive, she knew they'd have a devil of a time trying to get to her. 'I thought, *I'll be helpful and start pulling myself up*. I started to lift myself up the cliff a bit more, but there was a great big rock and I wasn't strong enough to lift myself over it.'

Now well and truly stuck between a rock and a hard place, she turned to Abby. 'I said to her, "Go and find Daddy!" She always does at home, but she wouldn't leave me. I guess she thought I needed her.' Twice more, Sue asked Abby to return to Mike, but the devoted dog wouldn't budge.

She hadn't felt any pain initially, but it didn't take long for it to well and truly kick in. Sue started to lose consciousness, but every time she faded Abby would nudge her to keep her awake.

Finally, however, the pain became overwhelming and Sue lapsed into unconsciousness. When she came to, the afternoon sun blazed overhead. She wasn't sure how much time had passed, but she realised Abby had vanished.

And in her place sat Irene Gleeson.

The presence of her dearly departed friend seemed entirely reasonable. 'She just talked to me like she was really right next to me. She said, "You silly girl!" She was telling me off the way she always did, with her big heart,' Sue says. 'I thought, *Really? At Gleesons Landing!* It's just the sort of thing Irene would do. I'm sure she's up there bossing Jesus around.'

In Irene's spiritual company she felt safe and peaceful, though she was dimly aware that her situation was grave. 'One per cent of me thought, *I don't know what to do, I'm going to be here a very long time*, but we just sat and watched the beautiful scenery.'

The scenery soon faded to black once more as Sue passed out again. The next time she awoke, she couldn't see Irene, though she could still feel her presence. Abby hadn't returned either.

But this time she could hear a faint sound in the distance. It was Mike and he was calling her name.

Moments later, Sue looked up to see him peering down at her from the cliff top. Abby was by his side.

'I tried to lift my leg up and said, "I think I've broken my leg,"' she recalls. As she did, her foot twisted further in the wrong direction. It was excruciatingly painful, but Sue didn't care.

Only one thing mattered at that point: Abby had found Mike.

Another wave of relief crashed over Mike as he spotted his wife. But just as before, it was immediately followed by panic. Sue was lying halfway down a cliff, bent and clearly broken. They were effectively in the middle of nowhere; the nearest hospital was at Yorketown, more than 60 kilometres away.

His first instinct was to scramble down the cliff to be by Sue's side, but he quickly rejected the idea. 'He thought, *If I go down there there'll be two of us with broken legs*,' says Sue.

Instead, Mike pulled out his phone and called emergency services – but that proved to be frustrating. 'He called 000 and that was painful because they wanted a proper address, and of course it was a remote camping spot with no specific address,' she says. 'He gave up and went back to the car.'

Flustered and on the verge of panic, Mike was hoping to find a spot with better mobile reception, and ideally see someone else who could help or raise the alarm. But on his way back to the car he spotted an approaching vehicle and flagged it down. Its occupants were two young women who ran a local surf school; they were taking a group of teenagers for a surfing lesson.

While one of the girls stayed with Mike and helped him place a second triple-0 call, the other climbed down the cliff to Sue.

'She brought me a jacket to shield me from the sun and some water – it was going to be pretty hot waiting all afternoon,' says Sue. 'She just sat, talking with me, doing the diversion therapy thing. I just went with it.'

After another forty-five minutes, an ambulance arrived. Paramedics promptly delivered a 'green whistle' – a morphine inhaler – to help dull the pain of Sue's injuries. A police car and a State Emergency Service (SES) team were also on the scene.

'I was in and out of consciousness. I had quite a few people helping me. They all worked together. It's just beautiful,' she says.

Her chief helper, Abby, was safely ensconced in Sue and Mike's car, though Sue has no doubt the tenacious dog would have preferred to be by her side. 'Poor little Abby was sitting in the car all this time. Michael had put her there so she could have water and shade, and because he didn't want her to get in the way of the paramedics,' she says. 'She must have been feeling just lost because she didn't know what was happening with Mummy and Daddy.'

It took the emergency services workers nearly two hours to retrieve Sue from the cliff face. Ultimately, she was taken further down the cliff so that paramedics had a flat area to load her onto the stretcher. Only then could they make the precarious trip back up.

'They dragged me up to the top of the cliff and then I went into an ambulance back to where our car was so the helicopter could land,' she says. 'The roads were too rough and my injury too severe to drive me to hospital, so I got a helicopter ride.'

She had left for her walk around 12.45 p.m. Paramedics arrived at 2.30 p.m. and it was 4.15 p.m. before Sue was loaded into the helicopter and flown to the Royal Adelaide Hospital, a 100-kilometre flight. Mike and Abby made the 260-kilometre, four-hour journey by road. Once at hospital, the full extent of Sue's injuries was revealed. She had severely dislocated her left foot, broken two bones in her lower left leg and ruptured the ligaments around her ankle. She had surgery the next day to repair the broken bones with pins and a metal plate. This was followed by two more operations over the next few months to remove bone chips and tighten ligaments.

'It took me a couple of days to realise what I'd actually done. I think I'd thought, *Oh well, a couple of broken bones – no big deal.* It was a little while afterwards that I realised this wasn't going to be an easy thing,' she says.

Sue spent five days in hospital and during that time she was hit with the magnitude of what Abby had done for her. Half crazed with pain on the cliff side, Sue hadn't felt at the time that her situation was too serious – but Abby knew it was.

'Because it was such beautiful scenery and all the spiritual stuff was happening, I thought I was good – though I didn't know how I was ever going to get Mike to know where I was,' she recalls. 'That was my main worry. It was just me and Abby, sitting on the cliff together. I never thought that she would actually find her way back to Dad.'

When Mike had peered over the cliff edge, Abby by his side, Sue had only dimly recognised that she must have led him there. 'Of course I was a bit dozy at the time, but when I saw Abby up at the top of the cliff and heard Mike's voice I thought, *She must have done it – or how did Mike know where to find me?*' she says.

'I thought about it more later on, in the days to come, when things had calmed down. It sunk in more and more the more I heard about it. I just loved her so much.'

As she began her long road to recovery, Sue and Mike pieced together as best they could exactly how their clever little canine had managed to raise the alarm.

When Sue and Abby didn't return from their walk and he couldn't see them on the beach below, where they'd promised to wave to him, Mike grew worried. He packed up his fishing gear, got in the car and set out to try to find them.

At the same time, Abby had scrambled back up the cliff and raced back to where Mike had been fishing – only to find, of course, that he wasn't there.

The couple suspects that Abby, confused, then made her way to the highest point she could find – the sand hill – to see if she could spot her master. By a stroke of luck, he spotted her first.

Mike showed Sue pictures of Abby that he had taken during the rescue mission. 'When he told me what he had gone through, I was worried for him. He showed me pictures of Abby in our car with my cut-up Asics shoes and my favourite tracksuit pants, which had been cut off by the paramedics,' says Sue. 'When I saw her sad little face and her head on the side I thought, *Oh my gosh.*'

Sue can't imagine how long she may have lain, immobile and in agony, on the side of that sun-baked cliff if Abby hadn't been there that day. Thanks to her brave, rescued red heeler, she doesn't have to.

Abby's devotion to Sue that day wasn't a one-off event. During the seven months she spent recuperating at home – when she couldn't work and had to walk first with a frame and then crutches – Abby rarely let her mistress out of her sight.

'Especially when I first got home from the hospital, she was just so excited to see me. Mike filmed it when I came home: I was in my music room, sitting on the piano stool. I had the frame protecting the leg,' she says. 'Abby came in, saw me and stopped – then she just went absolutely berserk.

'I'd lie on the couch with my leg up and if I started to fall asleep she'd come over and nudge me to make sure I'd wake up.'

Even now, with Sue fully recovered and back at work, Abby is a constant, concerned presence.

'When I go to the toilet she'll come and sit with me and then make sure I get back and settled again. She follows me around the backyard now as much as she does Mike,' she says. 'With Mike too, if he's unwell she just makes sure that we're okay. If you're sitting watching TV and you haven't spoken to her for five minutes, she'll pop up and say, *Hi, I'm here!*'

Sue's confidence took longer to recover than her leg. 'I used to climb up on chairs and fix this, fix that, change light bulbs. I can't do that now; I'm too scared,' she says. 'Walking up and down the stairs, I use the guard rail. I think the reality of it suddenly hit me.'

But Abby doesn't even mind that her walks are fewer and further between these days. 'I get too scared on the back roads in case Abby runs off after a rabbit or a snake, so we just throw the ball around for her instead,' says Sue.

On the plus side, the accident has helped Sue to become even better at her job. 'I've got a lot more empathy for the residents at work. I only used a frame for a short time, but they've got this pain forever, and the fear of falling,' she explains. 'I'll never push anyone fast in a wheelchair again. My gosh, the things you learn.'

There were a lot of lessons learned that day on the cliff side, and in the months that followed. It was a crash course in resilience, patience and the power of a spiritual soul.

Most of all, though, it was a lesson in love; a textbook example of how the ones we rescue often rescue us right back.

SARGE KESTER

RESCUED HUMAN: STEVE WARWICK*

Strictly speaking, Sergeant Kester isn't a rescue dog. At least, he doesn't fulfil all of the criteria that many people expect of adopted pets. The handsome blue heeler wasn't abused, neglected or abandoned. He wasn't taken in as a stray or plucked from a cold council pound. He has thankfully never known the sting of being tossed away by humans who moved house, changed jobs or had a baby.

But Sarge, as he's known to pretty much everyone, didn't come to his forever human via a pet shop or a newspaper classified ad either. His owner may not have 'adopted' Sarge in the way most people would describe it, but neither did he purchase his canine companion. Sarge *has* known several different homes in his young life, and he's had to call on the adaptability and resilience that rehomed pets are famous for.

* Name has been changed.

Sarge came from Whiskey's Wish, a Brisbane-based charity that provides trained assistance and psychiatric support dogs to veterans and ex-emergency services personnel all over Australia. Whiskey's Wish sources dogs from both rescue groups and trusted breeders. Sarge happens to hail from the latter, but who knows? Perhaps only fortuitous timing stopped him from ultimately finding himself with the former; working dogs, even purebreds, are among the breeds most commonly surrendered to pounds and rescue groups. (In fact, the charity's namesake, the dog that inspired founder Scott Jackman to start Whiskey's Wish, was a purebred blue heeler found tied up and abandoned outside a pet food factory – chances are Whiskey originally came from a breeder, too.)

His origins aren't the important part of Sarge's story anyway. What's most important about Sergeant Kester is that he is unequivocally a rescuer.

He literally saves Steve Warwick's life every single day.

Steve has endured more threats to his safety and experienced more trauma in his fifty-three years than most people do in a lifetime. He started his working life as an apprentice in the Australian Army, but a serious accident meant he was medically discharged after eighteen months. His injuries not only left Steve with ongoing physical difficulties, but psychological scars as well.

He didn't have time to properly address those issues, however, because Steve went straight from the Army into a security position with the New South Wales Police Force. Though he was not a sworn police officer himself, he worked closely with the officers in the internal affairs (IA) unit, known today as Professional Standards Command. It was the 1990s – not long after the heyday of notorious crooked cops like Roger Rogerson and high-profile organised crime figures including Arthur 'Neddy' Smith – and IA was a busy place indeed.

'I've seen some very frightening things. Really, really nasty stuff,' Steve says simply.

As a security operative, he was essentially the front line of defence for IA officers. One acquaintance of Steve's was officer Michael Drury, who claimed that Rogerson attempted to bribe him to change his evidence in the heroin trafficking trial of a convicted Melbourne drug dealer. Drury refused the bribe, and was shot twice through his kitchen window in June 1984. He survived and alleged that Rogerson was involved in the attempt on his life, though the disgraced officer was later acquitted at trial.

Incidents like Drury's shooting were a stark reminder for Steve that placing himself in extreme peril was a hard fact of his professional life. His job required him to suppress the fear that was his constant workday companion.

'We had a room for what we called intercepts: there was a Telstra technician in there and we could listen to basically any telephone in Australia,' he says. 'There was a multi-level car park opposite that room and somebody went up there and fired at the room. The bullet got lodged between the first and second pane of glass.'

Later, Steve became a special constable, and foiled an attempt on the life of his patrol partner. 'We caught these two blokes trying to jimmy the door on a café. One had a huge screwdriver,' Steve recalls. 'He turned around and saw the pair of us and tried to stab my partner, but I tackled him to the ground.'

But it was a later incident that had the gravest impact on Steve's physical and mental health. He was involved in apprehending a member of a well-known Sydney crime family who was later convicted of counterfeiting bank notes.

'I caught one of them red-handed with counterfeit fifty-dollar notes. He ended up getting two years in jail because counterfeiting is a federal offence,' he says. 'I had to chase him down through a car park and crash tackle him. I busted my knee up very badly, and my back, and spent nearly three months in hospital. Then I got a staph infection in my knee and very nearly lost my leg.'

What ultimately drove Steve out of NSW Police, though, wasn't the assaults or physical injuries; it was the threats. 'Let's just say that not only myself, but my family were getting death threats. Living with that as a consequence has been pretty hard,' he admits.

The entanglement with the crime family triggered a state of hypervigilance in Steve that is a common symptom of post-traumatic stress disorder (PTSD).

'I've got cameras everywhere. You won't find me in any phone book or on any electoral roll because of the nature of the threat from my previous job. I had to take extreme measures to protect myself,' he says. 'Hopefully with time the threat will diminish a bit, but given the nature of the people involved I'm not optimistic.'

Steve left the police in the late 1990s and started working in education security. His job was to patrol high school and TAFE campuses in Sydney's southwestern suburbs in the wake of a spate of computer thefts.

It seemed straightforward, perhaps even a little dull, a welcome change from the drama and threat of working for the police. But as Steve had by now come to expect, the reality was a lot more complex. He soon realised that many of the thieves he was encountering were drug affected to some degree.

'We found one bloke with a laptop and a couple of wallets stuffed down his underwear. When we searched him, he actually had syringes in his shoe and when they got him back to the station he started getting all jittery and they had to call doctors for him,' he says. 'I've seen some terribly sad things, too: homeless people camping out underneath school buildings and stuff like that.'

His experiences inspired a passionate hatred of drugs. 'Seeing that sort of thing as often as I did, it's given me a real set against drugs, especially hard drugs. One of my pet hates is drugs like ice,' says Steve. 'I have a zero-tolerance policy – I've got no time for it because I've seen what it does to people.'

The cumulative effect of years of daily trauma and terror, coupled with his lingering physical injuries, started to take a severe toll on Steve's mental health. The symptoms of his then-undiagnosed PTSD began to flare with crippling regularity.

'You see all sorts of things, and I suffered for many, many years with flashbacks of very bad things that I'd seen. It's a mix of a lot of things. There are particular incidents that I don't like to talk about because it takes me too long to get over them,' he says. 'There's one that if I revisit it I'd have to go and take Valium.'

As he wrestled with the demons that seemed to be tightening their grip with each passing day, Steve became alienated from his family. His constant state of high alert drove a wedge between him and his three daughters.

'I had to know where my kids were every hour of the day, because I was so worried that they were going to get caught up with the wrong crowd or something bad was going to happen to them,' he says. 'When you see really bad stuff like that, and you see the effect it has on people – especially when you have to go and tell someone that one of their family members has been killed – you can't help but wonder, *How would I feel if that was my kid?*'

His daughters, however, did not appreciate their dad's intense concern for their safety. 'I had those thoughts for many, many years, because I did not ever want to get that knock on the door. I was overbearing, I can admit that, and my kids started to resent me.'

Eventually, Steve was unable to keep working. His knee and back injuries, plus his deep psychological distress, meant he was assessed as being permanently disabled in 2001 and deemed eligible for the Federal Government disability support pension and Department of Veterans' Affairs disability pension. An official PTSD diagnosis followed in 2012.

He began taking medication and seeing both a psychiatrist and a psychologist, but Steve's thoughts grew progressively darker. He continued to be plagued by flashbacks, as well as terrifying nightmares. He was constantly exhausted. His world became smaller as he isolated himself from those closest to him in a bid to keep them safe from what he perceived as ever-present threats.

'I was in a very, very bad place. I was seeing faces I hadn't seen for twenty years,' he says.

In his blackest moments, Steve considered ending his suffering permanently. 'I'd spend hours contemplating ways to do away with myself. I'd spend my days making nooses and stuff like that. That's not an easy thing to admit.'

Steve felt desperate. He needed something to pull him back from the brink, but he couldn't imagine what that something would be.

He was about to find out.

In 2016, Steve's psychologist suggested during one of their fortnightly appointments that he might like to think about applying for a service animal.

At first, he was skeptical: what could a dog possibly do for him? How could a wagging tail or a lick on the nose possibly calm the storm roiling inside his brain? A dog wasn't going to stop his flashbacks or take away the terrors that stalked him in the night. It would just be one more creature for Steve to disappoint.

And yet, just as his doctor had encouraged, Steve *did* find himself thinking about it. In spite of his apprehension, he found himself imagining sharing his home with a four-legged friend. Perhaps it would be nice to hear the pitter-patter of paws around the place. It could be fun. Maybe having a canine companion would help him feel a little less alone.

It had to be worth a try. One thing was certain: Steve had to do *something* to try to manage his spiralling mental health. His life quite literally depended on it.

'The more I thought about it, the more I realised it could be a good idea,' he says. 'I was willing to give anything a shot.'

Research shows that psychiatric support dogs are indeed a good idea for people experiencing mental illness. While there currently isn't a lot of data that focuses specifically on veterans, the studies that do exist, combined with anecdotal evidence, suggest that assistance dogs can have a remarkable impact on the lives of returned service men and women with PTSD. Many veterans say they're likely to better manage their PTSD symptoms after being paired with a service dog, improving their overall quality of life. They also report being more likely to return to activities that their illness may previously have rendered impossible, including employment, study, and socialising with family and friends. Veterans with dogs also say they're less reliant on medications that have side effects such as drowsiness, which in turn makes them feel more engaged with the wider world.

Steve had always been a dog lover. He was just five years old when his first canine pal joined the family, a terrier called Tovarish. He didn't appreciate it until years later, but Tovarish displayed some fairly distinct PTSD-type behaviours himself.

'He was a little bit averse to fireworks and if you had a sparkler in your hand he'd probably bite you,' he laughs. 'We had to train him when we had fireworks night as kids, because he would quite literally run up and grab a lit firework and run around with it in his mouth. He would be going ballistic at the end of the chain.'

Steve decided he *would* like a dog, for company if nothing else. He recalled reading about a program at a local jail, which saw inmates training assistance dogs for injured soldiers in conjunction with a veterans' charity.

That led him to Whiskey's Wish and its founder, Scott Jackman. Scott had served in East Timor and Afghanistan before being medically discharged from the Army in 2013. He had severe PTSD, and receiving a psychiatric support dog that had been trained at the jail marked a turning point in his battle with mental illness.

Sadly, Scott's dog, Whiskey, died in 2014, just a year after they had been matched. Scott was devastated by the loss and decided to channel his grief into launching his own charity, Whiskey's Wish, which trains psychiatric support dogs for diggers and first responders. His charity would be different from existing organisations, Scott vowed, because it would stick with its clients for life, not just the life of the dog.

'I thought, *Well, I'll give it a go.* I contacted Scott, applied and was accepted, and they gave me Sarge,' Steve says.

Sarge was one of the first fully trained Whiskey's Wish dogs to be placed with a veteran. He was a favourite of Scott's, who had named the boisterous blue heeler after one of his best friends, Sergeant Michael Kester. The human Sergeant Kester was a former US Marine, a veteran of Desert Storm and several other US campaigns, and an Australian Army soldier. He suffered from PTSD and passed away in 2015.

Training a psychiatric dog costs Whiskey's Wish around $12 000 and takes between twelve and eighteen months. After leaving the shelter, rescue group or breeder, each dog spends six months or so with a foster carer learning basic obedience commands such as sit, drop, stay, walk-to-heel and toileting on cue. The dog then dons his L-plates – the red 'in training' jacket that affords access to places where dogs are often not permitted – and goes to live with his designated veteran. According to Scott, this is the prime age for developing a strong dog–human bond.

The pair trains as a team until the dog is around fourteen months old, when he takes his Public Access Test (PAT). Passing it earns him the blue jacket of a fully qualified assistance dog and means he can go almost everywhere his owner can.

Sarge was about sixteen months old when Steve became his owner in late 2016.

If he had any lingering doubts about taking on an assistance dog, they were laid to rest the very first night.

'One of my big issues is nightmares. Before I got Sarge it was just making my life so very, very difficult. I was lucky to be getting four hours of sleep a night, if that,' he says. 'On the first night he woke me from a nightmare by licking the back of my neck.'

Sarge's midnight wake-up calls quickly became a comforting nightly occurrence. 'He sleeps on a rug on the bed next to me. I've got a queen-sized bed and one half is his and one half is mine,' says Steve. 'If I'm tossing and turning with a nightmare, he'll be trying to wake me. He'll lick my neck or he'll put all his weight on me with his two front paws, and I'll wake up.'

It's just one of myriad ways a psychiatric support dog can assist his owner. Whiskey's Wish trains its dogs to carry out 'veteran specific' tasks based on the particular needs of each owner. A dog might confirm the safety of a room by patrolling its perimeter, for example, so that a combat veteran feels it's safe to enter. They can remind the veteran to take medication, prevent him from being startled by nudging him when someone is approaching, or physically block a person who is coming too close.

For Steve, Sarge is part guard dog and part balm for the soul. As well as helping to keep his nightmares at bay, Sarge also detects when Steve's stress levels are rising or a panic attack is imminent. He will use distracting behaviours to bring Steve back to the here-and-now before his anxiety spirals beyond his control.

(Author's note: as Steve talks about some of the incidents that contributed to his PTSD, Sarge suddenly starts barking.)

'He's circling me at the moment because he can see my stress levels starting to rise, because I'm talking about stuff I don't normally talk about. That's why he's barking, to try to distract me,' he explains. 'If he notices that I'm starting to get stressed, he'll pick up his ball and put it on my leg like, *Let's go do this instead!*

'He's very in tune with what's going on and he knows when I'm in a bad mood. He's great because he causes me to re-focus: I'm more focused on him and his wellbeing. Sarge does his job really, really well.'

Not only is Sarge extremely obedient, Steve says he's also highly intuitive. 'He knows who's who. He watches me for my cues. If a person comes to the front door he will bark to let me know somebody's there, and he will know by the tone of my voice whether it's a friend or a foe,' he says. 'He checks in with me every second of the day. There are a few people that he knows quite well and that he's got no problem with.'

Two of those people are Steve's young grandsons. Since taking control of his PTSD, Steve has slowly begun to repair his relationships with his daughters.

'With the passage of time my kids have forgiven me, my eldest in particular. Sarge loves my grandkids. He seems to understand when people are part of the family unit. I don't know how he gets that, but he does,' he says.

With Sarge by his side, Steve is able to get out of the house more often. He and his dog are a familiar sight around the small NSW town where they live. They have even taken holidays together, something Steve hadn't done for many years.

While the spectre of the person who threatened him still looms, with Sarge by his side Steve feels much more secure today than previously. 'I would have panic attacks when I was in public. I'm always looking over my shoulder with regard to that individual and his family; I have to. That's always in the back of my mind whenever I'm out,' he says. 'With Sarge I notice I don't do it as often – I don't have to because he watches my back. It's just a little bit of reassurance that he's there and that everything's all right.

'He just gives me that peace of mind and a little bit of security.'

Their outings are also important to Steve because he believes Sarge deserves plenty of opportunity to just be a dog. At just three years old, he has the youthful exuberance of a teenager – and he needs time 'off the clock' to burn off that blue heeler energy.

Sarge loves other dogs and is especially fond of swimming in the dam on Steve's friend's farm – even though, as Steve had the misfortune to discover, the water has a high cow manure content.

'My mate's got a big dam that the cattle get into – the mud in that dam would be three-quarters cow poo. Sarge got into that muck and I had to hose him down before I put him in the car because he smelled so bad,' he laughs.

But when his blue jacket goes on, Sarge is incredibly dedicated to his job. 'When I put the jacket on he knows it's work time: *This is serious stuff, I can't be silly.*'

Amazingly, Sarge also seems to sense Steve's physical pain. 'I don't know how to explain it, but he seems to know that my left knee is not good – he licks it like mad,' Steve says. 'I used to think he was just getting the salt off my skin, but I know now that he understands that I've got a sore knee and he's trying to fix it.'

But for all his impressive obedience and the long list of tasks he can complete, what Steve appreciates most about Sarge is simply his quiet, comforting presence.

'I think the biggest benefit is that I've started to realise just how in tune we are. He doesn't judge me. He doesn't talk back to me. He doesn't say, "Oh, why don't you go and do this." People always want to give you advice and too often it's bad advice,' he says. 'Sarge mitigates my disability and he does that without even speaking.'

It is often the case that we don't fully appreciate how unwell we were until we get better. For Steve, the realisation of how close he came to ending his life only dawned on him after his dog helped him rediscover how much he wanted to live it.

'Since I've had Sarge, my life has changed. He's literally saved my life and I don't say that lightly,' he says. 'He's basically what keeps me going. Getting him has turned out to be one of the best decisions I've made.'

We can't know what life may have been like for Sarge if he hadn't found his way from his breeder to Scott Jackman, then to a foster carer and finally to Steve. Maybe Steve rescued him from an unpleasant fate; maybe he didn't.

But Sergeant Kester rescued Steve, there's no doubt about that – and he continues to rescue him day after day.

'To sum up what Sarge does in just a few words,' says Steve, 'he chases the demons away.'

MORE INFORMATION

OSCAR

Oscar's Law

www.oscarslaw.org

BUDDY

Dogs Without Borders Australia

www.dogswithoutbordersaustralia.wordpress.com

CLOVE

Instagram: @thebullhikes

CAESAR

Australian Defence Force Trackers and War Dogs Association

www.aussietrackers.org

CAOIMHE

CJ Animal Rescue

www.facebook.com/CJ-Animal-Rescue-260286790702466/

ABBY

Sunraysia Animal Rehousing Group
www.sarg.net.au

COLT

Instagram: @servicedogcolt
YouTube: Service Dog Colt

SARGE KESTER

Whiskey's Wish
www.whiskeyswish.org.au

ACKNOWLEDGEMENTS

I can't adequately explain how grateful I am that the wonderful owners of these remarkable dogs have trusted me to tell their stories. To each of you who gave your time and spoke to me candidly about some of the worst times in your life, thank you so much. I appreciate your generosity and your bravery, and I feel enormously privileged to have the opportunity to play a small part in carrying on your dogs' legacies.

Thank you to Kimberley Atkins and Johannes Jakob at Penguin Random House for your ongoing indulgence of my crazy dog ladyness. And thanks to cover designer extraordinaire James Rendall.

And as ever, my biggest thanks are reserved for my husband, Mark, and our daughter, without whom I would literally never get anything done.